Morita Psychotherapy

DR. SHŌMA MORITA (1874-1938)

Morita
Psychotherapy

David K. Reynolds

University of California Press

Berkeley • Los Angeles • London

1976

University of California Press
Berkeley and Los Angeles, California

University of California Press, Ltd.
London, England

CONTENTS

PREFACE

The reader deserves to know the relevant background of an author, particularly when there is little accessible literature available against which to compare the content of his material.

This book is based on fieldwork of nearly two years' duration — sixteen months in 1967-68, one month in the summer of 1972, and six months in 1973. The fieldwork was supported in part by a National Defense Education Act Title VI Fellowship (1967-68), and a Fulbright-Hays Postdoctoral Fellowship (1973). A year's collaboration with Kenshiro Ohara, M.D., a Morita therapist and visiting scholar at the Suicide Prevention Center in Los Angeles, California, preceded my research in Japan. Between trips to the field I have maintained contact with Moritists in Japan and in the United States. I am in the enviable position of receiving sharp, learned criticism on my publications from the very people I work with and study. My papers and articles have been published in Moritist journals and magazines. I have also written several English-language journal articles with Morita therapists.

While in Japan I made extended visits to all the noted Morita therapy hospitals in the Tokyo area and shorter visits to hospitals in Chubu, Kinki, and Kyushu areas. Discussions with psychiatrists and laymen who use Morita therapy primarily on an outpatient basis proved useful as did observations in the inpatient wards of Jikei University and Okayama University. I participated in Moritist group therapy sessions from Hokkaido to Shikoku. In sum, to my knowledge there was no major site of Morita psychotherapy which escaped observation.

During two of the research periods I was Research Associate at Japan's National Institute of Mental Health. There I enjoyed fruitful discussions with various staff members and frequently took advantage of the excellent library facilities. Visits to various mental hospitals (some having no connection with Jikei University) helped to round out my view of non-Moritist psychiatric hospitals in Japan, and visits to various university departments of psychiatry added depth to my understanding of the broad spectrum of Japanese psychiatry. Of course, such an investment of time and interest does not preclude the possibility of errors of interpretation and understanding, but it has allowed the breadth and historical depth of contact necessary for the undertaking of this book.

To Dr. Takehisa Kora, his staff, and the patients of Kora Koseiin I owe a special debt of gratitude; they taught me, by word and deed, the Moritist way of life.

Also Dr. C. Suzuki and the late Mr. K. Mizutani, as well as Drs. Nomura, Usa, Fujita, Koga, and Noda — all Moritist hospital directors — were kind enough to open their hospital and clinics to my investigation, patiently answer my questions, and cooperate in various ways according to my needs.

Dr. N. Shinfuku, chairman of the Department of Neurology and Psychiatry at Jikei University School of Medicine, gave freely of his time to help my understanding of Morita therapy, as did his colleagues Drs. Abe, Iwai, and A. Kondo. Discussions with Drs. Ikemi, Shinfuku, and K. Ikeda during my visit to Kyushu University provided much useful information. Dr. Yokoyama and his colleagues showed me informed kindness at Okayama University. Drs. Kasamatsu, Kato, and Murase at Japan's N.I.M.H. helped me "situate" Morita therapy within the panorama of Japanese psychotherapy.

To my Moritist guides and friends — Drs. Kenshiro Ohara, Jong He Kim, and Chiga Mizutani — I wish to acknowledge another personal and intellectual debt.

English words seem somehow inappropriate for thinking wise, kind, old-young Oteru Okusan for permitting me to spend productive months of analysis and writing in the peaceful beauty of Hongakuin Temple in Ueno. Dr. Fukui, of Hasseiso Hospital, provided the financial means and freedom for me to continue through one difficult phase of the research.

To my dissertation committee, who offered mixed encouragement, enthusiasm, and prodding, I am understandably grateful.

Dr. David Clark and the late Dr. William Caudill extended encouragement and assistance based on their own extensive knowledge of psychiatry in Japan.

The staff and members of the Seikatsu no Hakken group, particularly Mr. Yozo Hasegawa, Dr. Aoki, Mr. Tanishima, and Dr. Ishii, invested themselves in my efforts to understand recent developments in the Moritist mental health education movement.

My thanks to Eleanor Kwong for patiently typing (and retyping) a lengthy and often revised manuscript.

Finally, to a brave family and hopeful friends I acknowledge gratitude that can express itself properly in years of deeds.

D. K. R.

INTRODUCTION

Morita psychotherapy is a Japanese method for treatment of neurosis. Developed in the early twentieth century, it is still practiced with success among the Japanese people. This book is about Morita therapy in theory and in practice. After presenting an overview of the therapy in chapter 1 and an in-depth look at how it operates in a single setting in chapter 2, I turn to broader issues in the remainder of the book. In chapter 3 I speculate about the fit between Japanese neurosis and cure and the culture and character of the Japanese people. In chapter 4 I look at changes in Morita therapy over the fifty years of its history and try to relate those changes to concomitant developments in Japanese culture over that same period of time. In chapter 5 I compare Morita therapy with other forms of therapy, both Eastern and Western. Finally, some theoretical issues about the psychotherapeutic enterprise are raised in chapter 6, issues that come into focus as a consequence of the similarities and contrasts revealed in the preceding comparative efforts.

The reader will be interested to know my purpose in writing this book. Let me begin by denying that I have wholeheartedly "bought" the lifeway of Morita therapy. Admittedly, I find the elaborately developed themes intellectually fascinating, and I find some of the principles personally useful. But I see Morita therapy in its cultural context, a context that is shifting toward acceptance of many Western values that counter the Eastern world view underlying the Moritist ideology. I am equally uninterested in trying to "sell" Morita therapy to Western psychiatry. But I am eager to present to Western psychiatrists the outlines of a carefully and rationally formed non-Western psychotherapy. We need to be aware of therapeutic alternatives in order to expand our clinical armamentarium and to bring into awareness our own taken-for-granted assumptions and blind spots.

Morita therapy's appeal to my experience (and appeal to the client's experience is strongly emphasized by modern Moritists) does not blind me to the contradictions in theory and behavior of therapists and patients. The reader is forewarned, however, that I emphasize the presentation of Morita's arguments in a form that makes sense to me. As best I can determine, this is the form that also makes sense to modern Moritists. This modern position may be slightly different in emphasis from Professor Morita's original position — frankly, it is difficult to know whether it is substantially different — so I shall present what appears to be Morita's original argument in chapter 4 within the discussion of historical process and cultural change and allow the reader to decide for himself the issue of essential changes in ideology.

There are several ways one might present this therapy to Westerners. One way would emphasize the Oriental quality of technique and theory. The therapy would appear mystical, Zen-like. (Such an approach could possibly sell more books to one sort of audience.) Following such a tack, I could imply that I had plumbed the depths of this esoteric Japanese art. Another form of presentation would emphasize the aspects that are readily understandable to most Westerners (perhaps, to most humans). As I have adopted this latter approach, I shall very likely be accused by some of watering down, altering, or unwittingly misinterpreting what Moritists say and do. At least I shall be seen by some as serving the interests of the Moritists who wish to make the therapy international in scope. Below, I present Morita therapy as I have understood it, both as an anthropologist and as a human being. I have been able to communicate with Morita therapists for seven years with only occasional blank looks and adamant disagreement. Some Moritists say and write publicly that I understand their ideas and practices better than any Westerner. My ability to communicate that understanding in English is the issue that concerns me most. If I succeed, the therapeutic system described in this book will "make sense" to my reader whether or not he chooses to adopt it personally or professionally.

The issue of whether or not Morita therapy is useful for treating non-Japanese can only be determined experimentally. And experiment can only follow a balanced descriptive presentation of Moritist theory and practice in Japan.

One experimental test of the efficiency of this treatment form is currently under way at the Los Angeles County Psychiatric Hospital Adult Outpatient Clinic. The results are not yet in.

I   MORITA PSYCHOTHERAPY: GENERAL

---

*Suppose I accept the principle that suffering is universal
and expect to suffer sooner or later; suppose that this is no
longer important to me. Suppose also that I accept that all
things change if I do not fix them. The Zen master had
said in effect: Look and see into yourself and your inner
pains may leave. He did not say my pains would leave; he
did not say they would not leave. What may happen is that
I no longer care whether pains continue or cease. It may
no longer be possible to care about that. If I once see that
there are things that I cannot predict or change, then I can
no longer concern myself with those things. And, con-
versely, when I know what things I can predict and if I
know what to do about them, I shall be very much
concerned with them.*

Jack Huber, *Through an Eastern Window*

MORITA'S THEORY

The formal beginnings of Morita psychotherapy can be traced to an
article with the unwieldy but descriptive title (in translation), "The
True Nature of *Shinkeishitsu* [Neurasthenia] and Its Treatment,"
written in 1917 by Professor Shōma Morita of Jikei University
School of Medicine in Tokyo, Japan. His form of psychotherapy was
designed to treat a neurosis found commonly among the Japanese
and characterized by interpersonally oriented symptoms such as
obsessive shyness, oversensitivity, and feelings of inferiority.

There follows in this section a description of Morita's theory as it has been set forth by Morita therapists themselves in a few English articles and in a vast literature in Japanese. The setting forth of Morita's theory in English is, of course, subject to distortion in language as well as to misinterpretation by those of different cultural background. The task is further complicated by ambiguities in the language and in the theory and by the various interpretations among Morita therapists themselves. Nevertheless, the essentials of the theory are rather simple and straightforward, however complicated the psychological referents of the terms. The Moritist argument flows logically and reasonably if certain assumptions are accepted. The assumptions I consider to be characteristic of Moritist thought have been made explicit below.

Morita's theory was founded on the introspective reports of his patients as well as on his own neurotic experience. It is consequently couched in terms difficult to assess objectively. Rather, the appeal is to the reader's own subjective experience; that is, "Don't you find these psychological principles and tendencies operating within you, too?" Of course, the reader may object to Morita's formulation of these principles and tendencies as the only ones operating in neurosis. Actually, very few Japanese patients seem to object along this line since they are caught up in the wonder of the new insights offered by Morita.

Although somewhat artificial, it is most convenient to divide the exposition of Morita's theory into two sections, the theory of the etiology of neurosis and the theory of cure.

Morita's Theory of Neurosis

Sei no yokubo (Self-actualizing tendencies). — Neurosis is a special condition arising out of the natural characteristics one can find in any man. We all have self-preserving instincts. That is, we fear death. We all have a deep desire to live life fully, to be self-actualizing, to utilize our potential to our own advantage as well as in the service of our fellowman. Morita therapists call this desire *sei no yokubo*. We have tendencies to avoid threats to our physical and psychological safety, to join into relationships with other men, to devote ourselves to worthwhile tasks — all these tendencies are subvectors within the overall directing of energy toward living life fully. Looked at from a

Western analytic perspective, *sei no yokubo* has physical, psychological, and social components.

Men do vary, however, in the strength of their impulse to fulfill themselves. Some people seem almost driven to produce much, to experience widely, and to live at deep levels of emotion and awareness. This is nothing more than an observation we have all made, the Morita therapists argue.

Morita's theory does not seek to explain the variance among men; it seems to be taken as "given." This point is the first of several at which Morita theorists are provisionally satisfied to accept a phenomenon as given, whereas others — for example — Freudians, are more inclined to speculate and explore the possibility of explaining the phenomenon on deeper levels. This difference in the level at which one prefers to begin accepting phenomena as given need not interfere with one's acknowledgment of these observations about man on this level. Sei no yokubo is the basic foundation on which both healthy and neurotic life-styles are built.

Hipocondori seikicho (Hypochondriacal temperament). — It seems that in Japan certain people are possessed not only of a strong desire to live fully but also of a character similar to what Westerners call "introverted." Literally translated from the Japanese, the term used here is "hypochondriacal temperament." Such people are overly concerned not only with their bodily state, but, more generally, they are overly concerned with themselves. They tend to be introspective, perfectionist, self-conscious, and shy, and, on the whole, quite literally self-centered.

Explaining how these people got this way is something of a problem. Some Morita theorists hold that self-centeredness is an inborn characteristic. Studies in Japan have found that from 15 to 31 percent of neurotic patients have one or both parents who are also disturbed (Miura and Usa, 1970). Other theorists consider over-discipline or overprotection in infancy and childhood to be the cause. Still others feel that pervasive elements of Japanese culture expressed in the institutionalized family structure and educational system foster its development. Most believe (as Morita himself believed) that all these factors in some complex way produce self-centeredness (N. Shinfuku, personal communication). However it comes about, we can readily observe this characteristic in many Japanese and perhaps, to some degree, it can be found in all men.

Now, persons in whom the qualities of a strong desire to live fully and the hypochondriacal tendency combine are in a difficult position. Their drive for personal success is opposed by their over-sensitivity to their own shyness, self-centeredness, and other personal limitations. They are acutely aware that these qualities of character hinder the full development of a rich, worthwhile life. It is important to reflect here, too, that all men face the same dilemma to some extent. The Moritists argue that we are all aware of some personal handicaps and that we are all troubled that these handicaps hamper the achievement of our aspirations.

At this point the characterological groundwork for the development of *shinkeishitsu* neurosis has been sketched in. There remain only a precipitating circumstance and the working out of several universal human psychological mechanisms to produce full neurosis.

Chokusetsudoki (Precipitating circumstance, literally, "direct motive"). — The person who is characterologically ripe for neurosis eventually undergoes some unpleasant, frustrating experience that serves to trigger his symptoms. Some accident, some chance remark, some minor illness that would be passed off as trivial by the normal person, is fixed upon and provides the kernel that will develop into neurosis. An example of such an experience is offered by Kora (1964). He writes of a young man who, after a long bout of drinking and playing the Japanese game of *go* with his friend, stood up and felt an attack of vertigo along with an acute headache. He reacted to his distress with anxiety palpitations, so a doctor was called. After that experience a morbid fear of fainting prevented him from leaving his home. The psychological mechanisms between the precipitating experience (the vertigo and headache, in this case) and the ultimate neurosis (the fainting phobia) are the next elements of Morita's theory to be discussed.

Seishin kogo sayo (Attention and psychic interaction). — That which is in our immediate consciousness, our focus of attention, naturally tends to flow along from object to object, from word to word. Even when we pause to think about some topic we tend to see it in relation to a shifting flow of related objects and ideas. It is when our attention becomes fixated on something, when we become obsessed with an idea or a goal or a problem, that we have trouble functioning in daily life. This definition of peak mental functioning in terms of a "flowing mind" is Taoist and Buddhist.

When a child loses his first front tooth he initially pays close attention to his new facial feature. He may stand in front of a mirror for long periods of time. He is likely to be very sensitive to any references about teeth, holes, and so forth. It is almost as if his tooth has become a magnet for his attention. To pursue the figure, it is as if his attention is being attracted back again and again to the locus of the loss. But eventually the magnetism wears off, and he neither pays much attention to his loss nor is so sensitive to it. Thus it seems that attention and sensitivity are related in a positive way. Teachers and parents quickly learn that distracting a child from overattention to his new cavity (or his skinned knee, or his bloody nose) will pay off in decreased sensitivity to it. Professor Morita offered the illustration that the mother of a sick child may be awakened by a slight cough but not by loud thunder. Her sensitivity to sound lies in the direction of the locus of her attention, her child.

Now suppose someone begins thinking a lot about some bodily condition, say headaches. His attention may have been drawn to the topic by a particularly severe headache, but he begins to worry about headaches, to be concerned with when and where and why they strike. He is gradually building up a sensitivity to the topic, and shortly many cues in many varying situations will call the subject of headaches to his mind. And the more sensitive he becomes to the topic the more it is called to mind and the more he focuses his attention on it. The result is further sensitivity and so on in an ever-narrowing spiral of consciousness until the subject HEADACHE stands out as a figure against the background of much of his daily life.

Within this spiral of attention and sensitivity, Morita therapists point out, attention is the more controllable of the two. In other words, one cannot will to be insensitive, but one does have some indirect control over the phenomena toward which one directs one's attention. Therefore, in the next section, dealing with strategies for cure, we note that therapy is directed toward breaking the destructive spiral by changing attention, with subsequent effect on sensitivity.

A closely related observation that Moritists have made is that we experience emotions in wavelike progressions. The deepest depression has some moments of less intense affect. Fear peaks and then recedes. Joy intensifies and fades. These natural cycles of feeling operate provided that the feelings are not restimulated by new experiences. For example, the girl who continues to see her estranged boyfriend repeatedly provokes her feelings of upset and despair. The man who again and again relives in his imagination the terror of an automobile crash may remain in a state of anxiety for an extended period of time. Properly directed attention will allow these feelings to run their natural course quickly without unnecessary restrictions on behavior.

Shiso no mujun (Conflict of thoughts). — There is a tendency in many people to try to overcome a fault directly. For example, some people are afraid to speak in public, but they feel they ought not to have such a fear. They recognize it as irrational and try to get rid of it rationally. Though they feel their internal conflict should not be there, it *is* there. The more they are conscious of the fear, and the more they try to deal with it directly by trying to rationalize it away or will it away, the worse they become.

To some extent all of us try to arrive at some resolution between the world as it is and the world as we would like it to be. We experience conflicts between our feelings and our rational minds, between what we expect on the basis of our intellectual understanding and what we experience in daily reality. Even on the perceptual level our eyes play tricks on us. Saint Paul wrote, "I do not understand my own actions. For I do not do what I want, but I do the very thing I hate" (Romans 7:15 RSV). There may be contradiction between our intentions and our actions.

Sometimes we can match reality with our ideals; often we cannot. The person who struggles inordinately to bring reality into line with his fantasies, his wishes, his view of the way things ought to be, is headed for neurotic suffering.

Moritists do not call for passive acceptance of all that life brings. As Morita put it, "When it's raining and you have an umbrella, you use it." It would be foolish not to do so. But it is equally foolish to put off cleaning one's room when it is raining outside simply because one prefers to be active on sunny days. Telling someone not to worry when he is worrying and doesn't want to but can't help it is the same sort of foolishness.

Conflicts of thinking are closely related to the themes of controllability and fixation. In our earlier example the fear of fainting was clearly uncontrollable by any direct means, and so attempts to deal with it directly would be a waste of time and energy. Furthermore, such attempts at controlling fear district one's attention from the natural flow of experience and fixate it on the fear itself. Fixated attention leads naturally into psychic interaction with the resultant vicious cycle already described.

Summary — To summarize, Morita therapists view the neurotic as a person with a particularly strong need to live a full life, perfectionist tendencies, and extreme self-consciousness — a person not unlike many Western adolescents. This person encounters some unpleasant event that focuses his attention on a particular problem; blushing, headaches, and constipation are typical examples. He becomes quite concerned about the problem, and he becomes increasingly conscious of its effects on his life. He becomes caught in a spiral of attention and sensitivity which produces a sort of obsessive self-consciousness. His efforts to overcome the problem directly by his will serve only to exacerbate his fixation. By the time he arrives at a Morita therapy clinic such a person is generally very shy and sensitive; he is unable to function socially, preferring to spend his life in his room withdrawn from the world outside. He is immobilized by the storm of counterconflicts and pressures raging within his psyche.

Put another way, from Morita's perspective, the problem of neurosis is that too much "self" stands out as figure against the background of the perception of the external world. When self-consciousness fills our attention we cannot attend to the other aspects of our world which require our interest and attention.

For "self" we can substitute terms like "pain," "anxiety," "fear," "sorrow," and the like because in a phenomenological sense (and Moritist theory operates from a phenomenological perspective) these experiences *are* the self. Later, in chapter 4, I talk about the original protective and adaptive functions of fear and anxiety, but the point is that regardless of the positive effect of these phenomena (now or in the past) they force the neurotic person to view himself as object rather than to lose himself in his perceptions of external reality.

Comments. — The Moritist's view of his neurotic patient allows the patient to see himself in a positive light. The emphasis is on how much he is like other humans. Indeed, in some respects, he has potential to become a superior person.

The neurotic person shares with nonneurotics the desire to live fully. It is the strength of this desire, when properly directed, which can produce a better than average existence. Similarly, he realizes that awareness of his limitations is a common human trait. It can be used to weed out the lacks and faults that can be corrected. He learns that all of us have had upsetting accidents, shocks, and the like. He comes to understand that all of us become more sensitive to those areas of our lives to which we direct our attention. The Moritist patient learns these truths both intellectually and experientially.

He adopts a coherent view of his psychological functioning within a life philosophy that emphasizes his productive potential (Reynolds and Yamamoto, 1973, pp. 219-221).

These elements of Moritist theory work to counteract the feelings of inadequacy and worthlessness commonly found in neurotic patients. The patient learns that he is suffering because he possesses some quite admirable qualities. It is precisely because of his strong desire for perfection and advancement in life that he is obsessed with his own faults. It is precisely because he has an extraordinary amount of drive and a strong will that he has tried to mold himself into an ideal person. These traits, when directed properly, can produce not merely an average person, but a superior one.

In an era which some psychologists and sociologists are turning to theories that emphasize the similarities rather than the differences among men (men who act differently in different situational contexts), Morita's view of neurosis may provide a fruitful vantage point.

Morita's Theory of Cure

Diagnosis. — Diagnosis generally precedes treatment. In Morita therapy, however, as in many forms of psychotherapy, fuller diagnosis may come after treatment has already been initiated.

Diagnosis is particularly important in Morita therapy for a number of reasons. One reason is that treatment seems to be maximally effective for the *shinkeishitsu* type of neurosis described above. A second reason is that certain elements of treatment may actually be harmful for certain diagnostic categories of patient. Cases of suicide during the absolute bed-rest period of therapy have occurred on occasion. These suicides are usually ascribed to misdiagnosis of depressed patients. Another reason for the importance of diagnosis is that certain types of patient must be screened out. Some sociopaths, psychopaths, or psychotics, if admitted to the hospital, would destroy the therapeutic milieu, making the treatment of any patient virtually impossible.

Morita distinguished among psychogenic disorders, depression, and character disorders. He classified psychogenic disorders into neuroses and psychoses and further subdivided the neurotic category into *shinkeishitsu* and hysteria. He considered hysterics to be emotionally sensitive, like *shinkeishitsu* neurotics, but extraverted rather than introverted.

According to Morita therapists (Ikeda, undated; Kora, 1965;

Miura and Usa, 1970), the *shinkeishitsu* neurotic patient usually has the following diagnostic characteristics:

a. a comparatively strong will and desire to recover;

b. the ability to achieve some (Moritist) insight into his condition;

c. hypochondriacal tendency;

d. asocial but not antisocial tendencies;

e. no evidence of intrinsic intellectual disturbance or dulling of feeling

f. general pattern of development of symptoms as discussed above from precipitating experience through psychic interaction and perfectionism to full neurosis. (The reader is reminded that Morita's theory of neurosis is in large part a distillation of his *shinkeishitsu* patients' retrospective and introspective accounts.)

g. There is some debate in Moritist circles about this point, but, generally speaking, no person under fourteen years age receives *shinkeishitsu* diagnosis.

Morita further classified *shinkeishitsu* neurosis into three clinical subcategories:

a. *Ordinary neurasthenic state.* The symptoms are most often bodily complaints such as fatigue, headache, tension, insomnia, heavy feeling in the head, ringing in the ears, tremor, impotence, frigidity, and vertigo, but also poor memory, poor concentration, inferiority complex, shyness, inability to read or study, and others.

b. *Obsessive-phobic state.* Symptoms include fear of looking other people in the eye, fear of being unable to perform perfectly, fear of omens, fear of blushing, fear of people, fear of disease, fear of dirt, persistent doubting, and persistently wandering thoughts. Although the terminology here is Freud's, the clinical patterns encountered by Morita therapists are somewhat different. The phobic symptoms among Japanese *shinkeishitsu* neurotics are less severe and closer to normal, adaptive fears. They tend to be more clear-cut and situationally flexible (Ikeda, undated). Within this subcategory there is a complex of symptoms related to difficulties in social interaction. They include fear of blushing, worries about having an unpleasant body odor, inability to meet another person's gaze, shyness, and the like. They are usually grouped together under the term *taijinkyofusho* or anthropophobia. This disorder is perhaps the most common one treated by Morita therapists.

c. *Anxiety state.* Some sort of fit is usually involved, such as a palpitation attack, a dyspneic fit, or vomiting. (Again, the term is used here in a slightly different manner from that in the West. The referent here is a fear reaction to a rather specific problem or anticipation rather than a vague generalized anxiety.)

Frequencies of various symptoms as they appeared at the psychiatric clinic of Kyushu University and as presented among inpatients at Kora Koseiin Hospital are recorded in tables 1 and 2.

THE PATIENT POPULATION

Morita therapy is practiced in several different ways: in hospitals and outpatient clinics, through a group mental health movement, and by correspondence. The characteristics of patients who take advantage of these differing settings vary somewhat. In addition, there have been some changes within the patient population over the fifty years in which Morita therapy has been practiced. Changes per se are discussed in chapter 4.

The hospital setting. — Kora Koseiin is one of the most famous Morita therapy hospitals. The patients' characteristics by sex and diagnosis are presented for the years 1958 and 1968 in table 3. As is common in Moritist hospitals, males outnumber females, although the male-to-female ratio is decreasing.

Kato (1964) reported on anthropophobic patients treated at "S" Hospital in Tokyo during two time periods. His description of these patients is found in table 4. Again we see that among the largest subgroup of obsessive-compulsive neurotics males outnumber females but with a decreasing male-to-female ratio. The reader will also note that the Morita therapist in the hospital setting tends to work with a young patient group. About three-fourths of these patients are under twenty-five years of age.

Caudill and Schooler (1969) carried out a factor analysis of 717 Japanese psychiatric patients admitted to four Tokyo hospitals in 1958. They found a factor characterized by "tense interpersonal relations and phobias" which they labeled *shinkeishitsu.* Even after eliminating the data from the one Moritist hospital among the four, they found the same factor appearing "essentially unaltered" in their Japanese patient data. Some of the reasons for this characteristic difficulty in the interpersonal sphere are discussed in chapter 3.

TABLE 1

Symptoms in 817 Cases of *Shinkeishitsu* Neurosis Treated in the
Kyushu University Psychiatric Clinic, 1928-1937

Symptom	Number of cases	Percentage
Ordinary neurasthenic state	*515*	
Feeling of pressure on head	217	41.8
Poor memory	186	35.8
Disorder of sleep	159	30.6
Headache	99	19.1
Physical and mental fatigue	45	8.7
Dizziness	44	8.5
Poor concentration	45	8.7
Difficulty in thinking, making decisions, and understanding	37	6.6
Impotence	34	6.5
Languor	30	5.8
Feeling of clouding of consciousness	27	5.2
Irritability	27	5.2
Tinnitus	25	4.8
Nocturnal emission	25	4.8
Tension feelings in shoulder	24	4.6
Premature ejaculations	18	3.5
Abnormal sensations	15	2.9
Gastrointestinal complaints	15	2.9
Obsessive-phobic state	*262*	
Fear of disease	85	32.4
Fear of people	43	16.4
Fear of blushing	33	12.6
Fear of dirt	26	9.9
Persistent doubting	26	9.9
Fear of ugliness	15	5.7
Persisting unwelcome thoughts	14	5.3
Fear of committing crime	11	4.2
Fear of being watched or stared at	8	3.1
Fear of acting	7	2.7
Fear of pointed objects	5	1.9
Fear of bacteria	6	2.3
Fear of spaces	4	1.5
Fear of high places	3	1.1

TABLE 1

Symptoms in 817 Cases of *Shinkeishitsu* Neurosis Treated in the
Kyushu University Psychiatric Clinic, 1928-1937 (Continued)

Symptom	Number of cases	Percentage
Anxiety state	*40*	
Fit of palpitation	23	57.5
Fit of difficulty of breathing	8	20.0
Fit of dizziness	6	15.0
Fit of vomiting	4	10.0

Source: Adapted from Ikeda (undated, fig. 2, p. 4-5.

TABLE 2

Major Symptoms of Inpatients at Kora Koseiin Hospital, 1950-1952

Symptom	Number of patients
Anthropophobia	380
Heavy feeling in head	108
Anxiety state	88
Insomnia	54
Pathophobia	43
Timidity and oversensitivity	37
Writer's cramp	33
Fear of being unable to be perfect	22
Excessive fatigue	22
Gastrointestinal complaints	20
Paresthesia	19
Fear of desultory thoughts	18
Fear of inability to read properly	17
Fear of own unpleasant body odor	12
Inferiority feelings	10
Mysophobia	9
Fear of stammering	9
Others	5

Source: Adapted from Kora (1965), table 1, p. 613.

The outpatient clinic setting. — Data from the Jikei University
outpatient clinic in Tokyo for the period 1949-1953 are presented in
table 5, which shows that males greatly outnumbered females. But,
compared with the hospital populations presented above, the outpatients included higher percentages of middle-aged and older
persons.

TABLE 3

Patient Population at Kora Koseiin by Diagnosis, Sex, and Year
(Figures in parentheses are percentages.)

| | 1958 | | 1968 | |
Diagnosis	Male	Female	Male	Female
Ordinary *shinkeishitsu*	57(28.2)	16(22.5)	22(21.0)	16(25.8)
Obsessive-compulsive *shinkeishitsu*				
a. Anthropophobia	102(50.5)	21(29.6)	45(42.9)	31(50.0)
b. Other	15(7.4)	11(15.5)	17(16.2)	6(9.7)
Anxiety *shinkeishitsu*	24(11.9)	13(18.3)	19(18.1)	6(9.7)
Other	4(2.0)	10(14.1)	2(1.9)	3(4.8)
Total	202(100.0)	71(100.0)	105(100.0)	62(100.0)

Source: Ohara, Aizawa, and Iwai (1970), p. 86.

TABLE 4

Anthropophobic Patients at "S" Hospital by Age and Symptoms

	1953-1955	1962
Male: female ratio	Ca. 4:1	7:3
Age		
10-19	91	91
20-24	133	121
25-29	49	32
30 and over	17	26
Symptoms:		
Blushing	127	152
Body odor delusions	121	128
Concentration problems	97	103
Shyness with opposite sex	84	112
Conversation difficulties	82	106
Eye contact phobia	77	95
Feelings of inferiority	55	115

Source: Selected items adapted from Kato (1964).

A two-part paper covering the same university's outpatients in 1953 and 1962 (Takeyama et al., 1966; Ohara et al., 1966) reveals that somatic problems were the most frequently presented complaints among all age categories of neurotic patients, particularly

TABLE 5

Jikei University Outpatient Clinic Neurotic Patients, 1949-1953, by Age, Diagnosis, and Sex

Age	Number	Male				Female			
		Ordinary neurosis	Anxiety neurosis	Obsessive compulsive	Total	Ordinary neurosis	Anxiety neurosis	Obsessive compulsive	Total
10 and younger	1	0	0	1	1	0	0	0	0
11-20	166	92	5	33	130	22	4	10	36
21-30	506	251	46	77	374	80	33	19	132
31-40	244	88	43	22	153	40	41	10	91
41-50	110	40	27	9	76	18	12	4	34
51-60	41	19	9	1	29	6	6	0	12
61 and older	9	7	0	0	7	2	0	0	2
Total	1,077	497	130	143	770	168	96	43	307

Source: Adapted from Yora, (1959).

among females. Forty-seven percent of the males and 41 percent of the females examined were in their twenties. Diagnostic categories were: ordinary *shinkeishitsu-sho*, 35 percent; obsessive-compulsives, 19 percent; anxiety neurosis, 11 percent.

Mental health movement setting. — The Seikatsu no Hakken Organization has a membership of some 2,000. The members subscribe to a monthly magazine and attend mettings, outings, retreats, and the like. From my observations of meetings throughout Japan I estimate that males outnumber females approximately 3:2 and that younger people are overrepresented.

A two-thirds random sample of the 678 persons who joined the Seikatsu no Hakken Organization in 1973 revealed the data shown in table 6. When we compare this population with outpatient neurotics we find that there is less tailing off with age, particularly in the neurasthenic and obsessive-phobic diagnostic categories. Teenagers in both populations, however, show a lack of anxiety neuroses and relatively high rates of obsessive-phobic disorders. In this self-help group there are many more middle-aged and elderly members than in Moritist hospital populations.

Therapy by correspondence. — Morita therapy can be carried out by mail. Dr. Ishii of Seikatsu no Hakken advises a wide range of patients through letters. Some patients initiate only a single exchange of letters, whereas others continue a program of correspondence. Ishii published excerpts from his exchanges with eight persons in 1973. They were equally divided by sex; four were in their twenties, one in her thirties, and three in their fifties. It appears from a follow-up study by Ishii (a study we shall touch on again when we consider the effectiveness of Morita's treatment form) that anxiety neuroses are relatively common among his patients in comparison with those of other treatment modalities.

An estimate of the characteristics of neurotic persons in the Japanese population as a whole would do well to take into account the letters received at the Seikatsu no Hakken Organization after two articles concerning neurosis and Morita therapy appeared in the newspaper, *Asahi Shimbun*. The letters, coming from all parts of Japan, included 54 from Hokkaido, 131 from Kyushu, and 71 from Shikoku. As could be expected, the largest centers of urban Japan contributed the largest numbers of letters: from Tokyo came 760 letters, and from Osaka-Kobe-Kyoto, 545 letters. The total number of letters received in response to both articles was 2,579.

TABLE 6

Membership of Seikatsu No Hakken Organization, 1973, by Sex, Age, Symptoms, and Occupation

(In percentages)

Sex	Males	Females			
	60	40			
Age	20 and younger	21-30	31-40	41-50	51 and older
	6	31	25	21	17
Symptoms	Obsessive/phobic	Neurasthenic	Anxiety	Psychosomatic	Psychotic	Other
	50	25	9	4	3	9
Occupation	Worker	Housewife	Student	Self-employed	Unemployed	Other
	49	16	14	7	13	1

As table 7A indicates, females actually outnumbered males in responding to the 1972 article and in requesting information or admitting to symptoms. These data support the hypothesis that neurotic persons are approximately equally distributed between the sexes. Males, however, are more likely to present themselves for hospitalization or outpatient treatment because of their greater freedom and mobility and because of certain values associated with sex roles. These values are discussed when we look at the fit between neurosis and treatment and Japanese culture. Reynolds and Kitano (1970) found no significant differences between Japanese college-age males' and females' scores on a scale measuring neurotic symptoms, but they found clear differences between the college students' scores and those of hospitalized neurotics.

Table 7B shows a pattern of age distribution somewhat similar to that of outpatients and, to a lesser degree, to that of hospitalized patients. The twenty-year age groups are modal with gradually decreasing frequencies in the thirties, forties, and older age groups.

As in the patient population, anthropophobia was the most common complaint within the obsessive-compulsive group for both males and females and for all age groups. Specific symptoms within the anxiety neurosis and ordinary *shinkeishitsu* diagnostic categories were much the same as those described in table 1.

To provide the reader with some sense of *shinkeishitsu* neurosis

TABLE 7A

Type and Sex of Respondents to Two Newspaper Articles on
Neurosis and Therapy, 1972 and 1973

Type ·	1972			1973		
	Males	Females	Total*	Males	Females	Total*
Those seeking information about Seikatsu no Hakken but mentioning no symptoms	178	244	437	498	433	949
Those admitting to symptoms	198	281	479	214	214	430
Those writing about a third person's symptoms	102	66	14	51	38	95

*Includes "Sex unclear."

TABLE 7B

Diagnosis and Age of Respondents to Two Newspaper Articles on Neurosis and Therapy, 1972 and 1973

Diagnosis	1972						1973					
	20 and younger	21-30	31-40	41-50	51 and older	Unknown	20 and younger	21-30	31-40	41-50	51 and older	Unknown
Obsessive-compulsive	53	67	22	14	3	50	26	34	24	14	4	61
Anxiety neurosis	21	23	20	14	8	70	2	11	11	9	5	27
Ordinary *shinkeishitsu*	3	10	13	7	11	36	6	21	24	16	11	60
Mixed types	29	13	4	2	5	97	2	11	8	2	1	80
Nonneurotic	0	4	3	1	1	14	0	1	2	1	1	2
Total	106	117	62	38	28	267	36	77	69	42	22	230

and its private meaning to the individual patient, I include the following translated excerpt from an introspective account by a typical anthropophobic patient (a young male patient at Kora Koseiin) of his neurosis:

Rather than "illness" I would call this condition "suffering." I shall write about the changes in my suffering and how I encountered distress again and again. I feel that it is also necessary to write about matters not directly, but indirectly, related to my distress. Everything important can't be explained in detail, and some events have slipped from my mind. With this as an introduction I'll turn to the main subject. It is just like me, in trying to write cleverly, I have made the introduction too long.

In the latter part of the ninth grade I began to become self-conscious about looking people in the eye. I felt that when I entered class everyone was watching me. My body became tense. It was awful! However, when I went walking outside of class, I didn't feel tense at all.

Then I entered high school. Basically, I was uncoordinated, lacked spontaneity, and was timid and hesitant. But since it was so disagreeable to pay attention to these qualities I tried not to think about them and identified with the heroes of various novels. Then I thought I'd try to become class president. I campaigned and, frankly, I lost. It was my freshmen year.

Besides that, when I talked with my classmates my attitude bordered on haughtiness. So I couldn't make friends. I suffered from my loneliness. This loneliness caused my greatest distress during high school.

Every night I thought about my isolation. It was too painful, too sad; often I ended up crying. I was an absolute weakling! In order to conquer my loneliness I read many books on the art of making friends. To some degree I revised my way of thinking and tried to achieve something like unaffected openheartedness. But I completely failed. My isolation was complete.

Furthermore, gradually my excessive self-consciousness grew stronger. When I entered class I became quite tense. My movements lost their naturalness and fluidity. And I couldn't respond properly when called on in class. On top of that, even walking along outside of class became painful.

Next, I began to be morbidly afraid of meeting anyone else's eye. I became oversensitive to people standing beside me. It was terrible! Around the end of my senior year in high school I began to be self-conscious about my facial expression. When called on in class I had the feeling that my teacher was watching my mouth. My mouth was frozen! Horrible! Even when I left the classroom my mouth felt tight, so I'd practice opening it properly in front of a mirror.

I took the examination in physical science at T. University because they had a special course in astronomy there. I wanted to be an astronomer. Certainly, I had a strong interest in space, but more than that I thought I could avoid interpersonal misery in that profession. But again I failed . . .

EFFECTIVENESS

It is difficult to assess the effectiveness of any psychotherapeutic activity that aims at more than behavior change. "Cure" and "improvement" have various and specialized meanings for Morita therapists, and these meanings have changed, I believe, over the fifty years of development of the therapy. The patient who still suffers yet carries out normal daily activity is considered cured by some. Other see cure as improved behavior plus elimination of extraordinary subjective disturbance.

A number of studies have looked at pre- and posttreatment psychological test results. Several studies including follow-up questionnaires have been reported. Other studies rely on the therapists' evaluations of treatment results in a consecutive population of patients. None of the studies utilizes blind or double-blind research design. With the obvious opportunities for unintended bias and selectivity of respondents in mind, we shall look at some of the better evaluations of effectiveness.

Yokoyama (1968) reported the results of a questionnaire sent out to the 136 patients he had treated by Morita therapy during a three-year period. Of these, 110 responded (a response rate of 80.9%). The results were as follows: 37 persons were free of symptoms, and 42 persons still had symptoms but were not apprehensive about them and their daily life was not disturbed. Yokoyama labeled these persons "cured" (71.8%). In addition, 28 persons (25.5%) had symptoms remaining and were apprehensive but found daily life possible, and thus were called "improved." Only three persons (2.7%) were unable to carry out their daily tasks owing to their suffering. Yokoyama also asked when the first two groups of former patients felt they had been cured or improved. The replies were: during hospital residence, 32.7 percent; soon after discharge, 19.8 percent; within six months after discharge, 21.8 percent; and over six months after discharge, 25.7 percent.

In a similar study, Suzuki (1967) queried 824 former patients and got a response rate of about 77 percent (633 replies). (The percentages here are recomputed from the raw data presented in Suzuki, 1967.) Using the same definitions, 63.0 percent were cured (symptom free, 28.6%; no apprehension, 34.4%); 28.2 percent were improved (symptoms and apprehension but daily life functioning); 3.6 percent were still unable to function; and 5.5 percent did not reply. As the reader can see, Suzuki and Yokoyama got similar results from independent questionnaires. These two studies show cured and improved rates of 97.3 and 91.2 percent, respectively. If we assume that all those who did not reply were not in the cured or improved category (a rather unjustified assumption), the cured and improved rates drop to 79 and 70 percent, respectively. Of course, those who responded could be trying to please the therapist by their responses, but that is a potential danger in follow-up studies of any psychotherapy.

In the same study Suzuki found that complete cure came, on the average, after 27.6 months had elapsed following the beginning of treatment. In other words, hospitalization, if it occurs at all, is only the first step in the life discipline which reaches maximal effect more than two years after it has begun.

Ikeda (undated) reported on a mixed population of inpatients and outpatients treated by Morita therapy in 1951. Seventy-six percent were cured and 8 percent were improved after a mean of seventy-three days of treatment. In a second study of thirty-five inpatients treated in 1959, Ikeda found 57 percent cured and the rest improved. The treatment period of four-fifths of the patients was less than three months. When followed up from half a year to seven years later, Ikeda found some symptom relapse in three of the twenty cured patients, and two of the improved patients were completely cured.

Yora (1959), in a follow-up mail questionnaire sent out four to five years after outpatient treatment, got a response rate of 37.6 percent from 406 responding ex-patients. Overall he found 63.3 percent cured and 16.2 percent improved. The best results were realized among males suffering from anxiety neuroses (80.0% cured, 16.3% improved, N = 55) and the worst, among obsessive-compulsive males (49.0% cured, 22.6% improved, N = 53). Yora found no significant differences in success by age or education for the group as a whole.

Morita's own research results from a population of 301 neurotics treated between 1919 and 1929 are reproduced in table 8. Morita reported that 68.5 percent of the completely cured were discharged

TABLE 8

Results of Treatment by Morita 301 Neurotic Patients
between 1919 and 1929

Diagnosis	Number	Percentage cured	Percentage improved	Percentage not cured
Obsessive-compulsive	147	54.4	36.4	8.2
Ordinary neurotic	125	60.0	32.0	8.0
Anxiety neurotic	29	62.1	37.9	—
Total	301	53.8	29.7	6.7

Source: Ohara, Aizawa, and Iwai (1970).

between ten and forty days after admission, and that 61.3 percent of the improved were discharged between ten and forty days after admission.

Eleven other studies reported by Ohara, Aizawa, and Iwai (1970) over a period from 1919 to 1960 (patient populations ranged from 29 to 1,317 per study, with a mean of 336) showed that, on the average, 84 percent were cured or improved. Bearing in mind the Moritist definitions of "cure" (which means not necessarily "symptom-free' but no longer bothered by symptoms) and "improvement" (bothered by symptoms but able to carry out normal functioning daily behavior), and recognizing that these studies were carried out without comparable control groups and without double-blind designs (some evaluations of cure were based solely on the clinical judgment of the treatment therapist), we cannot dismiss the opportunities for unintended bias in the results.

On the other hand, it is quite clear that some patients consider themselves cured by Morita therapy. Some, after undergoing treatment in the Moritist tradition, have tried various other religious, philosophical, or medical treatments before finding release from their suffering. Furthermore, as I have argued elsewhere (Reynolds, 1972) and as I do again in chapter 6, there are considerations other than symptom removal or even symptom control which we would do well to take into account in evaluating psychotherapies. Even if the efficacy of Morita therapy in Moritist terms were documented to our complete satisfaction, the results would not be comparable to the results of psychoanalysis or behavior therapy because the treatment goals are different.

Whatever one's definition of "cure," a number of studies suggest that patients undergoing Morita therapy tend to change in expectable ways. I refer here to studies using standardized psychological and physiological tests before and after treatment. Again, double-blind design and adequate controls are generally absent. Let us look at some of the better-known studies most often cited by Moritists in their journals.

Kora (1965) cites studies by Yasuda and by Nakae carried out on patients at Kora Koseiin at time of admission and discharge. Using the Extraversion-Introversion Index, Yasuda found increased extraversion in patients at discharge. Nakae found no differences in degree of personality integration between discharged patients and normal controls using the Rorschach projective test. Between admission and discharge, Nakae found a decrease in repressive tendencies, an increase in internal stability, self-assertive tendencies, and a more objective attitude in responses to the inkblots.

Abe (1960) administered the Thurstone Temperment Schedule to sixty-nine inpatients between 1957 and 1959 at admission and discharge. Scores increased significantly (beyond the .01 level of confidence) on five of the seven scales: vigorousness, impulsiveness, dominance, emotional stability, and sociability. The last three scales no longer showed significant differences from standardized norms at the time of discharge.

Takano (1961) tested forty inpatients with the Rosenzweig P-F Test. The patients ranged in age from seventeen to forty-six; thirty-one were males and nine were females. Takano also tested a group of thirty slightly younger normals (sixteen males and fourteen females, age range sixteen to thirty-two). He found significant differences between neurotics and normals and between admission and discharge scores with some of the scores entering the normal range at discharge.

Miura and Usa (1970) cite Kataguchi's finding that Morita therapy, compared with nondirective therapy, did not result in major changes on the Rorschach test. Usa, in a pretreatment-posttreatment design, found evidence of improvement in emotional integration in posttreatment Rorschach responses.

Two minor studies of physiological change during treatment revealed nothing extraordinary. Takahashi (1960) carried out various tests on urine specimens collected from thirty-eight neurotic inpatients before and during three stages of treatment. The researcher found some differences between neurotics and clinical norms and some expectable changes during the absolute bed-rest period of treatment but no correlations with success of treatment. Okuda (1960) conducted Mecholyl tests on sixteen neurotics (nine in-patients at admission and discharge and seven outpatients at first and second visits). The differences between tests were small or non-existent. The author offered no statistical evaluation of the differences found in fourteen of the sixteen patients, presumably because of the small population size and the smallness of differences in most cases.

THE SETTINGS

Once the patient has been diagnosed as appropriate for Morita treatment and the logistical arrangements have been worked out, he is admitted to an outpatient program or to a Moritist hospital. Whether the patient is assigned to inpatient or outpatient treatment is determined primarily by whether or not he is capable of working at his regular job on the outside. If he can carry out his work, however painfully, he is encouraged to stay out of the hospital. Lesser factors include financial status, time commitment, available space in the hospital, family opinion, and so forth.

Inpatient Care

Morita therapy was originally carried out on an inpatient basis in the home of Professor Morita. The patients became, in a sense, temporary members of his family. Therapy was carried out within this family setting on an informal basis. As Morita worked alongside the patient, as they strolled in the garden, or as they sat talking after the evening meal, the therapeutic instruction was given.

The modern Morita therapist may or may not live on the hospital grounds, but there is still an effort made to keep some familylike warmth and informality within the hospital milieu. For example, rather than calling patients into his office for interviews, the doctor is more likely to go out and talk with the patients as they work or play. Work within the hospital is usually of a domestic sort such as the care and maintenance of gardens and buildings, washing clothes, heating the bath, and preparing meals.

The four stages of inpatient treatment. — The four phases of inpatient treatment may blend into one another, particularly during the latter phases, but they do represent conceptually meaningful periods to the Morita therapist. Each period, according to theory, lasts approximately one week, so the entire course of hospitalization ideally lasts about a month.

The first stage is called the period of absolute bed rest. During this period the patient lies quietly in his room alone. He is not permitted to read, chat, smoke, listen to the radio, write, or engage in any pastime. He is permitted to eat three times a day, to wash his face and brush his teeth, to defecate and urinate as necessary, and to bathe (generally once or twice during the week). His therapist may make brief visits daily to check his progress. The remainder of the time is to be spent simply thinking whatever thoughts come to mind and feeling whatever feelings well up without resisting them. His instructions might sound like this (Kora, 1964, p. 17):

> 1) You can think of anything you want to think of. As a matter of fact, it is better that you ruminate your thoughts as much as possible. If you are worried about your symptoms and conditions, go ahead and worry. If you are suffering from them, suffer to your your hearts content.
>
> 2) During the course of bedrest, you might get bored and feel the strong urge to get up. You might feel this treatment of staying in bed doing nothing to be unbearable, or even ridiculous. You might even come to wonder if you would be cured by just lying in bed like this. You might just want to leave the hospital. Whatever mood might grip you, lie in bed as you are told to and keep it up believing it to be your duty.

Patients most often seem to experience drowsiness for a couple of days, followed by wakefulness and much doubt and suffering, then by increasing boredom for the last few days.

Two patients' retrospective accounts of their bed-rest experience are relevant here. The first wrote concerning his sixth day of bed rest: "I have nothing more to think about. I have no way of passing the long day doing nothing. I'm now at my wit's end; I don't care what would happen now . . ." (Kora, 1964, p. 18). The second wrote of his fifth day of bed rest: "The ennui is so unbearable that even going to the toilet is now a great pleasure. I have never experienced such a great joy in my life"(Kora, 1964, p. 18). Other patients write of their boredom, their suffering and struggling with memories and symptoms. Bed rest tends to evoke strong emotional responses.

The bed-rest period serves a number of purposes, according to Moritist theory. Any emotion, even anxiety or fear, declines in intensity over time, provided it is not restimulated. During the bed-rest period the patient's extreme fear reactions diminish gradually, thus preparing him for further treatment. Bed rest also serves as a standardized condition for diagnostic observation. Patients who cannot follow the bed-rest restrictions, as well as those who do not react to bed rest with increasing boredom, are diagnosed as non-*shinkeishitsu* or mixed types and receive somewhat modified therapy.

By obeying the instructions to accept his feelings and thoughts as they are the patient reduces his perfectionistic struggle against them, facilitating the breakdown of the vicious cycle of attention fixation and oversensitivity. Again, the patient learns through his own experience that inactivity and withdrawal run counter to his nature, that emotions decline over time when allowed to run their course, and that psychic interaction only restimulates and exaggerates his neurotic distress. The ennui of bed rest motivates the patient naturally to desire activity and work. And it is work that will dominate the remainder of the treatment process. Thus, bed rest provides an experiential benchmark of inactivity against which one can measure an active life, as illustrated in the following diary entry: "The work wasn't much fun, but when I think about bed rest, moving my body is pleasant."

A final use to which the period of absolute bed rest has been put by modern Morita therapists is as an opportunity to establish a positive relationship between therapist and patient. Any social contact, however, brief, is welcome under conditions of isolation. These are the important ways in which therapists and patients view absolute bed rest. Alternative perspectives — bed rest as sensory reduction, a condition for extinguishing anxiety, an initiation ritual, and so forth — are covered in chapter 5.

When the patient rises from his bed-rest experience he may feel somewhat euphoric. Some notes in translation from a patient's diary give an indication of his feeling of elation: "I got up at 5:30. Quickly I washed my face and went out into the garden. What a beautiful day! I wandered around in a dream. It was wonderful feeling my body move. First I swept up the fallen leaves and trash with a broom. Until the breakfast chimes I worked as if in a dream. . . . I simply wasn't aware of the passage of time. After lunch I washed clothes. I climbed up on the clothes-drying roof and just looked around slowly. After that I wiped the flowers' leaves one by one. I've never encountered anything like this. They call this *work*!" Another wrote, "I feel like a child now. Everything I see seems strange to me. . . . Never in my life did the world look so beautiful to me."

This euphoria provides the therapist with an opportunity to make an important point. The patient must learn that his pleasant emotions as well as the unpleasant ones will decline with time. His feelings and moods are constantly shifting and impermanent ("like the Japanese sky"), so he would do well to base his life on something more stable than his emotional state; that is, he must build his life on his behavior, not on his feelings.

A period of light work is the second stage of treatment. During this period the patient is given light physical tasks such as sweeping, raking leaves, and washing clothes. He is permitted to stroll in the serene, well-kept gardens, observing nature and taking in fresh air and sunshine. He is still prohibited from casual conversations, reading, leaving the hospital, and accepting visitors. He is not permitted to sleep more than seven or eight hours, nor is he allowed to retire to his room during the day.

During this period the patient begins to absorb the formal instruction of Morita's theory. Through the diary, *kowa* lectures, meetings, and discussions (described below) he begins his formal indoctrination into the Moritist world view. But the main purpose of the period of light work is to consolidate and further the gains made during the preceding bed-rest period. While the patient's body is gaining in strength his attention is consistently directed away from himself and toward the task at hand. Whatever he is doing, he is required to do it purposefully and carefully. His experience soon teaches him that as his attention is directed outward he does not "notice" his symptoms so much.

During the next stage, the period of heavy work, the patient engages in tasks requiring greater physical output. He may or may not be given more latitude in his choice of work, but the appropriate tasks include gardening, carpentry, and cutting fuel. By this time the patient has begun to develop confidence and joy in his accomplishments. He is more job-oriented. His symptoms have receded. He does not notice the passing of time because he is fully occupied in his work. He has been a member of work groups of patients and has found it increasingly natural and pleasant to interact socially. He is working without pay, so he begins to realize the satisfaction and feelings of self-worth which spring naturally from contributing to social ends.

Dr. T. Kora (1964, p. 16) offers this advice in conducting work therapy within the Morita therapy hospital setting:

> The patient is guided to put hands on, tackle, and complete anything that has caught his attention and that needs to be done. I tell the patient that "Work is born there and then when you find something that is not in good order." An example would be a stalk of a chrysanthemum that is falling. The falling stalk is something that is not in good order and so there and then the work is born of giving it support and preventing it from falling. If a patient walks down the narrow land in the garden of the hospital and finds a small puddle obstructing his path, he finds before him the work of filling it with the ground he can find nearby. When the patient has acquired this attitude and this frame of mind, he can find work anywhere, and he will be so busy that he will feel the day to be very short. Once he has reached this stage, the symptoms diminish at a rapid pace.
>
> At times, the patient complains that the work is not interesting. When we hear such complaint, we explain as follows: "You do not do any work just because it is interesting; work is something that should be done even if you do not like it. Work is not play where you enjoy yourself." In this manner, we make the patient understand the true nature of work. At the same time, we make him experience that if he does the work regularly as he finds it, a rhythm will be born in his work and the work will no longer be so disgusting or uninteresting.
>
> The patient sometimes takes the attitude that he is doing all this work for the sole purpose of trying to cure his disease. But it must be noted here that this kind of attitude still has his mind directed upon his own self, prevents him from dealing with concrete objects of the outside world, and makes it difficult for him to apply himself to or to be absorbed in work.

The attitude Moritists try to foster in their patients is less one of "Do what you need to do" and more one of "Do what is there to be done." As Suzuki remarked, "One of the characteristic features of the *shinkeishitsu* neurotic is the tendency to criticize the value of an activity . . . for example a student only thinks about the effect of his study and does not commit himself to the study. I direct him to experience and acquire the attitude *not* to inquire about the effect of his study simply [*tada*] " (quoted in Davis, undated, p. 13).

There appear to be three distinguishable values related to work in Moritist thought. First, work is good in itself. Second, the effects of work are good both for society and for the growth of the individual. Third, work allows the self-centered person to "lose himself," that is, to transcend himself. Of course, these values are interrelated. But the last two are intellectualized; they sooth the understanding. The spirit of Morita therapy emphasizes the first — one works because the work is there to be done.

The kinds of work done in Moritist hospitals are more often physical than mental. They include such tasks as filling an oilstove, burning trash, wiping a ceiling, dusting an office, raking a garden, sweeping a path, and other jobs requiring body movement and effort. Reading, proofreading, making lists for shopping, and so forth may be assigned, but, barring patients with some genuine physical disability, no one finds himself sitting much of the day once the bed-rest period is completed. Historical changes in the kinds of work done by patients are discussed in chapter 4.

Reading is generally permitted by the third stage of therapy. Certain restrictions are placed on the type of literature allowable; escape literature such as novels is prohibited, but books directed toward reality, such as history, geography, and popular science, are permissible. When reading, the patient should make no particular effort to understand or remember the text. Extreme effort might result in a new cycle of obsessive attention and sensitivity. Visitors may be allowed during this period, but extended or frequent visits are discouraged.

The final stage of treatment is a period of preparation for return to normal life. The patient gradually takes on the privileges and assumes the responsibilities of everyday life. Errands and visits outside the hospital are encouraged when necessary and purposeful. Sometimes this period is extended so that the patient can go to work or attend school outside the hospital while living within the security of the hospital milieu.

The emphasis in this stage is on broadening the base of attention-directed activities so that the transition following discharge will be a smooth one. The following account of a fairly typical day in a hospital, emphasizing Zen Buddhist aspects of Morita therapy, was written in 1969 by a patient, Dr. S. of a northern Japanese university medical department. It was published the same year in *Ima ni Ikiru*, volume 9, number 2, on the inside back cover. It is translated here with some of the description of the content of the therapeutic lecture omitted.

A Day of Morita Therapy

February 17th, my thirty-sixth day in the hospital.

I got up to the sound of clacking wood blocks at 7:00. After the usual cleaning from 7:10, I went with Mr. Y. to pick up the charcoal briquettes. After breakfast I lined up with everyone at 8:30 for the brief visit with the doctor. Before 9:00 I participated in the physical exercises broadcast over the radio, and then there were thirty minutes of quiet Zen sitting.

I used a rag to clean the frame dirtied, I guess, by the snowfall two days ago. Once you start going from one task to the next one you spot you just don't rest at all. Around 9:30 I watered the flowers in the greenhouse, using the watering can. Then I went to help correct a manuscript in the reception room. The proofreading wasn't finished until after 3:00. I had to pay close attention to little details like improperly written characters and syllabary endings. The manuscript was the magazine, *Living in the Present*, number 32. It was Dr. Suzuki's special anniversary issue. Since there were contributors from all walks of life, the content was interesting and I was engrossed.

From 4:00 P.M. I had cooking duty. I washed vegetables and washed the rice in the special tub. There is no sound so pleasant as the well-liked sound of rice swishing around the tub. Everyone working in the kitchen was somewhat tense so we moved briskly.

Oh, yes, the doctor's lecture was at 1:00 P.M. It was about Professor Morita's advice to patients when their thoughts were opposed to what the doctor said. In such a case, even though you think differently, try to do as the doctor says for a while. This is obedience. When obeying it is important to carefully integrate your own thinking with that of the other person. If you had no thoughts of your own, you'd be a machine, obeying blindly. For example, in learning Occidental music from a teacher you can easily understand the principle involved. At first, when the teacher corrects your singing, you just can't figure out what he means. But resigning yourself and doing as you've been told, before long you'll come to realize your mistakes. Thus, the doctor introduced us to Professor Morita's story.

The doctor said that in some sense it's fine to have doubts and reservations on entering the hospital. Up until now we've been trying to understand by our own intellectual stores; we've been bumbling along, but no matter how hard we tried we couldn't understand and solve our own problems. So now we've promised to give the Morita method a try, even in the midst of our doubting. Anyway, to obey the hospital rules and to live actively — that's what is important. When we do that we can, like Morita, add to our understanding from our own experience. Mr. K. had the duty of heating the bath and he didn't hear much of the lecture. He came in near the end and was caught immediately (sneaking in late). When I'm heating the bath I want to hear the doctor's lecture — my mind tries to be on two things. That's the way our minds are. . . .

At 4:30 P.M. I again joined the group in physical exercises by radio broadcast. Then after dinner our diaries with the doctors' notations were returned. After quietly sitting in Zen posture from 7:00 to 7:30 I was summoned to the reception room and there wrote "A Day of Morita Therapy."

To give the reader a view of the hospital experience over time, I have selected several diary entries from the account of a patient who was seventeen years old, a junior in high school. His chief complaints at admission were lack of ability to talk with people comfortably, frequent distraction of attention, insomnia, strong inferiority feelings, and fatigue. The account is from Ohara and Reynolds, 1973 (a slightly different translation of the same diary account appearing in Kora and Ohara, 1973, p. 68).

Diary opening: "I am nervous by nature. I hear that when I was a baby I used to cry out frightened by any little sound. Since I was a child I have suffered greatly from feelings of isolation, humiliation, and suspicion at home and at school. As an early teenager I had already developed many of my symptoms and distortion of character. Now I am bothered by anthropophobia, low efficiency, timidity, anxiety, insomnia, fatigue, as well as such persistent difficulties as mythophobia, pathophobia, inferiority feelings, difficulty in concentrating, tics, body tremors and a fear of sudden noises. Can someone like me really be helped by Morita therapy? If I find relief it will be a miracle."

The first day after absolute bedrest: "I left my bed for the first time. But everyone here is unfamiliar and I am not thinking clearly. When my symptoms emerged as usual, I worried about them alone in my room. But after lunch I began to get accustomed to the people's faces, met some people, and worked a little. But I felt anxious about their eyes as I've felt before. Although the doctor said in his lecture that there is no need to be a great man I still have an earnest desire to be great. Even now I intend to conquer my neurosis through Morita therapy and then I may improve my personality through Zen or Yoga. But I'm afraid this intention is wrong. Certainly, when I am in a group I enter into rivalry with the others. What a fix I am in! Furthermore, since I am very clumsy how will I be able to do the handicrafts? If I do, my work will be worthless. I am completely lacking in self-assurance. But today's harvest was that by not running away I was able to establish friendly relations with almost all of the people here by evening."

The seventh day after absolute bedrest: "This is the most painful time for me. I must get through this period at any cost and advance toward the future. I am such a contradictory being. I am caught in a circle and cannot stir an inch. Last night I dreamed that I was caught in the web of a gigantic spider. The spider came and said to me, 'It is no use struggling. You can't escape.' The dream reflected my present state of mind. Now I am beginning to look on the bright side of things. If I do as the doctor tells me I will gain something at least, however trifling the gain is. I will let things take their own course."

The thirty-third day after absolute bedrest: "I filled the oil heater. This was my first time doing it so I couldn't do it very well. When I finished my hands were stained by oil. Took care of the birds. Today a lovebird egg hatched, two days late. Next I cleaned the garden. Read. Played ping-pong. Then I saw my mother off at Takatanobaba Station. I had my watch repaired in a watchmaker's shop. Although I had to struggle with myself to enter the shop I opened the door in spite of my apprehension. After supper I was visited by Mr. A., a former patient here, and we went into Shinjuku to buy books and have a snack. It was pleasant to see Mr. A. again — it seems so long ago that he was discharged. I felt some self-consciousness, but everything went well. Then I picked up my watch at the watchmaker's shop. Then I delivered a book that I had earlier promised to lend to a fellow patient. She was in the hospital's crafts room with a number of other women. I have a strong desire to be respected and loved, which is one of the characteristics of anthropophobia. According to Morita therapy I should recognize this strong desire and accept and use it rather than focusing on my symptoms. But I fear that if I do so I will become passive, stereotypic and artificial."

The forty-eighth day after absolute bedrest: "Today I shall end my diary at Koseiin Clinic. I am filled with emotion. I have gradually come to understand the word 'arugamama' (accepting one's self, one's symptoms, and reality as they are; literally, 'as it is'). No matter what my ideals, ideas, and feelings may be it is most important to accept reality. In fact, I can't help responding to reality. Looking at it one way I am thankful for having been an anthropophobic patient. I have advanced one step, and now I want to go on advancing endlessly. In sum, I dimly begin to realize that this neurosis was like a spring board which enabled me to develop myself. I desire to understand myself fully and then to use that knowledge in a practical way. Thanks to my mastery of life through Morita therapy I have become aware of my true self now. I find it gratifying that my true self is not so much inferior as it is great. I really thank you for your long-range guidance."

At the time of discharge the patient may still have fears, unhappiness, or other symptoms. If, however, his behavior has changed, if he is capable of carrying out his living regardless of his symptoms, he is qualified for discharge. It is occasionally remarked that in some cases symptoms are likely to show substantial decline only years after discharge. The patient is expected to apply Moritist principles to his daily behavior during those years. But Morita therapists have consistently stressed that acts, not symptoms or feelings or moods, are most important for living fruitfully and therefore that changed behavior, not changed feelings, is the key criterion for discharge.

Discharge, however, is not necessarily the act that severs all ties to the hospital. Well over 3,500 ex-patients receive Moritist magazines published by the larger hospitals. Some patients maintain contact through outpatient treatment; some attend meetings at the hospital for ex-patients; some participate in group excursions sponsored by the hospitals. And a number maintain contact simply through occasional visits, letters, and gifts.

Characteristic elements of inpatient treatment. — Having sketched in the four stages of hospital treatment, I turn now to the special methods by which Morita therapists instruct their patients in intellectual and experiential acquaintance with Morita's theory.

Here, too, the focus is on what Morita therapists say about their methods, leaving until later the description of their actual practice. The eight characteristics particularly associated with Morita practice are the familylike setting, absolute bed rest, work therapy, the annotated diary, the *kowa* lectures, the *Kojiki* readings, hospital magazines, and ex-patient meetings. As the first three elements are discussed above, I begin here with the annotated diary.

On the first evening following the bed-rest period the patient begins his diary. He is instructed to write a page or more each evening. The diary is to cover what the patient saw and did during the day. He is not to write about his symptoms or his subjective feelings. He is to focus on his behavior, especially on the work he accomplished.

The diaries are collected each morning and turned over to the therapist. He reads them during the day and makes appropriate comments in red. The diary provides a means by which the therapist can keep himself informed of the patients' progress while providing them with guidance and encouragement.

Aside from the conveniences of this form of communication in terms of the doctor's being able to schedule his time "with" each patient, the record-keeping advantages of the diary both for the staff and for the patient (who takes the diary with him when he returns home after discharge) and the ease with which more than one therapist can respond to a single diary entry (minimizing transference [Caudill and Doi, 1963]), there is a peculiarly Japanese benefit in this method of interaction. A shy, sensitive patient may find it easier to communicate his inner doubts, his anxieties, and his disagreements with an authority figure through indirect contact. The Japanese people have a long tradition of diary writing, and since the turn of the century the "I novel," a kind of lightly fictionalized auto-biography, has been popular in Japan. I have more to say about the cultural fit of the therapy as a whole in chapter 3, but here let me simply point out that the diary form allows both patient-writer and therapist-respondent to control carefully the content of the message within a limited range of channels (word choice, handwriting style, length of message, accuracy in writing characters, and the like) and allows time for careful thought about the message and the message format which is not available to persons interacting in face-to-face speech. The Japanese are very concerned about what might be called "signal management" in interpersonal contacts. The *shinkeishitsu*-neurotic person is even more concerned about signal management than the ordinary Japanese. The diary (like letter therapy) gives him the time and distance and channel control within which he can communicate with minimum discomfort.

The *kowa* lectures are another important part of Morita therapy. Although therapists counsel and guide patients informally through-out the day, some sort of formal meeting is generally held at least once a week during which patients gather to hear a lecture and its specific appliation to individual cases. During the *kowa* the therapist may read from a book, question patients about symptoms and progress, explain the meanings of various calligraphies hanging on the walls of the hospital, or he may simply talk from his experience in treating neurosis. The kind of material appropriate for the *kowa* lectures is illustrated in the following translation (Kora, 1968, p. 322):

> When a man of average income loses twenty-five dollars he feels bad. And even though he intellectually accepts that this is a fact of life, the bad feeling lingers for awhile. If he loses ten times as much

the feeling remains somewhat longer. However, there are people who try to use their wills to force the bad feelings away at once. They don't understand the special characteristics of emotion and are trying to do the impossible. The result is conflict. We can with comparative freedom select our *behavior*, but as for *emotions*, it is difficult to direct them with our will.

Among the special features of emotion, another important one is the fact that no matter how high the wave of emotion, in time it will fade. If this were not the case our lives would be destroyed. If the tragic feeling of some heavy blow were to stay with us at its original strength indefinitely no one would be able to continue living. Depending on the importance of the event, its special characteristics, and the personality of the individual, in the end, when left alone the ups and down of the waves of emotion diminish, whether we like it or not. This fact is of great benefit to us, but sometimes it has a negative result. When, after some tragic experience, we vow to hold to some new good habits, our resolutions may last only a short time, like a "three-day monk."

During the stages two through four for a few minutes just after rising and just before going to bed each day the patient may be instructed to recite a poem or read from a classic chronology of Japanese history called the *Kojiki*. When reading the patient should not be concerned with the meaning of the difficult characters but only with his accuracy in pronouncing the phonetics written alongside them. This procedure frees the patient's consciousness of worries and stray thoughts and facilitates his getting up and relaxing at the appropriate times. We have all experienced the inner debate regarding getting out from under warm covers on a cold morning. Such inner conflict short-circuits our action with the result that we continue to lie in bed deciding. The reading or recitation frees the mind from just this sort of conflict and allows one to respond spontaneously to the necessity of the situation. It is also said to develop alert, controlled thought processes.

The magazines published by various Moritist hospitals are professional-looking journals which appear at least twice a year. Circulation of a single issue may be as high as 1,800 copies. The forty pages or so in a typical issue contains articles about Morita therapy by therapists and patients, excerpts from diaries, *kowa* notes, records of symposia, testimonies, advice, poetry, slogans, news of meetings and trips, and human-interest stories about inpatients and therapists. Popular books related to Morita therapy and back issues of the magazine are advertised. The hospital's address, phone number, and sometimes a brief description of the facilities and admission procedures are included. Special issues commemorating important events in the hospital's history may be published with photos, extra pages, articles by guest contributors from among the ranks of famous Morita therapists, and so forth. The magazines serve the dual function of maintaining contact with ex-patients and recruiting new patients.

In the survey of 610 former patients referred to earlier (Suzuki, 1967), questions were asked about the hospital magazine. Of the 601 persons who replied to these questions, 56.1 percent said that they read the magazine; 42.9 percent said that they do not. The main reasons given for reading were self-improvement (79.6%) and the desire to know more about *shinkeishitsu* (10.5%). The most common reasons given for not reading the magazine were that the respondent was too busy and forgot (29.3%), that he could get along without the magazine despite his symptoms (27.6%), that he did not know that it existed (16.3%), and that because he was cured he found the magazine unnecessary (16.6%). Moritists would smile with satisfaction at all the reasons for not reading their magazine, except for not knowing about its existence.

Ex-patient meetings are still another characteristic element of Morita therapy. The term "ex-patient meetings" is used here because former patients make up the bulk of those attending, but inpatients, outpatients, inquirers, therapists from various hospitals, and special guests and guest speakers may attend the meetings as well.

These bimonthly, quarterly, or semiannual meetings are generally held on Sunday afternoon. Tea and cakes are served. The program consists of lectures, testimonies, question-and-answer sessions, and panel discussions. A variation of these meetings is an all-day group outing. A trip, perhaps a picnic, with group singing, games, and hiking is a highlighted event held at irregular intervals.

The bylaws of one ex-patients' group states that its purpose is to plan reunions, promote individual personal development, and aid in the proper understanding and dissemination of Morita therapy. To accomplish this purpose the members agree to attend meetings, publish notices, sponsor social events, promote recreation, and so on.

Before discussing other settings for the practice of Morita therapy, it would be well to summarize and comment upon Morita's theory of cure as presented above. Morita therapy is most effective for *shinkeishitsu* neurotic patients and is potentially harmful for some others; thus, careful diagnosis is extremely important. Inpatient treatment occurs in a familylike milieu under the active, managing guidance of the therapist. The treatment properly consists of four temporal phases: absolute bed rest, light work, heavy work, and final preparation for discharge. Discharge is determined primarily on the criterion of changed behavior, not feelings, but discharge need not cut the ex-patient's contact with the hospital. The outstanding features of Moritist inpatient treatment procedures include the familylike setting, absolute bed rest, work therapy, the annotated diary, *kowa* lectures, *Kojiki* readings, hospital magazines, and ex-patient meetings. A summary of information from seven major Moritist hospitals is found in table 9.

At this level of generality the treatment procedures make sense in terms of Morita's theory of the etiology of neurosis. The patient learns to accept himself — including his symptoms and his anguish — as he is, without direct struggle. At the same time his attention is directed outward and away from his own problems. Yet, even at this level puzzles begin to appear. If the fundamental principles of Morita's theory are easily understood, why must education continue after the hospital period? Don't meetings and magazines, testimonies and illustrations, direct attention toward symptoms in empathic response? Other puzzles emerge later as we examine the actual practice of Morita therapy in more detail.

Outpatient Care

Morita therapy on an outpatient basis is fairly widespread throughout Japan. In part, the popularity of Morita therapy as an outpatient treatment form is owing to the expansion of the meaning of the term to include any advice to an outpatient to try to live an active life in spite of his symptoms. A few persons with some training in Morita therapy are practicing privately or in counseling centers or other institutions.

Most Moritist hospital directors also see outpatients in their hospitals. In addition, there are some ten general psychiatric hospitals and university clinics where physicians responsible for outpatient treatment place strong emphasis on Morita therapy. The patient is generally seen once a week for thirty to forty-five minutes. Data from Jikei University's Outpatient Clinic (Ohara et al, 1966*b*)

TABLE 9

Seven Moritist Hospitals: Selected Responses to a 1968 Questionnaire

Item	Hospital						
	Mizutani	Suzuki	Usa	Kora	Nomura	Koga	Fujita
Year hospital built	1960	1964	1927	1938	1954	1928	1963
Maximum patient capacity	20	40	50	24	15	10	8
Actual number of patients on day of questionnaire reply	15	40	57	15	10	4	8
Number of staff	9	16	17	7	10	6	5
Average period of hospitalization (days)	40-60	40-120	?	30-50	100	?	?
Cost per patient per day, in yen(360 yen = $1.00)	1,200	1,500	1,200 / 2,400	2,500	1,000	4,000	1,500
Percentage of patients sent to hospital under family pressure	10-20	20	20	36	30+	?	25
Percentage of patients cured or improved (therapist's estimate)	70	95	80-90	90	97	75	50
Percentage of patients who escape	Some	5	3-	0	1	1-	?
Percentage of patients who commit suicide	0	0	0	0	1-	1-	?
Percentage of patients murdered	0	0	0	0	0	0	0
Do you think Moritist hospitals are like families?	Somewhat	Very	Very	Somewhat	Somewhat	Very	Somewhat
Nurse is like what role group(s) — (fixed choice)?	Friend	?	Aunt	Aunt, elder sister	Aunt, mother, friend	Mother, friend	Mother
Doctor is like what role group(s) — (fixed choice)?	Elder brother	?	Uncle	Father, elder brother	Uncle, father	Father, friend	Father

indicate that 44 percent of outpatients are seen only once; 38 percent are seen two to five times.

These patients receive an intake interview and, in the time remaining, are counseled according to Moritist life principles. They may receive medication and/or referrals to Moritist hospitals. Japan's national health insurance program pays the therapist only the equivalent of $3.33 for the patient's first visit and $2.40 per treatment thereafter, a rate that Hasegawa (1974b) indicates is on a par with a barber's fee.

Group Therapy

In 1957 K. Mizutani founded a Moritist organization called Seikatsu no Hakken Kai (literally, "The Discovery of Life Group"). After Mizutani's death in 1970, Y. Hasegawa took over the leadership of the group during a period of expansion and development in the direction of self-help and group therapy outside the hospital.

Hakken Kai has three major group thrusts.* Twice a year retreats are held (called gasshuku gakushukai) for four or five days each. A total of 115 persons had attended these live-in study experiences by 1974. The most popular retreats were held in a mountain temple where participants were able to work together, cook, and hike as well as learn about Morita therapy through lectures and discussions. Diaries are an integral part of the learning experience. The emphasis is on application of Moritist principles to life within the study group and on opening oneself to other group members through mutual verbal sharing of past experiences. As could be expected, those attending are mostly young people, primarily males.

A second group therapy format is the shudankai (literally, "group discussion meeting"). In 1974 there were seventeen shudankai groups scattered across Japan from Sapporo in the north to Fukuoka in the south. The shudankai assemble once a month in a public hall, a hotel meeting room, or the like. The 100 yen to 500 yen (40 cents to 2 dollars) each member pays covers the cost of renting the meeting place and providing light refreshments. In the nine major shudankai I attended the modal number of participants was seventeen, including one or more lay leaders. Usually one or two

*I am indebted to Dr. Ishii (1974) for his fine summary and analysis of recent Seikatsu no Hakken Kai activities.

professional persons with special interest in Morita therapy led the meetings.

The format of the meetings varies somewhat from city to city but generally packed into the four hours are self-introductions including occupation, age, descriptions of symptoms, how the person came to know about Morita therapy, his treatment experience, and how he learned of that day's meeting. In addition, visiting and regular therapists comment on various cases, ask questions, answer questions directed to them from the neurotic participants, and give lectures. The meetings are relatively informal (by Japanese standards) and time is provided for conversation and planning social get-togethers. Responsibilities for setting up the room, preparing refreshments, keeping the roll, and so on are passed around from member to member.

The therapists use typical Moritist style when communicating with members about their symptoms. They emphasize concreteness in time, place, and type of complaint. They reinforce verbalizations that indicate the member can see his problem in Moritist perspective. They use key phrases and terms associated with Morita therapy. They predict (almost always successfully) other symptoms on the basis of what the member has divulged. They emphasize the similarity of one member's symptoms to those of other members as well as to those of persons cured by Morita's method. They offer simple, clear advice for overcoming particular problems. They direct the discussion to clarification of the member's own errors and failures rather than to what happened to him, how others influenced him, or how the external environment affected him. They focus on work — what he has accomplished, what he can do at the time, and what he wants to be able to do. I have heard some therapists at these meetings guarantee cure and even predict the course of improvement over time. They certainly speak with confidence and authority.

It is both sensible and politic for the Moritist who is not a physician to refer a new member to a physician so that any physical source of his problem can be ruled out. As one lay therapist put it, once the member has been properly labeled neurotic by a physician, he feels relieved to know what kind of problem he has and is eager to begin work on it.

The therapists at these meetings support one another's stated opinions and advice. They present a solid ideological front. Professor Morita's sayings and writings are referred to as historical authoritative sources of the theory and practice presented to the members. At one meeting a photo of Morita was prominently displayed during the proceedings. Similarly, elderly persons who had been treated and cured by Morita himself are given an honored place and receive respectful attention when they speak.

I consider the *honbu gakushukai* (literally, "main branch study group meeting") to be a variant of these *shudankai*. The main differences are that the *honbu* group meets more often (weekly for three months) and that the members maintain diaries for discussion and written comment.

All these meetings are publicized in the organization's monthly magazine, *Seikatsu no Hakken*. This publication is representative of the third group thrust, use of written media to maintain current members and recruit new ones. The seventy-five-page monthly magazine is similar in format to the Moritist hospitals' magazines. It includes articles by noted therapists, accounts of members' experiences, transcriptions of tapes from *gasshuku gakushukai* and *shudankai* meetings, notices of meetings, advertisements of Moritist books, and a list of hospitals and clinics, with addresses and phone numbers, where Morita therapy is practiced.

The Seikatsu group makes use of newspaper publicity to a degree previously unknown in Moritist circles. Efforts are made to have notification of *shudankai* meetings published in local newspapers. The national *Asahi Shimban* has printed two articles on Morita therapy, including the Seikatsu group's address, as a public service. The resulting response swelled the ranks of the membership. More than simply another setting for Morita therapy, this organization represents a trend toward egalitarianism, rationalism, and broadening of impact of Morita therapy. The historical and cultural concomitants of this trend are dealt with in chapter 4.

Letter Therapy

Although T. Ishii is the name most prominently associated with correspondence therapy, many therapists occasionally offer advice and guidance to patients through the mail. Letter therapy has the same advantages as the diary exchanges discussed above: convenience, control of the medium, permanent recording, and the Japanese tradition of freedom to express inner conflicts and feelings through writing. In addition, the correspondent can maintain a distance and the anonymity uniquely available through this method. Telephones are not used extensively for this purpose as yet.

The content of some of the letter exchanges between Dr. Ishii and his clients has been published in a series of articles in the *Seikatsu no Hakken* magazine. The letters are typical of the didactics of Morita therapists in any setting. The client presents problems, complaints, questions, details of his progress, and the like. The doctor gives advice, explains, seeks information about specific problems, and so forth.

STYLES OF THERAPY

Lest the reader gain the impression that Morita therapy is uniform in practice throughout Japan, we turn to a series of brief descriptions of the various "styles" of this form of psychotherapy in the late 1960s. The development of Morita therapy along several lines was apparently promoted by Morita himself. He took several of his students aside and suggested areas that needed special investigation. And as Morita's ex-patients, students, and colleagues grew old and trained a corps of young psychiatrists, further elaboration took place.

There is no formal association of Morita therapists or Moritist hospitals to standardize methods. Few therapists have been in more than two or three Moritist hospitals. Accurate comparative statistical data are nonexistent. No one has attempted a comprehensive study along the lines of this book.

The Seikatsu no Hakken organization has begun to be a focal point for communication among the scattered therapists. Similarly, the celebrations in honor of Professor Morita's hundredth birthday in 1974 brought together a number of theoreticians and practitioners of Morita's method. Yet the styles remain individualistic. And perhaps stylistic variety is most fitting for the therapeutic projection of a life philosophy that stresses self-acceptance as one is without making the impossible effort to please everyone else all the time.

It would be misleading to use the term "schools" in this description because the total number of Japanese therapists whose major specialty is Morita therapy is probably in the neighborhood of thirty. A style in the sense used here may represent only one therapist, but each variation is well represented in the form of books and articles, by the patients cured, and so on. Since each style recognizes its intellectual debt to Professor Morita, there is much overlap among them. Yet each emphasizes a different aspect of Morita's therapy and most claim that because of their particular emphases they are more effective and truer to Professor Morita's intent than the others. We encounter a circumstance not unlike that in the development of Freudianism. A number of these styles and some of the practical aspects of their theoretical differences are discussed below.

The Zen style. — The two largest Moritist hospitals, Dr. Usa's in Kyoto and Dr. Suzuki's in Tokyo, place strong emphasis on the relationship between Morita's theory and Zen Buddhism. But in the practical application of Zen and Morita therapy to the treatment of neurotic patients, there are considerable differences even within this single style.

Dr. Suzuki's hospital is only a few miles from Kora Koseiin in Nakano, a busy section of Tokyo. The U-shaped hospital complex includes a large, modern three-story building with examination rooms, offices, parlors, patients' rooms, kitchen, and a dayroom. There is also an old-style wooden building containing the communal bath and some patients' rooms. Dr. Suzuki's home forms the third unit in the complex, which surrounds a central rose garden, ponds, and a general-purpose working area. In addition, the hospital owns a larger garden about 2 miles away. As in all Moritist hospitals, the buildings and grounds are in excellent condition because hospital upkeep is the main form of work therapy.

There are approximately forty inpatients at Suzuki Hospital, and a larger number of outpatients come to the hospital for treatment. The staff includes the director, the assistant director, a part-time physician, six nurses, three nursing assistants, and four general assistants. The high ratio of staff to inpatients (about 1:3 here) is a common feature of Moritist hospitals. The recruitment of staff from among ex-patients is also common, and Suzuki Hospital provides a neat progression of roles from patient, experienced patient, general assistant, nursing assistant, nurse, through chief nurse, illustrating the possibilities of working up within the Moritist hospital system.

As in most Moritist hospitals, there are many patients in their twenties, males outnumbering females. They are, for the most part, diagnosed *shinkeishitsu* neurotics, although there are some depressives. About half of the patients came to the hospital after having read one or more of Dr. Suzuki's books.

Dr. Suzuki was himself a patient of Morita's in the late 1920s.

During his initial period of bed rest he was cured of his neurotic condition. He is proud of the claim that his hospital is the strictest of all Moritist hospitals. He enjoys authority, snapping out commands, organizing, directing, moving people from task to task. The force of his character dominates the hospital milieu. When he enters a room or steps out into the garden the pace of work quickens, and people come running at his call. As Dr. Suzuki is fond of cultivating roses, there are hundreds of rosebushes on the hospital grounds. The patients soon begin to share Suzuki's fascination. Hours are spent caring for the roses (to the extent that umbrellas are placed over several prize bushes to protect their petals from a heavy rain), discussing their botanical names, their blooming seasons, and the various prizes they have won, arranging them, showing them to visitors, even writing about them. The roses not only distract patients from their neurotic self-rumination, but they also provide a neutral common ground for conversation among all patients, between patients and staff, and between patients and ex-patients.

In addition to his personal qualities, Dr. Suzuki is perhaps best known for his identification with Zen Buddhism. When he is asked to speak publicly or to write an article it is often assumed that he will include something about the relationship between Morita therapy and Zen. His influence as an ex-patient, a successful Morita therapist, and a graduate of Tokyo University Department of Medicine gives his ideas certain force among Japanese psychiatrists.

Suzuki is quick to point out Morita's belief that there was no direct relationship between his theory and Zen. Nevertheless, Suzuki believes that there definitely is a relationship, and a close one. Perhaps Morita feared that scientists would disregard his ideas if they seemed to be founded on a belief system. Suzuki notes many parallels between the two systems. The patient and the new monk come seeking answers to life problems. Depending on his sect, a Zen monk may be given a *koan*, a kind of puzzle with no rational solution, such as, What is the sound of one hand clapping? He is placed under social psychological pressure to solve the problem, and yet he cannot do so intellectually. He is forced to deeper levels of mental functioning. At these levels action becomes natural and spontaneous. Suzuki sees the patients' symptoms as a kind of *koan*. Their symptoms, too, are insoluble by rational understanding. The result is that the patient is forced to similar levels of functioning which ultimately free him from his obsessions and delusions and lift him to an above-average plane of existence.

Zazen (literally, "sitting Zen") is the meditative means of breaking through the *koan* into enlightenment, but there is also a lesser-known technique called "lying-down Zen." It corresponds in some degree to the absolute bed-rest period of Morita therapy. And just as the monk must make periodic appearances before his master in order to keep the master apprised of his progress and to be spurred himself to greater efforts, so the patient on absolute bed rest at Suzuki Hospital is required to present himself before the doctor in charge once each day. In both instances, it is said, one's progress is reflected in one's face and bearing so that a minimum of verbal communication (or none at all) is necessary. Even after the bed-rest period, patients at Suzuki Hospital sit together for *zazen* half an hour each morning and each night. Patients At Ushibuse Hospital in Numazu also "sit quietly" (*seiza*) twice daily in a formal posture, observing proper breathing control.

It may be noted in passing that, in pragmatic terms, *zazen* and *seiza* (like work therapy and absolute bed rest) keep patients controlled and out of trouble for long periods of time with minimal supervision. At the same time the patients feel that they are occupied in maximally meaningful and purposeful pursuits. In other words, patients move themselves toward cure at very little cost in terms of staff time and hospital space.

At Suzuki Hospital, other parallels remind one of life in a Zen temple: the clacking of wooden blocks to mark the progress of the daily schedule and the cooperative living arrangements, including cooperative cooking, cleaning, and preparing the bath. And, on occasion, a Zen monk is invited to the hospital to lecture.

There is, however, no intent to convert Moritist patients to the Zen faith, but rather to provide an auxiliary support for Moritist treatment. Support is meant in two senses here. First, Zen provides certain disciplinary techniques including *zazen*, walking properly, pouring tea properly, and so forth. These techniques can be used by the patient in rechanneling his attention and energies away from himself toward constructive behavior. The techniques may be carried out after discharge, too, thus providing the ex-patient with familiar exercises to augment his efforts at maintaining improvement outside the hospital. Second, Zen is used ideologically to support the world view of Morita therapy. The Morita therapist can cite common principles underlying both Zen with its historical prestige and Morita therapy with its immediate applicability to the neurotic problem at hand. We shall take a more careful look at the parallels between Zen and Morita therapy in chapter 5.

But one must be careful not to suggest a marriage of these two ideologies at Suzuki Hospital. Rather, the connection is metaphorically closer to the relationship between a wealthy European and his mistress. The relationship may be mentioned with pride in some circles, and the mistress's skills may be useful in achieving some of her lover's ends, but the two individuals must be careful to maintain separate existences.

On the other hand, something approaching a marriage between Morita therapy and Zen Buddhism did exist (and, to a lesser degree, still does exist) at the largest of Morita therapy hospitals, Sansei Hospital in Kyoto. It was established in 1927 in its present Zen Buddhist temple complex by a former Zen monk named Genyu Usa. He, too, was careful to give Morita sole credit for the development of Morita therapy, recognizing its formal independence from Zen, but he felt that both systems were founded on the same principle of living spontaneously. The founder of Sansei Hospital is said to have been a dominating, strict authority figure. His son, Shinichi Usa, who now directs the hospital, has preserved much of the Zen influence but projects a softer, more kindly image. The Japanese would describe him as *yasashii*.

Kyoto is a city of temples. It is a city in which one finds quiet eddies of the past just off the swirling current of automobile traffic. The atmosphere of quietness within Sansei Hospital is fostered by the surrounding temple buildings, the dark corridors, and a rule of silence. Here, too, the clacking wooden blocks mark the day's schedule. Those patients who desire Zen training go to a nearby temple, though only about a quarter of the fifty to sixty patients avail themselves of the opportunity. In the past *zazen* was a regular part of treatment, but now it is voluntary. The studied care with which every movement must be carried out until one walks and rises and works firmly and naturally is a legacy from Zen Buddhism, an integral element of therapy at Sansei Hospital.

The rules at Sansei Hospital are, along with its size and temple atmosphere, among its most noteworthy features. Because of the large number of patients, a printed brochure of rules and detailed information is distributed among inpatients. Some of the rule sheets and guidelines have been translated into English for the information of foreign visitors and for the two Western patients treated in the hospital.

The rule prohibiting speech at Sansei Hospital seems particularly restrictive. Not only during the bed-rest period but afterward as well, during meals and when working, conversation is discouraged. A sign prominently displayed in the dayroom reads, "People who converse will not get well." Although in fact there are long periods of silence at meals and during work periods, the rule finds many exceptions in practice. Chatting among patients, even between a patient on absolute bed rest and her roommate, has been observed. Similarly, the specified hours for submitting diaries for comments and the requirements for attending meetings are less rigid in practice than on paper. Discrepancies between stated rules and actual behavior in Moritist settings are discussed in some detail below. It is sufficient to say here that rules remain in perspective as means to the end of cure. They are enforced or ignored with human consideration.

Another rule forbids games and unproductive pastimes. The rationale is that Morita therapy is not recreation therapy but rather emphasizes work. On probing, I learned that work was interpreted very broadly by Morita. Neurotic patients, however, tend to seek escape from their symptoms in recreational fantasy, and Dr. Usa holds that this tendency must be suppressed for the patients's own good. Theoretically, it seems that one can use work as an escape, too, but practically work is a lesser evil because there are advantages to society and to the patient in a productive form of escape. On this point Morita therapists disagree. Recreation therapy plays a major part in some Moritist hospitals, as we shall see.

Dr. Usa feels that he has surpassed the number of admissions for maximal effectiveness of the treatment method. Sansei Hospital has room for fifty patients; in November, 1968, there were fifty-seven. Overcrowding is not unusual for Japanese mental hospitals. The problem is somewhat mitigated by the use of *tatami* mat floors and sleeping pads and quilts which are laid out on the floor at night. They allow some flexibility in room occupancy and the use of rooms for multiple purposes.

Sansei Hospital admits patients who pay by health insurance, including the national health insurance system. Insurance benefits are relatively small (in 1974, only $6.83 per day, less than the cost of a moderately priced hotel room), so the hospital must be kept at or above capacity in order to maintain itself economically. Furthermore, because the hospital cannot be overly selective in the types of patients admitted, a number of schizophrenics and depressives have entered the hospital. Neurotic patients may be discharged in fifty to sixty days, but psychotics and depressives tend to stay much longer. Thus the hospital's capacity for treating *shinkeishitsu* neurotics gradually diminishes as the number of long-term psychotics and depressives increases. The latter patients cannot fully participate in the Moritist program. The unhappy result is that those neurotics who can participate are more or less distracted by the alternative possibilities of action and treatment applied to nonparticipants. The Sansei Hospital seems to be caught in a destructive cycle initiated by economic necessity.

The analytic style. — Dr. A. Kondo is an unusual man with a special approach to Morita therapy. Having studied under Karen Horney in America, in addition to receiving training in Morita therapy at Jikei University, he is in a unique position for synthesizing the two approaches. Working with Westerners and Japanese on an outpatient basis, he is well aware of the cultural limitations as well as the cross-cultural applicability of Morita therapy.

Horney was among the psychoanalytic theorists called neo-Freudians who paid a great deal of attention to the importance of sociocultural factors in the development of neurosis. Although Horney found the cause of neurosis to be essentially a lack of security and affection in childhood, Kondo sees overaffection and overprotection as key factors in the development of neurosis among the Japanese.

Horney saw therapy as an active process in which the analyst is permitted to interpret the traces of an idealized self-image in the neurotic, get himself to see himself as he really is, and thus release his potential for healthy growth. Kondo translates this process into Moritist terms: the therapist offers his patient insight into his over-concern with ideals and perfectionism, gets him to accept himself as he really is, and thus releases the formerly symptom-directed *sei no yokubo* for healthy growth. Self-acceptance seems to be an element common to both theoretical systems; however, there may be differences between the two in what is meant by "self." In Horney's system the self is more of a conceptualized entity, whereas in Morita's system it is nothing more than a stream of experiences. Furthermore, according to Kondo (1961), both Horney and Morita require the therapist to accept the patient as he is, a fellow human, in order to demonstrate to the patient how to accept himself. And in order to be able to accept the patient, the therapist must be able to accept himself. For this reason, according to Kondo, the most effective Morita therapists have suffered from neurosis and have achieved cure through self-acceptance.

In his home-office Dr. Kondo uses illustration, advice, and direct influence on the patient's home and work milieu to achieve his treatment goals. The patient receives an explanation of his symptoms in Moritist terms. The explanation is effective, says Kondo, because it appeals to common sense, it works whenever it is tried, and it fits in with Japanese traditional thought.

For example, a student may come with the complaint that distracting thoughts bother him as he studies. The problem is so severe that he learns nothing at all, he feels he is a complete failure, and he wonders if life is worth living. Kondo asks what conditions would be best for studying, and after listening to the reply he points out that perfect conditions never exist for anyone but that people seem to get along without them. If the problem cannot be controlled by external means one must seek an internal solution. The student seems to think that he ought to be able to concentrate perfectly without drifting thoughts.

"Do you think I have no irrelevant thoughts as I talk to you now?"

"I suppose not."

"But I have. I am thinking at times about sitting uncomfortably, about dinner, about an appointment tomorrow, and several other things. But since I accept these thoughts without trying to control them, they cause me no trouble."

The patient subsequently learns that his problem is simply that he has allowed himself to be distracted from his goal. He began to think about suppressing his stray thoughts and so took on a new, sidetracking objective. And then he overestimated this single fault, feeling that it nullified all his chances to achieve anything. If he would look carefully at his idealized goal to become a great scholar and his perfectionist attempts to regulate his study setting and his state of mind, simply accept himself with his various faults, and cease struggling against drifting thoughts, he would no longer be neurotic. Therefore he is advised to study for a regular period each day whether he learns anything or not, all the while accepting distractions but keeping his eyes on the book. He may be advised to take up a hobby as another outlet for his strong need to succeed. But he will certainly hear in many ways that his desires for achievement are normal and strong, only misdirected, and that his neurosis is not a sickness but a phase of growth leading to fuller use of his capacities.

Kondo makes a remarkably plausible case for the proposition that Morita therapy, a method that seemingly avoids the assumptions of psychoanalytic insight therapy, is in reality a kind of insight therapy itself, one closely related to a recognized Western method of psychoanlysis.

The family milieu style. — This style of Morita therapy emphasizes the importance of a familylike setting for the cure of neurosis. The therapist, his family, and the patients actually live together under one roof, eat together, play together. The two hospitals classified within this category are Mr. Mizutani's and Dr. Koga's. Although differing in some important respects, these hospitals share the family-centered philosophy.

Mr. Mizutani was an ex-patient of Morita, a graduate of Tokyo University, and a former journalist. He received no formal medical training and was, to my knowledge, the only nonmedical Moritist hospital director. Mizutani Hospital employed five medical consultants (including Mizutani's son and daughter who graduated from Jikei Medical School). Mizutani's house could sleep a maximum of twenty patients plus his family of four. His wife prepared meals with the help of the patients; his son and daughter grew up working and playing alongside the patients. From many of the walls of the home framed photographs of Professor Morita looked down on the residents.

Mizutani emphasized that neurotic patients suffer primarily from a combination of selfishness and idealistic thinking. Much of his therapy was concerned with encouraging patients to work for the benefit of others. Thus, even outside the household, patients served the neighborhood by cleaning up and collecting old scrap wood. Almost daily a work party set off for a nearby shrine where the patients cleared away the undergrowth and beautified the area as a community service. Such service by means of down-to-earth physical labor was held to be especially beneficial for the patients.

The aftercare service at Mizutani Hospital was particularly well developed. An adjoining series of buildings could be rented from cooperative neighbors and used as halfway houses. Ex-patients stayed there from six months to a year, gradually readjusting to society under conditions in which they could readily get help and direction if necessary. Another feature of the aftercare service was the

ex-patient meeting. At Mizutani Hospital these meetings were frequent and well attended. The hospital magazine, too, had wide
circulation and a long history which climaxed in 1968 in a celebration marking its hundredth issue.

These features, along with Mizutani's special technique of group
diary analysis, were the main characteristics of the hospital.
Mizutani, the man, was something of an individualist. He was one of
the more popular authors of books about Morita therapy (along with
Dr. Kora and Dr. Suzuki). He expressed his attachment to the
memory of Professor Morita, which was quite strong, in a kind of
pilgrimage to Morita's home and tomb. Perhaps his attachment to
Morita is best considered a reflection of the larger familistic orientation of this therapist.

Mr. Mizutani died in 1970. Although his hospital closed down his
followers continued the Seikatsu no Hakken group he founded.

Dr. Koga was trained in psychiatry and internal medicine at Jikei
University. Morita asked him to devote his attention to the develop-
ment of Moritist theory in the field of psychosomatic medicine. Thus
Koga is the key figure in Morita therapy with specialized medical
training in a nonpsychiatric field. He practices internal medicine in a
Tokyo clinic but treats neurotic patients only in his home.

Koga's interpretation of the importance of a family setting for
Morita therapy has a special emphasis. He feels that young patients
are very idealistic and must be exposed to "raw" life. They must see
that even persons with high status get angry and depressed, that there
is grumbling and bickering at times in every family. The patients who
are temporarily "adopted" into the Koga home participate in life "as
it is" with no pretense, no formalities. There is no supporting staff,
but only the Koga family, as many as seven patients, a maid, and a
consulting psychologist and social worker.

The fee at Dr. Koga's hospital is the highest encountered,
4,000 yen ($11.11) per day, more than twice that of other Moritist
hospitals. The principal reason is that Koga specializes in treating
patients who are both neurotically and physically ill. In particular, he
treats patients suffering from complaints mimicking an early stage of
tuberculosis. Since special considerations within the family are kept
at a minimum, everyone must eat the same nourishing diet required
by these quasi-tubercular patients.

At the time of my last visit to Dr. Koga's hospital, his mother
had unexpectedly passed away. Patients were assisting with the

funeral arrangements. They, too, felt keenly the loss to the family.

Harmonization style. — Tanishima's theoretical approach emphasizes the concept of harmony in the treatment of neurosis. According to Tanishima, truth was defined by Morita as the harmonization of subjective experience and objective reality. When disharmony prevails, the neurotic person is not living in reality. Therapy aims at merging and harmonizing subjectivity and objectivity. Similarly, when a person experiences his anxiety as separate from himself he suffers from a polarization of feeling and self. When he immerses himself in his anxiety — that is, accepts it or harmonizes himself with it — the anxiety disappears.

At Ushibuse Hospital in Numazu, a similar approach directs patients toward merging with or harmonizing with nature's reality. Nature walks, systematic observations of natural phenomena, and meditation help the patient to see himself as part of the natural world and to place himself in harmony with it.

The eclectic style. — The hospitals belonging to two former chairmen of Jikei University's Department of Neurology and Psychiatry, Dr. Nomura and Dr. Kora, use the eclectic style. Both doctors continue to have a great deal of influence at Jikei University, admitting many of their patients on referral from Jikei's outpatient clinic.

These hospitals employ other (particularly Western) forms of therapy in addition to Morita therapy, interpret Morita's theory rather broadly, and admit a relatively wide range of diagnostic classes of patients. Recreation is emphasized as well as work, and a good part of the patients' evenings may be spent in watching television. These institutions seem to serve not only as Moritist hospitals for neurotics but as quiet convalescent homes for a few patients, such as psychotics in remission.

Forty-five minutes by train from central Tokyo, Dr. Nomura's hospital is located in a quiet suburb. It is a fairly small hospital even by Moritist standards. Patients number from nine to fifteen, but a series of recent building and remodeling projects have provided more than adequate space to meet the hospital's needs. As in most Moritist hospitals there are a number of outpatients who visit regularly. Dr. Nomura hopes someday to open an electroencephalogram clinic to augment even further his hospital's capabilities.

Nomura, aged and ill, has passed on most of the routine

responsibilities of running the hospital to a younger assistant director. He does, however, handle special cases, and he delivers a weekly *kowa* lecture on Sunday mornings. He emphasizes that Morita's ideas are a life philosophy applicable to the daily activities and orientation of every Japanese, not only neurotics. He remarks that it is the look of happiness and freedom on the faces of the discharged patients which assures him that his life was well spent.

Perhaps the most notable feature of Nomura's hospital, aside from the eclectic nature of the treatment is the influence of the nurses on the daily lives of the patients and on the general operation of the hospital. The two nurses are outgoing and energetic. They work and play with the patients and yet manage to perform their clerical and pharmacological duties, too. They show a genuine familistic concern for their patients. They are maternal but not overprotective, living out their interpretation of Morita's philosophy in purposeful activity. In this small hospital with rather unobtrusive doctors, the nurses seem to dominate the milieu — an arrangement agreeable to all.

Dr. Kora's hospital, Kora Koseiin, is merely touched on here, since its fuller description is the subject of chapter 2. In the West it is perhaps the best-known Moritist hospital, for here Caudill, Leonhardt, Wendt, and others gathered much of their data on Morita therapy. It is perhaps the most eclectic of Moritist hospitals, utilizing group therapy, counseling, electroconvulsive therapy, recreation therapy, hypnotherapy, medication, and convalescent care in addition to Morita therapy.

Perhaps because of Kora Koseiin's larger size (it handles up to twenty-four patients comfortably), staff-patient relations are somewhat more formalized than at Nomura Hospital. The personal characteristics of doctors and nurses at Kora Koseiin are such that the nurses do not overtly dominate the scene, as they do at Nomura Hospital.

The group therapy style. — Dr. Fujita's hospital is oriented toward the group therapy aspect of Morita therapy. Except for relatively brief contacts with Dr. Fujita, his wife, and two young psychologists, the group of patients under the supervision of a professional *tsukisoi* (a kind of private nurse) are left pretty much to themselves. The number of patients in the hospital is small, around seven or eight, but the patients represent a variety of diagnoses of which approximately half would be classified as psychotic.

The hospital features classes in sketching and cloisonné ware, psychodrama, group reading, and a group diary. Group life centers in a large room with a kitchen bar, central table, sofas, and a large amount of equipment for recreation, including a sewing machine, television, a stereo set, books, newspapers, magazines, a ceramic oven, and a guitar.

At Fujita's hospital the patients have as much freedom as at any of the Moritist hospitals, if not more. The freedom is particularly noticeable because of the dearth of medical supervision on the grounds during much of the day. Nevertheless, doors are open, the drawers containing patient records are unlocked and easily accessible, and patients are simply expected to treat the expensive equipment well, request permission before going into town for shopping or a bath or haircut, and so forth. The responsibility demonstrated by Japanese patients in Moritist hospitals (and in general psychiatric hospitals, for that matter) deserves examination in detail later. Is is worth mentioning in passing that it is not uncommon to see quite disturbed institutionalized patients with free, unsupervised access to expensive and potentially dangerous equipment, to items of decoration including glass-encased fragile dolls, and to the unaccompanied children of staff members. These children may be found playing freely among the patients even in locked wards of general psychiatric hospitals. The mentally disturbed patient's willingness to accept this responsibility not only eases the administrative burden on the staff but permits wider latitude in their choice of methods of treatment.

One feature of Fujita's hospital is a kind of group diary written in turn by selected patients. The diary includes a record of hospital events such as the menu, recreational activities, work accomplished, and visitors as well as notes on the weather, world events, and so forth. Records of group meetings are also kept in turn by the patients. These notes become public (group) documents available to all members of the hospital society.

The psychiatric ward style. — In a few large private psychiatric hospitals (e.g., Kaisei Hospital in Osaka and Mishima Morita Hospital), as well as in several university psychiatric hospitals, special buildings, wards, or rooms are set aside for treating patients with Morita therapy. The large majority of patients in these hospitals, however, are psychotic and are treated with chemotherapy and are under custodial care.

The atmosphere of these treatment settings is more like that of a hospital than like that of a family. A characteristic problem is that natural work is hard to generate, given the paid janitorial staff. In addition, the variety of severely disturbed patients living alongside neurotics makes it difficult to maintain the group cohesion found in other Moritist inpatient settings.

The narrow diagnosis style. — This style is conceptually contrasted with the neo-Morita style, to be dealt with next. The narrow diagnosis style is notable in the Kyushu area. It holds that Morita therapy is a specialized treatment for a special disorder, *shinkeishitsu* neurosis. Morita therapy is not indicated for other types of neurosis, such as depression and hysteria. Nor is it effective in treating psychosis, sociopathy, addiction, manic depression, or character disorders involving weak will. Differential diagnosis becomes extremely important, because therapists of this persuasion insist that disorders other than *shinkeishitsu* be treated by other forms of therapy. One effect of this treatment policy has been a general decline in the use of Morita therapy in this part of southern Japan because the pure forms of *shinkeishitsu*, as described by Morita, seem to appear less frequently among modern Japanese neurotics. Mixed forms of neurosis seem to be on the increase. These mixed forms provide complications for those who wish to use Morita therapy as an adjunct to other therapeutic measures. It is far easier to add an antidepressant drug as an adjunct to handle depression during psychoanalysis than it is to add Morita therapy to handle the *shinkeishitsu* elements of a neurosis while continuing psychoanalytic care.

The medical staff at Kyushu and Okayama universities generally hold to a narrow diagnostic indication for Morita therapy.

The neo-Moritist style. — This style centers in Tokyo, particularly among the younger psychiatrists at Jikei University. Its philosophy is basically the opposite of the narrow diagnosis style. From this perspective Morita therapy is seen to be of use in the treatment of nearly all psychiatric disturbances, from hysteria to schizophrenia in remission. Morita therapy may be used with both outpatients and inpatients. Furthermore, the possibility of application of Moritist principles outside Japan is seriously considered. In fact, in almost every direction possible the proponents of this style are broadening the boundaries and enlarging the scope of Morita therapy. Parallels with a number of Western psychotherapies are spelled out, and broad interpretations of both Moritist and Western psychotherapies are made in order to facilitate favorable comparisons between the two.

This style is slightly different from the eclectic style in that Kora and Nomura use various therapies simultaneously, but recognize them as separate. The tendency of neo-Moritists is to utilize these therapies, give them a Moritist-oriented twist and interpretation, and then call the synthesis neo-Moritist.

Summary — This section has emphasized the variations within Morita therapy. Possibly because of Morita's own individualism he recognized the individual needs of his patients and students and so modified his discussions with them to suit their cases. One supposes that on a metalevel there were consistent principles for tailoring the modifications to fit the patients, but these principles were not recorded. At any rate, the theory that is recorded is subject to vagueness and omissions and generally provides no clear-cut evidence to support one or another of the diverse interpretations of his patients turned therapists. The result has been styles so different in interpretation of theory that they produce diametrically opposite therapeutic practice.

For example, in a survey of Morita therapy hospitals and clinics (Ohara et al., 1966), three hospitals responded that they had a regular program of recreational activity as part of therapy but seven responded that they did not, some remarking that Morita therapy is a work therapy, not a play therapy. These results clearly reflect a basic disagreement. As mentioned earlier, some therapists forbid recreation because it is seen as an escape and a hindrance to the development of habits of single-minded attention to work. Other therapists interpret work as any activity involving concentration of one's attention outside the self. When games are permitted they are often fast-paced and absorbing. Examples are ping-pong and *hyakunin isshu*, a card game requiring quick recognition and fast reflexes similar in principle to, but more complicated than, slapjack.

Another area of opposing practice is in the discussion of symptoms by patients. Morita's theory states rather unequivocally that patients are not to write about their symptoms in their diaries or to converse among themselves concerning their symptoms. At some hospitals this rule is interpreted as a restriction on complaining about symptoms and not a blanket prohibition of the topic. At Kora Koseiin, for example, therapists point out the advantages of discussions among patients. The patients learn that they are not alone or "special" in having certain symptoms; they can discover that their feelings of shyness or ugliness or of having bad body odor are not directly noticeable by others.

On the other hand, Moritists with a stricter interpretation of theory claim that such discussion does little more than focus the patients' attention on themselves and their symptoms, the very thing Morita therapy is trying to eliminate. And at least one director interprets the prohibition so broadly as to limit casual conversation on any topic, as noted above.

Though basic ambiguity within Morita's theory may be the foundation on which the variations in styles were erected, the single main factor that differentiates the practice of one hospital from that of another seems to be the character and interests of the director and his assistant therapists. It is at Kora Koseiin that patients are drawn into an interest in golf, Dr. Kora's hobby; at Suzuki Hospital the director's fascination for roses is transmitted to the patients; and at Sansei Hospital Dr. Usa's devotion to Zen results in patient interest in the same subject.

Morita therapists represent a wide variety of character, from the effeminate to the masculine, from the humble to the egotistical, from the active and domineering to the withdrawn, almost schizoid, from the witty, polished cosmopolitan to the throat-clearing and slow-thinking philosopher. There continues to be a place for each of these individuals within the therapeutic approach of a great individualist. How consistent it is that these men, who learned and teach a world view valuing self-acceptance and productivity regardless of one's personal qualities, should so clearly reflect a wide variety of personal idiosyncrasy. In a society that stresses conformity they reflect no single personality mold, and each hospital reveals the distinctiveness of its founder.

II DETAILED ANALYSIS OF A SINGLE MORITIST HOSPITAL

Chapter 1 presents a broad perspective of Morita therapy and a slightly more detailed picture of the various styles of the therapy. Chapter 2 is devoted to the analysis of a single hospital, Kora Koseiin, as it existed in 1969. After a brief description of the physical setting, the emphasis is on the social setting, including official and unofficial roles and characteristic interactions.

THE PHYSICAL SETTING

Kora Koseiin is located in a residential and light industrial area in northwest Tokyo. From the transportation center of Shinjuki a ten-minute train ride to Shimochiai Station, followed by a ten-minute walk, brings one to the main gate of Kora Koseiin. The surrounding buildings are tall, fairly old, and dirtied by the polluted metropolitan Tokyo air. The neighborhood is crowded and busy, with narrow, snaking, much-used streets and no sidewalks.

In contrast with the surroundings, the hospital's entrance gate opens into a large shaded well-kept garden. A low wall, slightly more than 5 feet high, runs along the two sides of the hospital grounds facing the street, and a series of higher walls run along the irregular shaped boundary between the grounds and the adjacent neighborhood dwellings. About one-third of the hospital area is devoted to greenery. The impression is one of relative silence, peace, and order in the midst of a hustling lower-middle-class urban district. The sign at the entrance reads "Kora Koseiin," literally, "Kora's Revitalized Life Medical Institution."

As one enters the main gate and walks along the stepping-stones, to the right is a small wooden cottage now used for storage. Next is a functional modern two-story stucco building in which are located Dr. Kora's room and single rooms for fourteen patients; each room has a built-in closet and is simply furnished with a bed, a desk, and a chair. Behind this building is a bathing room with a large tub heated by a wood stove. The roof of the bathing unit provides one area for drying the wash.

The stepping-stones run on between the two story building and the administration building. The latter, a one-story, irregularly shaped wooden structure, contains a waiting room, an examination room, doctors' offices, nurses' office and quarters, dining room, kitchen, bathroom, storage rooms, a laundry room, and a small hothouse. At the far end of the administration building the path turns sharply left and a U-shaped complex of buildings surrounding a central garden comes into sight. The open end of the U is on the far side and contains the ping-pong area, the golf practice cage, and a small garden devoted primarily to roses. The bottom of the U is formed by the building that comprises the group recreation room, the office for the accountant-bookkeeper, and the occupational therapist's room. To the right is the work therapy shop and a long, narrow, Japanese-style *tatami*-floored ward housing four patients in single rooms. To the left is a wing of the administration building and another Japanese-style ward with facilities for three patients and the assistant cook's quarters.

Except for the single two-story building, the hospital complex is fairly old, having been rebuilt after the World War II bombing, but it is well cared for. The gardens contain paths, benches, goldfish ponds, and miniature golf course. The hospital is not isolated from its surroundings, but nevertheless it is set apart from them not only physically by the wall and the contrast in setting, but also psychologically and socially. Contact with other persons in the neighborhood is almost exclusively impersonal and economic.

THE SOCIAL SETTING

Within the walls of Kora Koseiin, there exists a small, complex society. According to Caudill (1958), the hospital's small society is governed by a hierarchy of formal roles crosscut by informal relationships.

Role Categories

Six broad, formal role categories form the social system at Kora Koseiin. They are doctor, nurse, work therapist, patients, semi-patients (including outpatients and discharged patients), and service personnel (including cooks, *tsukisoi*, and an accountant-bookkeeper). Each role category is further subdivided (these subdivisions are discussed later).

Doctor. — The doctor represents medical authority and knowledge at Kora Koseiin. He is a physician and an expert in Morita therapy. He may have other interests and expertise in the field of psychotherapy, such as a broad knowledge of modern psycho-pharmacological methods or of hypnotherapy. He may be proficient in arts and skills outside the medical profession, such as artistic design, drawing, ping-pong, and golf. But, though he can and does display these auxiliary talents within the hospital setting, he is above all a physician who is the teacher-guide Morita therapist.

His job is not time-bounded in the strict sense. He may be at the hospital late at night or he may accompany patients on a weekend outing. His job is difficult but varied and, for him, enjoyable. His satisfaction comes primarily from a genuine confidence in Morita therapy which develops as he watches patients "get well" in the Moritist sense. His role-fixed tasks include diagnosis, counseling, prescribing medication, making rounds, deciding about admission, visits, and discharge, administering specialized therapy such as electric shock treatments, correcting the patients' diaries, and running the hospital. He may also play with the patients, work with them (on rare occasions), assist them with crafts, help them obtain jobs outside the hospital, write articles for journal publication, and practice other forms of psychotherapy as his interests dictate.

The doctor role is divided into five subcategories: director, assistant director, part-time psychiatrist, research psychiatrist, and former therapist.

The director of Kora Koseiin is Dr. Takehisa Kora. He founded the hospital in his home in 1939. He treats some outpatients, plays with the patients, works with the patients, delivers the weekly *kowa* lecture, comments on the patients' diaries, and makes major administrative decisions. Since he is sixty-nine years old, the time and energy he has to invest in the hospital are limited. He has, in addition to his hospital duties, many outside obligations and interests such as writing and lecturing. Much of the daily contact with the patients, and many of the minor administrative details that require constant touch with the hospital situation, fall within the domain of duties assigned to the assistant director.

The assistant director is Dr. Abe. He is the second in command. It is understood that as Dr. Kora gradually retires from his responsibilities at the hospital Dr. Abe will take up the slack. He carries most of the everyday therapeutic and administrative load at Kora Koseiin. His position is secure and personally rewarding. The stability of his personality, the slow pace of the hospital routine, and the delegation of minor tasks to other staff members allow him to function smoothly in this demanding role. In contrast with the other doctors his interests outside the hospital are limited. The hospital is a large part of his life.

The part-time psychiatrist is Dr. Iwai, who visits the hospital twice a week. His tasks are essentially the same as those of the assistant director except that there is less administrative decision making. Dr. Iwai has many outside interests. He is a prolific writer; he practices hypnotherapy and lectures on the subject; and he is active in research at Jikei University. He is independently wealthy. He is an artist and an art connoisseur, numbers Europeans and Americans among his acquaintances, and reveals a romantic attachment to things Japanese. He brings a breath of the outside world into the hospital on his visiting days.

The research psychiatrist is Dr. Kim. He, too represents the outside world in that he is a Korean, heavily influenced by Korean Buddhism and Western dynamic psychiatry. He comes to the hospital three times a week. His tasks are essentially the same as those of Dr. Iwai, with two exceptions. He sees very few outpatients in consultation, and he leads a group psychotherapy meeting once a week. His position is somewhat ambiguous in that he is not paid for his services at the hospital; ostensibly he is there to learn about Morita therapy through practice, but actually, after nearly two years of practice, he is functioning as an experienced but unpaid Morita therapist.

Some fifteen therapists have received training in Morita therapy at Kora Koseiin over the years. Although they go on to other positions, they maintain their ties with the hospital and its director. In addition to scattered informal visits there is an annual gathering of these doctors around a banquet table in the administration building of the hospital.

Nurse. — If the doctor is primarily the trained guide of Morita therapy, the nurse is the service-oriented assistant. She performs the service tasks that connect doctor and patient. She carries the food tray to the patient on absolute bed rest; she prepares medication, answers the telephone, collects fees, keeps records, runs errands, and generally handles all the minor physical, economic, and social tasks that must be dealt with so that the process of therapy can proceed smoothly.

Her attitude toward the doctors is one of respect and obedience, but she may politely disagree and joke freely with them when the occasion arises. Her attitude toward the patients is one of casual friendliness. Patients will come and go, so she reserves her deeper friendships for other nurses, cooks, and a few people outside the hospital.

The nurse generally uses polite speech forms and honorifics. She uses the polite *san* for "Mister" when referring to patients; the doctors are likely to use the less formal, less respectful term, *kun.* Her role is somewhat complicated in that her sex (and, for a junior nurse, her age) carries low status in Japan, but her occupational role is slowly rising in status. In an extreme case, the demeanor of a young, junior nurse interacting with an elderly male patient is the end product of a balancing of several competing social vectors. The older male hospital director and the young female assistant cook encounter this social balancing problem to a much lesser degree.

The nurses live at Kora Koseiin. As with the doctors, their jobs are not time-bound, although they, too, have official duty nights. Occasionally they find time to play a game or two of ping-pong with patients, or they may join them for evening games. More likely, in the evenings they gather in one room or another and watch television or talk among themselves.

The nurse role may be divided into three subcategories: chief nurse, nurse, and junior nurse. These subcategories correspond to formal training, seniority at the hospital, and age. The chief nurse has more administrative duties and acts as chauffeur and private secretary to the director, but she shares in all the other nursing tasks as well. The two junior nurses, still in their teens, have friendly peer contact with the patients. The chief nurse and the nurse are both ex-patients. They, like Dr. Kora and Mr. Maruyama, the work therapist, have experienced neurosis themselves.

Work therapist. — The role of the work therapist is quite

different from that of the occupational therapist in American mental hospitals. Although there are some superficial similarities between the two, the work therapist role in Moritist hospitals is uniquely a product of Morita therapy as it has developed since Morita's time. The work therapist is a living example of the effect of following Moritist principles. At Kora Koseiin this position is filled by a paid ex-patient, Mr. Maruyama. At other hospitals, it may be filled by advanced patients, servants, nursing assistants, or even nurses. But in every Moritist hospital there is someone who energetically leads the patients in the everyday manual tasks necessary to the upkeep of the hospital, someone who knows what needs to be done, where the tools are kept, and what the proper method for accomplishing the chore might be. He is a kind of foreman for patients, but he is more than that. Dr. Kim calls him the "culture carrier of the hospital."

It is unlikely that in Professor Morita's hospital, Morita himself filled the work therapist role. But as advancing age and professionalization separate doctor and patient, the need for someone in close contact through cooperative labor with the patient, someone to serve as a model, became the necessity. The older therapists simply cannot engage in much physical labor, and the younger therapists are too busy with more professional, "cleaner" tasks to fulfill the modeling function.

Mr. Maruyama fills the role admirably. He has been at his job for several years, and he is well versed in the theory of Morita therapy. More than that, from his daily experience he knows the effects of living under the Moritist life philosophy. At times his tension and speech blocking and stuttering betray his former patient status, but, nevertheless, he carries out his tasks and teaching assignments with a single-mindedness of purpose which epitomizes the aim of Morita therapy.

The work therapist holds a pivotal role in many senses. He is the repository of a wealth of knowledge on the practical maintenance of the hospital grounds and buildings. He organizes the daily work groups. He is both student-patient and therapist-guide. He has more regular contact with the patients than any other staff member. He eats with the patients and attends the kowa lectures with them.

Although he is among the patients, he is not one of them. He forms no close ties with any of them, nor does he establish deep relationships with other staff members as the nurses do among themselves. His life is primarily one of getting his jobs done and, recently, of studying for the night school class in accounting which fills his evenings with meaningful endeavor.

He is most comfortable in work clothes, sandals, and a worn straw hat, working in the garden or talking about roses or fruits in season. His position in the status hierarchy at the hospital is somewhat ambiguous. That, too, is relatively unimportant to him. His work is near at hand, and that is where his attention is primarily directed.

Patients. — Patients form the least stable role category at Kora Koseiin. There is a constant stream of new faces passing through successive phases of treatment. The staff is well aware of the temporary quality of the occupants of the patient role. Staff members remark about the changing atmosphere of the hospital as different combinations of personalities form the core of the patient population. And, as noted above, they usually reserve their special friendships for role groups with less fluctuation in membership.

Selected background data on the patient population at Kora Koseiin in 1966 and 1967 are presented in tables 10 to 12. The data are presented by year because the variance between the years would be concealed if only combined data were presented. The patients were relatively young (table 10): over 60 percent were younger than thirty in both 1966 and 1967, and over 80 percent were younger than forty in 1966 (over 70 percent in 1967); median and modal ages were in the twenties. In comparison with the general Japanese population, young people and women of early middle age were overrepresented and elderly persons of both sexes were underrepresented. Males outnumbered females in a ratio of approximately 3:2.

Occupationally, more than 50 percent of the males were students or white-collar workers (table 11). Nearly a quarter of the females were students and nearly a half were housewives. In comparison with the Japanese population as a whole, students were overrepresented and farmers were greatly underrepresented (*U.S. Army Area Handbook for Japan*, 1964). Among the patients were physicians, teachers, attorneys, stewardesses, beauticians, printers, butlers, maids, farmers. There is some selective bias here, though, because the cost of hospitalization at Kora Koseiin is relatively expensive by Japanese standards. Since patients are not admitted under the national health insurance program, people at a lower economic level are unlikely to seek admission to the hospital.

TABLE 10

Kora Koseiin Inpatients by Age and Sex, Compared with Japanese Census Figures, in 1966 and 1967

Age	Males			Females			Total	
	General census figures for Japan	Kora Koseiin inpatients		General census figures for Japan	Kora Koseiin inpatients		General census figures for Japan	Kora Koseiin inpatients
		1966	1967		1966	1967		1966 and 1967
Age range		104	79		50	63		296
		16-73	16-61		15-59	17-78		15-78
Mean Age		28.3	30.7		29.7	33.6		30.4
Standard deviation		11.6	11.9		11.7	14.4		12.3
Age groups	%	%	%	%	%	%	%	%
10-19	11.4	21.1	11.3	10.7	22.0	20.6	11.0	18.5
20-29	18.0	45.1	53.1	17.5	38.0	26.9	17.7	42.1
30-39	16.3	22.0	15.0	15.6	14.0	25.3	16.0	19.5
40-49	10.2	1.8	10.0	11.9	14.0	14.2	11.0	8.7
50-59	8.6	5.7	7.5	9.3	10.0	6.7	8.9	7.0
60 and older	9.0	3.8	2.5	10.5	0.0	6.3	9.7	3.3
Unknown	0.0	0.0	0.0	0.0	2.0	0.0	0.0	0.3

Source: Bureau of Statistics, Office of Prime Minister, in Nippon, 1966, table 4-5, p. 37.

TABLE 11

Kora Koseiin Inpatients by Occupation and Sex in 1966 and 1967

	Males				Females				Total	
									1966 and	
Occupation	1966		1967		1966		1967		1967	
	N	(%)	N	(%)	N	(%)	N	(%)	N	(%)
Student	39	(37.5)	20	(25.3)	11	(22)	15	(23.8)	85	(28.7)
White-collar worker	26	(25.0)	30	(37.9)	8	(16)	4	(6.3)	68	(22.9)
Professional	3	(2.8)	7	(8.8)	0	(0)	2	(3.1)	12	(4.0)
Merchant	5	(4.8)	1	(1.2)	0	(0)	0	(0)	6	(2.0)
Skilled	6	(5.7)	2	(2.5)	3	(6)	5	(7.9)	16	(5.4)
Other	6	(5.7)	6	(7.5)	3	(6)	6	(9.5)	21	(7.0)
Unemployed*	9	(8.6)	10	(12.6)	25	(50)	31	(49.2)	75	(25.3)
Unknown	5	(4.8)	0	(0)	0	(0)	0	(0)	5	(1.6)

*Unemployed category includes housewives.

Geographically, Kora Koseiin draws its patients from almost all of Japan. Slightly less than 50 percent came from outside the Tokyo and nearby Kanagawa areas in 1966 and 1967. As would be expected from status consideration, females had somewhat less mobility than males (table 12) in those years.

The hospital specializes in the treatment of neurosis. This selectivity is revealed by the relative frequencies of neurotics and psychotics and others treated in 1966 and 1967 (table 13).

The mean length of hospitalization in 1966 and 1967, as presented in table 14 was about a week longer than the theoretical ideal. Those hospitalized for one week or less, and those hospitalized for six months or more, were not included in the mean calculation because they did not receive standard Morita therapy and their inclusion would needlessly have distorted the mean.

Among the patients social relationships naturally spring up. These patients are, for the most part, young people thrown together by circumstance, sharing a common anguish, a number of work and play interests, and a common goal. In such a setting friendships quickly form. Some of these ties survive the role changes

TABLE 12

Kora Koseiin Inpatients by Home Address and Sex in 1966 and 1967

Home address	Males				Females				Total	
	1966		1967		1966		1967		1966 and 1967	
	N	(%)	N	(%)	N	(%)	N	(%)	N	(%)
Tokyo	40	(38)	33	(42)	20	(40)	35	(56)	128	(43.2)
Kanagawa Prefecture	9	(9)	11	(14)	5	(10)	6	(10)	31	(10.4)
Other	55	(53)	35	(44)	25	(50)	22	(35)	137	(46.2)

Note: Range includes thirty three of Japan's forty two prefectures plus Tokyo, Kyoto, Osaka, and Okinawa, but not Hokkaido.

TABLE 13

Kora Koseiin Inpatients by Moritist Diagnosis and Sex in 1966 and 1967

Diagnosis	Males				Females				Total	
	1966		1967		1966		1967		1966 and 1967	
	N	(%)	N	(%)	N	(%)	N	(%)	N	(%)
Shinkeishitsu neurosis	78	(75.0)	68	(86.0)	35	(70.0)	50	(79.3)	231	(78.0)
Psychosis	11	(10.5)	5	(6.3)	8	(16.0)	8	(12.6)	32	(10.8)
Other	15	(14.4)	6	(7.5)	6	(12.0)	4	(6.3)	31	(10.4)
Unknown	0	(0)	1	(2.0)	1	(2.0)	1	(1.5)	2	(0.6)

accompanying discharge, and some survive geographic separation so that letters and meetings continue between patient friends for twenty years and more.

But even when no close friendships develop the patients at any given time feel an esprit de corps springing from a perceived mutual understanding of their neurotic suffering, the transference involved in confession and in the outpouring of deep feelings and cherished ideas, the shared work, kindnesses, and rewards in the hospital setting, and the common understanding of a new way of looking at the world and themselves. In this respect the patient relationships

TABLE 14

Hospitalization Period of Kora Koseiin Neurotic Patients
by Sex in 1966 and 1967

	Males		Females		Total
	1966	1967	1966	1967	1966 and 1967
PATIENTS INCLUDED IN MEAN DAYS CALCULATION					
Number of patients	68	61	27	39	195
Mean days of hospitalization	40.7	38.5	34.9	34.8	38.0
Standard deviation	27.7	28.7	19.7	23.3	26.2
Range (days)	2-342	3-457	1-457	3-154	1-457
PATIENTS NOT INCLUDED IN MEAN DAYS CALCULATION					
Length of stay unknown	0	0	0	2	2
Hospitalized one week or less	8	7	7	9	31
Hospitalized six months or more	2	0	2	0	4
Total number of patients	78	68	35	50	232

appear to be somewhat like those of monastic monks or military recruits in training.

If the patient role is to be described in a single word, the only suitable one is "student." The patient enters Kora Koseiin to learn about himself and his illness (as has been shown, these two issues are conceptually not wholly separate) and to be cured. He may have expected the knowledge itself to cure him, or medication, or whatever. But he is placed in the role of student. And with the therapist as teacher-guide, the work therapist as model, and the nurse as assistant the patient-student finds himself in a beneficial learning situation.

The role-fixed tasks of the patient are varied. He is normally required to clean his room, wash his clothes, attend to his minor personal needs, keep his tools straightened, and perform minor services for others such as errands, returning empty dishes to the kitchen sink, and so on. There is some leeway in carrying out these minor tasks, and the discrepancy between the compulsive straightening of slippers or tools which one reads about in the literature and the actual practice is at times extreme.

Each morning on a blackboard in the dining room the morning's cleaning assignments are listed. For example, on one May morning they were: doctors' offices (three people), first- and second-floor halls of the new building (two people), toilets (two people), recreation room (one person), old buildings (two people), crafts room (one person), garden paths (three people), dining room (one person), bath (one person). In addition to these assignments work groups are formed to plant or weed, pick and dry fruit, paint, and the like. These tasks are all seen as part of the therapy. There is a great deal of variation among patients as to how long they actually keep busy each day. Some patients do enough to have something to write in their diaries and satisfy the work therapist, then they chat, read, and rest in their rooms.

There are a number of subcategories within the patient role group. One can subdivide patients by symptom. Most patients can state their own diagnoses (although they do not know the name or dosage of their medication) and the diagnoses of the other patients as well. The interactions among patients include searching for similarities and differences in their symptoms and in their attitudes toward these symptoms. The typical neurotic patients, who compose the core group at Kora Koseiin are generally stiff, very self-conscious, overcontrolled, and lacking in spontaneity; and they have a tendency to retire to their rooms when under stress. Patients who do not conform to this description, particularly mildly schizophrenic patients who are occasionally out of contact and rather manneristic, stay on the fringe of the patient group. They are never rejected outright, but they are never forced to join in beyond their inclination to do so.

Another subdivision is between the new patient and the experienced patient. The new patient is expected to display gaps in his understanding of Moritist principles and in their application to daily life. His mistakes are tolerated and patiently and repeatedly corrected by other patients and by the staff. However, the experienced patient who continues to rebel by repeated questioning of Morita therapy's effectiveness, by complaints, and by slothful behavior gradually finds himself isolated from the patient group.

Should he finally follow instructions and begin to understand his disorder in Moritist terms, his potential for becoming an example noticeably increases.

"Examples" and "favorites" may be considered as subcategories of patients at Kora Koseiin. These roles are usually occupied by the same people, the patients who showed remarkable improvement during their hospital stay. They are emphasized in reports, displayed to visitors, and held up to other patients in person or by report. They are given special privileges such as taking trips with the director and going on shopping excursions outside the hospital for the staff. They are usually given more responsible and stimulating tasks than fall to the lot of other patients, who sometimes exhibit jealousy of the favorites. The only sign of potential physical violence among patients observed during my sixteen-month stay at the hospital was directed toward a favorite patient.

Semipatients — There are several subcategories of persons who are not in admission status for the full course of Morita therapy. Some are outpatients who have never been admitted for inpatient treatment, and others are discharged patients who maintain contact with the hospital as outpatients. Still others are ex-patients who are just visiting or persons who suffer from recurrent disorders (depressions, for example) and are admitted for only a few days or weeks at a time. Since these semipatients are all short-term visitors to the hospital, they cannot participate fully in the patient subculture.

Discharged patients who return to Kora Koseiin to visit find themselves warmly welcomed by the staff and held in high esteem by the patients. They are a self-selected group in that they have usually done well after discharge. Otherwise, they would probably be too ashamed to return except for rehospitalization.

Service personnel. — The cooks and the occasional professional *tsukisoi* are servants and companions to staff and patients. Their number fluctuates with the number of patients in the hospital, with the hospital's financial situation, and with the needs of particular patients.

The primary responsibilities of the cooks are the purchasing and preparing of food and the cleaning up after meals. They are likely to receive assistance in these functions from nurses and from female patients. Food seems to take on special importance in "total institutions," as Goffman (1961) has termed them. The patients at Kora

Koseiin often discuss the food and its preparation and wonder when it will be ready.

The senior cook is an old, motherly woman, dedicated to and experienced in her job. The junior cook is still in her teens. She sometimes participates in ping-pong and in the evening gatherings of patients, but her closest ties are to the junior nurses.

The bookkeeper comes and goes regularly and quietly with minimal participation in hospital social life.

The *tsukisoi* is a professional servant who cares for a patient on a private basis, often around the clock (Caudill, 1961). Patients who require *tsukisoi* attendants do not remain long at Kora Koseiin, but are soon transferred to other hospitals. Thus the *tsukisoi* has little opportunity for developing long-term relationships with the other role groups.

It seems strange to append a nonhuman category to a discussion of role groups, but animals do have an important socializing function within many Moritist hospitals, including Kora Koseiin. In some instances withdrawn, socially oversensitive people can at first relate more comfortably to animals than to humans. At Kora Koseiin there had been chickens in the past, and during the period of research there were a cat and a dog, several pairs of caged birds, a caged chipmunk, and various fish in the ponds. The dog was a particular favorite among the patients. Of course, the patients were responsible for caring for the pets as part of work therapy.

A Role Hierarchy

The relationships among (and within) the formal role groups at Kora Koseiin are to no little degree determined by a formal role hierarchy. Soon after my arrival at Kora Koseiin I developed a hypothetical hierarchy based on my background knowledge of status distinctions in Japanese culture. This hypothesized role hierarchy is found in table 15, column 1. The ranking was arrived at by using the criteria of (1) professional education, (2) male dominance, and (3) seniority in the hospital, in that order.

Of course, the authority associated with a role varies from situation to situation, and the relevant role from among those applicable to a given individual similarly varies from situation to situation. Nevertheless, it seemed possible to find some meaningful overall

TABLE 15

Formal Role Hierarchies

	Column 1 Hypothesized order	Column 2 Questionnaire order	Column 10 Behavioral order
Doctors	Hospital director	Hospital director	Hospital director
	Assistant director	Assistant director	Assistant director
	Staff doctor	Staff doctor	Staff doctor
	Research doctor	Chief nurse	Research doctor
	Anthropologist	Research doctor	Anthropologist
Nursing Staff	Chief nurse	Nurse	Chief nurse
	Nurse	Work therapist	Nurse
	Junior nurse	Anthropologist	Junior nurse
Auxiliary Staff	Work therapist	Junior nurse	Work therapist
	Cook	Assistant cook	Cook
	Assistant cook	Cook	Assistant cook
	Tsukisoi	Senior male patient	*Tsukisoi*
Patients	Senior male patient	Senior female patient	Senior male patient
	Junior male patient	Junior male patient	Junior male patient
	Senior female patient	*Tsukisoi*	Senior female patient

ranking of roles in this small hospital system. Two methods were employed to check the above hypothesis: one was a questionnaire; the other was to observe a set of social situations in which social ranking appeared to by symbolized. The results of these checks largely confirmed my hypothesis, but the discrepancies among the three sets of rankings (hypothesized, questionnaire, behavioral) also proved interesting.

The questionnaire. — The questionnaire listed fifteen persons by name with instructions to rank them in terms of their "degree of influence" at the hospital. ("Kora Koseiin no naka de mottomo eikyoryoku no aru hito no jumban wo bango de tsukete kudasai.") The completed questionnaires were collected under conditions of pseudo anonymity from two doctors, three nurses, one patient, and the work therapist.

The averaged rankings appear in table 15, column 2. There were no examples of unanimous agreement on the role's rank, but there was general agreement among the raters; Spearman Rho correlations are given in table 16. Discrepancies between hypothesized rankings and questionnaire rankings of two or more levels are marked with arrows (table 15). Let us examine some of the possible explanations for these discrepancies.

The chief nurse's high ranking is no doubt due largely to her informal close ties to the hospital director. She acts as chauffeur, companion, and private secretary to Dr. Kora. She serves, also, as an informal but efficient communication channel to the director in both official and unofficial matters. Thus, her informal social position places the chief nurse relatively high in authority. Similar conditions augmenting the influence of the chief nurse's role may also be found in many other mental hospitals in Japan.

The work therapist's formal training is limited, but his experience and broad responsibilities are not underestimated by the personnel at Kora Koseiin. The discrepancy in ratings of the work therapist's role led to my reexamining this role at the hospital and hence to a new appreciation of its function. Further investigation revealed persons with similar vital functions as social model in all Morita therapy hospitals.

It may be true quite often, as here, that the anthropologist overestimates his effect on the social system he is studying. Limitations in speaking ability (no interpreter was used) and a rather passive observer role in the early stages of research probably contributed to the lower estimate of the anthropologist's influence at the hospital.

TABLE 16

Interrater Correlations (By Spearman RHO)

Rater number	1	2	3	4	5	6	7	8
1	—	.413	.335	.411	.420	.229	.426	.130
2		—	.874	.799	.869	.799	.829	.945
3			—	.945	.926	.793	.898	.956
4				—	.912	.814	.873	.886
5					—	.840	.849	.895
6						—	.809	.818
7							—	.807
8								—

The senior female patient was ranked higher than hypothesized partly because, as a member of the patient role group, she moved up relative to the *tsukisoi* and partly because, in this instance, it seems that seniority was weighted more heavily than male dominance, placing her above the junior male patients. This finding provides some slight confirmation of the hypothesis that one's influence increases within the patient group as one moves toward discharge.

Finally, the *tsukisoi*, a professional servant, was seen by the anthropologist more as a professional and by the personnel at Kora Koseiin more as a servant. The researcher's misconception was to some degree fostered by an otherwise useful paper (Caudill, 1961) in which the status of *tsukisoi* may be somewhat overemphasized. The professional *tsukisoi* actually plays a minor, dwindling role in the tableau of Japanese psychiatric care.

Behavioral. — Relative social ranking may also be determined by examination of social situations in which privileges are allocated and/or authority is symbolized. Several such situations are discussed below.

1) Seating arrangements for the *kowa* lectures. The seating pattern divides the room into six authority zones. The hospital director, backed up by the doctors and the anthropologist faces the patients, with the chief nurse and the work therapist to the side. This "confrontation" seating arrangement is clearly not designed for the egalitarian or pseudoegalitarian group therapy session that is found more often in circular seating patterns in the West. The mixed nature of the social positions of the chief nurse and work therapist, both as ex-patients and as current staff members, is displayed beautifully by the seating plan. They are seated with the patients but off to the side.

The seating positions have symbolic meaning, but they also carry with them certain practical advantages and disadvantages. For example, the advantages for the other doctors include being out of the hospital director's range of vision (permitting drowsing or other inattentiveness), access to patients' charts and other privileged materials as the director examines them during the lecture, and a clear opportunity to listen to the patients' replies and watch their reactions during verbal exchanges between director and patient. Other practical advantages accompanying seating positions include the amount of space one controls, accessibility to room entrances, maximum viewing range, and minimum exposure of oneself to the view of powerful role groups.

2) Seating arrangements for the noon meal. The noon meal is the most public of the three meals at Kora Koseiin. Breakfast is eaten early, about seven-thirty, before visitors and outpatients begin to arrive, and dinner is served around five or five-thirty, after the public has gone. Essentially there are four eating areas: the doctors' table, the patients' tables (one for males and one for females), the kitchen, and the patients' rooms. Under normal circumstances the doctors' table is further subdivided into the director's side, the assistant director's side, the other doctors' side, and the empty side toward the television set. On occasion, however, the chief nurse eats with the doctors. No other staff member eats the noon meal with the doctors and the chief nurse at this table. The nurses are free to eat at the female patients' table or in the kitchen, but usually they choose the kitchen in order to converse and to cover the kitchen telephone in case of incoming calls. The work therapist eats at the male patients' table. Under special circumstances such as absolute bed rest, sedation, or physical disability a patient may receive a tray in his room; normally, he is required to eat at the patients' table. Of course, this privilege is not really role specific to patients because any role group member may receive a tray in his room when suffering physical illness.

3) The wearing of lab coats. Officially, the purpose of wearing a lab coat (*hakui*) is considered to be the protection of one's clothing. In this small hospital setting, lab coats are not usually needed as identification for the staff. Doctors usually remove their lab coats when playing, during meals, and after working hours when meeting with friends. The coat is always worn during *kowa* lectures and often during consultation with outpatients, when making rounds, and the like. Thus it seems to symbolize a formality-informality dimension as much as authority. Only staff members wear lab coats of any sort, even occasionally.

Only situations in which relative status is rather clearly delineated and parallel to the results of the hypothesized ranking and questionnaire ranking have thus far been presented. It is probably obvious to anyone who has actually analyzed role hierarchies in ongoing human communities that not all situations provide such consistently neat results. More specifically, humans not only have other things to do besides expressing role hierarchies, but they also have competing hierarchies, Furthermore, situational requirements such as physical limitations of humans or spatial limitations of buildings may prevent the expression of a hierarchy. At this point two additional situations are offered, the first reflecting a competing hierarchy, sex, which overrides the role hierarchy in one situation, and the second an unclear situation reflecting either sex or formal role distinctions or both.

4) The bath (*ofuro*). It is customary in Japan to fill and heat the bath once a day. The bathers, in order, wash and then enter the bath for warmth and relaxation. Of course, those near the end of the line must bathe in the coolest, murkiest water. The bathing order at Kora Koseiin is as follows: director, assistant director, anthropologist and research doctor and staff doctor (these latter three were told of the bath's availability at about the same time, hospital personnel leaving the bathing order of the three to negotiations on each occasion), work therapist and male patients, female patients, and, finally, nurses. Clearly, the primary distinction here is sex with male dominance. The relative order within the female group probably reflects the low status which formerly characterized nursing in Japan (and still does, to a lesser degree) as well as the work schedule of the nurses, whose duties extend somewhat longer into the evening than do those of female patients.

5) The arrangement of shoes at the entrance (*genkan*). It is immediately noticeable at the entrance (where one removes one's shoes and steps into the slippers provided by the hospital) that the shoes of males are lined up on the right and those of females on the left. There is also an assortment of males' and females' shoes in the center of the area; they are the shoes of outpatients, guests, and anyone who expects to be at the hospital for only a short time during the day. The placing of shoes against the right and left walls occurs every day, and when I purposely left my shoes against the left wall I would return to find them neatly lined up against the right wall. It seemed that a sex distinction was being made. Upon questioning the nurses, however, it turned out that from their perspective a formal role distinction was being made, doctors to the right, nurses to the left. Unfortunately, the other role groups in the hospital do not leave their shoes lined up at the front entrance, and so the critical examples of the work therapist and male patients could not be observed in the natural setting. However, a fictional

case was utilized to check the nurses' interpretation of shoe arrangement.

With the aid of a small diagram, several nurses were queried independently: "Where would a female physician who came to do research at Kora Koseiin place her shoes at the front entrance, on the left or on the right?" The response was unanimous. She would place her shoes on the right with those of the doctors. One wonders, of course, if in actual practice a visiting female physician would be able to discern the role distinction being made by the nurses without responding to the obvious sex distinction suggested by the styles of the shoes. The issue remains clouded.

Five situations have been presented above. Although they are not uniform in their symbolization of social ranking, or unambiguous, they do provide additional confirmation of the other two rankings. A simple method of notation (with no claims of mathematical precision) for recording them is as follows:

1) Seating during *kowa* lectures: doctors (director/assistant director/anthropologist + research doctor + staff doctor) + chief nurse + work therapist/patients (male/female).

2) Seating during noon meal: doctors (director/assistant director/anthropologist + research doctor + staff doctor) + chief nurse/nurses + cooks + *tsukisoi*/work therapist + male patients/female patients.

3) Wearing of lab coats: doctors + nurses + chief nurse + work therapist/auxiliary staff (cooks + *tsukisoi*) + patients.

4) Bath order: Males (doctors (director/assistant director/anthropologist + research doctor + staff doctor)/work therapist + male patients)/females (female patients/chief nurse + nurses).

5) Shoe arrangement: Males (doctors + anthropologist)/females (chief nurse + nurses) *or* doctors + anthropologist/chief nurse + nurses.

One possible composite arrangement of all the above notations is as follows: staff (doctors (director/assistant director/anthropologist + research doctor + staff doctor)/nursing staff (chief nurse/nurses))/auxiliary staff (work therapist/cooks + *tsukisoi*)/patients (male patients/female patients) (see table 15, column 3).

The overall intermeasure correlations (comparing the hypothesized ranking, questionnaire ranking, and behavioral ranking) were very high (table 17) and mutually confirming.

TABLE 17

Intermeasure Correlations (By Spearman RHO)

Type of ranking	Hypothesized ranking	Questionnaire ranking	Behavioral ranking
Hypothesized ranking	—	.989	.998
Questionnaire ranking		—	.992
Behavioral ranking			—

It should be made clear, however, that although this formal role hierarchy of power and privilege held for the most part, exceptions did occur. For example, one wealthy young female patient who used the hospital during convalescence from periods of severe depression received special treatment despite her low formal role as patient. Nevertheless, the Japanese are usually quite sensitive to the over-stepping of one's position, and such complications are probably kept to a minimum.

Crosscutting role divisions. — The formal role within the hospital is not the only relevant dimension for analysis of social interaction in that small society. One dimension that crosscuts some of the formal roles — that is, sex — has already been encountered.

At Kora Koseiin males bathe before females and generally sit at separate tables. It is also true that patients spend more time during the day with persons of their own sex and that there is some division of labor by sex. For example, only female patients were observed to help out in the kitchen.

Friendship ties also form crosscutting divisions. The friendship ties between director and chief nurse and between junior nurses and junior cook have already been mentioned. Another one worth noting is a warm friendship between the assistant director and one of his ex-patients who is now a professional psychologist.

Age seems to be an important factor too. Although young and middle-aged patients seemed to fraternize, the few older patients tended to segregate themselves from the younger groups. Very young and very old patients, regardless of their length of stay at the hospital (seniority), seemed to receive particular attention from staff as well as from other patients. Particularly strong friendship ties seemed to develop almost exclusively between people in approximately the same age bracket.

Interactions at Kora Koseiin

Some hints about patterns of interaction within the hospital have already been offered; here the patterns are described in more detail. The hierarchy of formal role groups is outlined above, then cross-cutting role divisions by sex, friendship, and age are detailed. For the analysis of interactions a number of categories may be useful. Dyadic relations between role groups are commonly used in such analysis; similarly, work groups, play groups, and formal and informal meetings are common settings for interactions. An example from each of these interactions has been selected for purposes of continuing my analysis of the hospital social system.

There are a number of settings for doctor-patient interaction: during informal rounds, through diaries, and in group meetings.

Each day he is at the hospital a doctor makes his rounds. This routine is not so formal or ceremonious as it is in some Japanese psychiatric hospitals. At Kora Koseiin the doctor simply makes certain that he has a chance to talk with each patient every day. For the most part, these exchanges are conducted outside the doctor's office. The garden, the patient's room, the recreation room, or the crafts room is the natural setting for the interaction. The patient may be engaged in constructing a box or an umbrella stand, he may be waiting his turn at table tennis, or he may be discussing neurosis with other patients at the time the doctor approaches. Usually no one stands or bows or takes a more formal sitting position when the doctor arrives. Some questions may be directed to the therapist. There is usually laughter or other signs of informality, but the tendency is strong for the interaction to evolve quickly into one in which the doctor lectures while the patient listens or questions.

The content of the conversation varies considerably, but the patient could be told an illustration like this: Your mood is changeable day by day like the Japanese sky. If your mood is cloudy, don't worry; it will clear up. If it is sunny, don't rejoice; it will become cloudy again. Whether it is cloudy or sunny be disappointed only when you don't work. If you accomplish your task be satisfied whether your mood is cloudy or clear. Don't base your life on uncertain, uncontrollable moods; behavior is certain and controllable.

When the conversation lags the doctor may move on to another patient. His pace is slow and his movements are usually unscheduled. His pace seems to conform to a natural rhythm in the situation.

Key patient-therapist interaction also occurs via the patient's diary. As described above, the patient usually writes a page or two each evening before retiring. This task may require from ten minutes to nearly an hour. The next morning the diaries are collected and delivered to the therapist's office. The doctor reads and corrects the diaries in red ink as his schedule permits, allotting from five to twenty-five minutes per diary depending on the length of the entry, the number of diaries, the overall amount of time available to him, and his particular habits. The communications contained within the diaries are quite controllable in the sense that the channel is single (written), the receivers are a known limited pair (ordinarily doctor-patient only), and the time for careful construction of a clear message is not much of a limiting factor. The patient takes his diary with him at the time of discharge.

Content analysis reveals that much of the patient's written material deals with his daily activities at the hospital. The time he arose, the meals taken, the work and play around the hospital, the conversations with fellow patients, and remembered words of the doctors fill the diaries. Another large topic is the patient's physical and psychological state both during hospitalization and in the past. Occurring less frequently are confessions ("I was ashamed. People like me think only of our own condition and hardly ever the other things.") and apologies ("Doctor, I'm sorry. I slept in until nine o'clock. I even missed breakfast. I'm sorry, but I cannot take the proper course in this matter. I'm a heck of a guy, aren't I?"), complaints and doubts ("Every day I think about *arugamama* and my basic purpose and understand them, but *arugamama* doesn't fill my mind."), appeals for advice and reassurance ("I think, Doctor, that people are isolated. In the other hospital someone told me that this is probably so. Please instruct me in this matter."), compliments ("Whatever Dr. Abe does he is skillful at it."), and self-praise ("Although I was somewhat anxious, not being one who gives up, I continued with the hospital's work"; and "I went out with a brave heart.").

On the other hand, the communications from the doctors are, for the most part, evaluative statements or advice. Evaluative statements may be positive ("Good." "Exactly." "Correct." "You certainly improved." "You have become active." "Well done." "You have completely recovered." "You understood well.") or negative ("Don't." "Regrettable."). There is a writing convention within the hospital related to evaluation, too. The doctor may draw a line alongside a phrase or sentence by way of calling special attention to it. If the line has a circle at its head, the meaning becomes, "Important and good."

The advice covers many aspects of the patients' lives, but several focuses — purpose, work, and anxiety — occur particularly often: "Without controlling your anxiety, leaving it as it is, the important thing is to concentrate on your purpose which is to accomplish the task." "If there is anxiety, that's all right. . . . Accomplishing your purpose is most important." "The purpose of the bath is to get clean and warm. Fasten onto this purpose as you would cling to a rock. . . ." "When you are dizzy or anxious accomplish some task anyway. . . . Do what needs to be done." "When you want to work, work; when you don't want to, work anyway. It's something you must do." "The results of your efforts will live after your work is finished." The content and even the phrasing of this sort of evaluation and advice are rather stereotyped and, although in a single diary there is some variation, after reading five or ten diaries the forms become more or less predictable. But the advice can be more specific, too, recommending more social interaction ("Meet with many kinds of people, those you feel comradeship for and those you don't, in disturbing circumstances and calm ones."), giving instructions regarding the diary ("Write what you did each day, not about your feelings."), offering suggestions as to medication ("When you can't sleep at night call the nurse."), and inviting the patient to further discussion ("Let's talk later.").

Occurring less frequently are reassurance (". . . but *your* life is surrounded by parents and faithful friends and is certainly not isolated."), direct suggestion ("Your condition is relatively easily cured." "You can do anything. Carry around your mature attitude toward life here. If you can do it here you will certainly be able to do it when you return home."), information with instructions ("This is the heaviest snow in Tokyo in seventeen years. Look around and see it." "Now there are few patients, so take up the work slack."), definitions ("That's *arugamama*." " '*Arugamama*' is not 'a calm spirit.' It is rather the spirit of working no matter what your mental condition is, no matter how painfully."), corrections of omissions or improperly written *kanji* characters made by the patient, and questions ("Why"?). Such is the content of communications via the diary at Kora Koseiin.

Work and Play Groups

One of the striking features of life at Kora Koseiin is the informality of the system. There are no regular staff meetings; no deluge of mimeographed bulletins, forms, memos, and the like clutters up the time and space of this hospital. Information may be passed along during the noon meal by word of mouth. The communication system is sometimes inefficient, but generally it is adequate to maintain the hospital at a functioning level.

The pace within the hospital is almost always slow. For any job there are likely to be more than enough willing hands. Occasionally, the outpatient interviews keep the doctors busy into the lunch hour. On those days the nurses, too, may be quite active filling pre-scriptions, answering the phone, and greeting visitors. But the pace never becomes harried; the load never overburdens the capacities of those on duty plus those that can be called upon to help.

The nurses prefer to work together in teams. Their routines and their work allocations are smooth and basically unchanging from week to week. The work therapist's duties vary with the seasons and with the structural repairs needed. He may work alone or with patients, but even in a group the work therapist seems more en-grossed in his work than aware of the presence of others. The doctors' general duties remain the same from day to day. Doctors work as individuals with patients rather than as a team (although they do provide one another with feedback on the patients' conditions and their treatment), so they can be quite flexible in their hours and in their methods.

The patients' lives, too, are only minimally regulated by their work load (in contrast with the situation in some Moritist hospitals). At Kora Koseiin the morning's work assignment can usually be finished by ten-thirty. After that the patient is expected to find work, to study, or to play as his circumstances require. On occasion, special afternoon work groups may be formed.

Play groups form around table tennis and the miniature golf course when weather permits. Small impromptu tournaments are held for table tennis players, and course records are kept on the number of strokes taken around the nine-hole golf course that runs through the gardens. Patients and staff play together when the work load permits.

Special excursions to temples, gardens, and parks in the Tokyo area are enjoyed by patients. About once a year longer trips are taken in the company of ex-patients and staff. One of the shorter trips was to Inogashira Park and Kichijoji Temple in the spring of 1968. On this outing the work therapist was the leader; five male patients, two female patients, and the anthropologist accompanied him. Other patients either had not received permission to participate or had elected not to go. It takes courage for a shy neurotic patient to commit himself to train and bus rides, to crowds of people and picnicking in public. The trip was officially defined as an outing and only that. It was undertaken in order to explore the park and the temple, not as practice in socializing, not as a test of the patients' progress.

During the trip only one patient showed inappropriate behavior, exhibiting compulsive movements and tics. The other patients joked, laughed, and chatted appropriately in every public setting. One heavy patient, in fact, displayed less anxiety than I did while we rowed about on a lake together in a shallow-draft boat. We were sitting well down in the water. Everyone appeared fatigued at the end of the active, but leisurely paced, day. Observations were checked against the patients' reports of the trip in their diaries:

> Mr. K. wrote, "Today was a happy one. Everywhere we went my illness was gone."

> Mr. S. wrote that he wasn't much interested in looking at flowers and was only tired by the trip.

> Miss H. wrote that Mrs. M. cried when she saw the kindergarten children in the park, for she was thinking of her separation from her own children.

> Mrs. M. wrote of wanting to return to her home right in the middle of the trip, but she didn't write of her crying.

> Mr. M. didn't write of his symptoms even though they were noticeable enough to attract some slight attention from other passengers on the train and the bus.

It seemed that the patient group had provided sufficient emotional support for the members to behave appropriately, and even for some members to forget their self-consciousness long enough to enjoy the experience.

Formal Meetings

These gatherings are formal to the extent that they are set up by the staff, all patients are automatically and publicly invited, and the time is roughly scheduled. The primary meetings of this sort are the ex-patients' meeting, the English conversation class, the group therapy meeting, and the *kowa* lecture.

At Kora Koseiin the *kowa* or therapeutic lecture takes place every Thursday afternoon in the dining room. It generally lasts about an hour. The term *kowa* is the same one used for a somewhat similar instructive lecture among Buddhist monks. The purpose of the *kowa* is to provide an official time in which the director can give the patients instruction and personal guidance.

The seating arrangements are described elsewhere, but basically Dr. Kora, backed by the doctors, sits facing the patients with the chief nurse and the work therapist on the patients' flank. The meeting begins when the director, having finished his outpatient consultations, seats himself at this small table.

The form of the *kowa* may vary somewhat from time to time, but it nearly always follows the same general pattern. Dr. Kora, with the patients' charts and diaries for reference, asks the new patients and then the continuing patients individually about their condition, listens, then replies with stories, advice, witticisms, or somewhat simplified technical lectures on psychiatry. Next he answers questions, gives a final lecture, and signals that the meeting is over. There follows the customary group bow, *Domo* ("Thank-you"). The director stands, and the meeting is dismissed. Observed variations included Dr. Kora's reading an article from one of his books, reading a short passage from a patient's diary, and explaining the mottoes carved on plaques by the patients. On one occasion he had the patients read by turns from an article about Morita therapy.

The communication is this situation is predominantly either a lecture from Dr. Kora to the group or a person-to-person exchange between the director and a single patient; there is almost no patient-to-patient communication. Dr. Kora may ask the patients if they understand a fellow patient's complicated explanation of his feelings or if they think he gives off a bad odor as he believes he does. Even then the reply is directed ostensibly to Dr. Kora; he figures in nearly all the communication exchanges. This system is certainly not intended to be an egalitarian group therapy experience. In the West, a similar form of therapeutic lecture seems to have been historically a transitional step to group therapy (David Clark, personal communication). At Kora Koseiin, however, the value of listening to a learned and respected *sensei* remains high, and the group sharing experience can take place under other circumstances, both formal and informal.

The following excerpts are offered as examples of the content of therapeutic lectures:

You *can't* control your likes. You *can't* make yourself like snakes. But you *can* control your behavior. That's important.

If we're not skillful at doing something it doesn't mean we're bad people or failures.

If you can't *gaman* ("stick it out") you can't be cured.

You're not getting better because you're not sticking it out.

Many people have trembling hands. [A patient had said that he thought he was the only person whose hands trembled in social situations.]

Don't focus so much on the past. Turn your attention to what you will do from now on.

If you're always talking about yourself you can't listen.

On the night before last there was an all-star baseball game. Nagashima didn't get a hit although he's a big slugger. Some days our condition isn't good — it can't be helped. We can't stay in top form for *every* game, *every* day.

We *all* feel afraid of cancer. It's sensible to fear cancer. People die from cancer, and we don't want to die. But we can work anyway.

In a recent article, Dr. Kora discusses (1968, pp. 317-318) his favorite illustrations for use in the therapeutic lecture:

> As I talk to the patients I begin with easily understandable concrete examples. For instance, when you grow a chrysanthemum you prepare the soil, plant the seed, water, and fertilize. You remove insects, provide supporting sticks, and protect the plant from wind and rain. Your results may be poorer than those of an expert, but you will undoubtedly have a deep love for the chrysanthemums you grew yourself. The important thing is the fact that by taking care of the flower with your own hands you developed a love for it. . . .
>
> There is a saying that retarded children are most lovable. This is the result of the long period during which the parents care for the child. . . .
>
> *Concerning anxiety, fear, and pain.* Neurotic persons abhor unpleasant feelings and sensations just as much as normal people. But ordinary people realize either consciously or unconsciously that such distress is an inevitable aspect of living and cannot be completely avoided. They know that it is useless to try to resist such natural and necessary thoughts and feelings. In other words, these experiences cannot be helped. But there are many neurotic persons with the idealistic attitude that they should not have such unpleasant feelings or that having them, they can somehow get rid of them. For this reason, they may become easily caught by a contradictory over-consciousness to their own anxiety and pain.
>
> Nature is not man-centered. Natural calamities occur every year; bacteria harmful to man propagate, and vegetables, when planted and left alone, are harmed by weeds and insects. Similarly, though society was created by man, it doesn't exist for any particular man's benefit. Competition is severe so we must exert outselves or fail. Sickness, accidents, death, interpersonal conflicts, and economic losses threaten us. We must clearly realize that such anxieties accompany human life, but that we are stimulated by them to constructive efforts resulting in a meaningful, worthwhile life.
>
> Even in sports without anxiety over the possibility of defeating one's opponent or the pain of being defeated we probably wouldn't practice diligently. And when the opponent is so weak that we are sure to win there is no interest in the game at all. If we had no fear there would be no response to avoid an approaching car. Again, if we had no sense of pain we wouldn't be able to protect ourselves from injury. Only when we recognize the necessity of our fundamental fears and their usefulness can we free ourselves from the conflicts involved in opposing them.

In order to influence the patients by the methods Dr. Kora employs in the therapeutic lecture, it is first necessary to attract and hold their attention. This is a particularly important problem with these neurotic patients because their attention is likely to drift to their own subjective reactions to the lecture and to their own feelings and thoughts. Thus holding their attention is not only a means for therapeutic gain but also a kind of therapeutic end in itself.

Dr. Kora is well known as a good lecturer and storyteller. His talks with patients are filled with vignettes, reminiscences, quotations, and current events, all with points of relevance for the patients. Although it is only indirectly possible to measure his success (by observing eye movements, appropriate responses to jokes and questions, and references written later in the patients' diaries), his techniques for holding attention seem to be effective.

Informal Meetings

In the evenings the patients gather in groups of three or more. The nature of these informal groupings depends on a number of heterogeneous factors, including the number and individual characteristics of the patients, the day's work load, the weather, and the heating facilities for different rooms.

Casual evening pastimes are watching television and playing cards, but on special occasions informal meetings may be called. On holidays, for example, there may be fireworks and special foods. For a while social dancing was practiced informally in the evenings, and the doctor on duty, the nurses, and the work therapist attended along with the patients.

The *sobetsukai* is a celebration honoring someone who is departing. In the hospital a *sobetsukai* may be set up informally by the patients in honor of one of their number soon to be discharged. In most respects the *sobetsukai* honoring Miss N. in the summer of 1968 was typical of these informal meetings.

The party was scheduled for seven o'clock in the evening. At seven o'clock several patients were finishing the repainting of the ping-pong table, and the work therapist was still out buying the cakes that each guest's donation of 50 yen (about 15 cents) had gone to buy. When the brushes were put away and the food had been prepared it was after seven-fifteen. No one had yet entered the recreation room. The cue for beginning the party was not the position of the hands on a clock but rather the personal, informal call that the party was ready to begin. A disadvantage of this casual summons system was that a special inquiry had to be sent out later to those who might not have heard it. And, in fact, three more patients did come about ten minutes late, after the second call. Those present totaled thirteen: the work therapist, nine male patients, two female patients, and the anthropologist. Other patients who did not attend sent explanations in terms of their illness, medication, and so forth. The nurses and one doctor were present in the hospital but had other plans and did not attend.

The party began with records and watermelon provided by the hospital. The guest of honor was shy, still suffering to some degree from anthropophobia, but she had chosen to continue her treatment on an outpatient basis. The patients discussed her improvement, particularly her improved attitude, which one young man described as "completely changed." They then discussed how long she had been hospitalized (fifty-four days, perhaps, she wasn't certain) and began to compare that figure with the length of stay of the other patients, good-naturedly joking about the patient who was still there after three months had passed. Miss N. remarked how the faces had changed as one by one friends had been discharged and new faces appeared.

There followed several party games with the work therapist in charge. First came the popular card game, *hyakunin isshu*, then a variation of "who's got the button," and finally "inspiration," which one young patient had learned at a nearby Protestant church. The games were full of spontaneity and laughter. Certainly, in no obvious way could I distinguish this group from any other group of Japanese young people enjoying themselves at a party. Sweets were passed around and eaten, and then the party was drawn to a close by the work therapist. Everyone bowed, *Domo arigato* ("Thank-you") and, to Miss N., *Ogenki de* ("Best wishes"), *Sayonara*. It was nine o'clock.

This *sobetsukai* points up several features of the social system at Kora Koseiin. One is the independence with which patients are permitted to carry on their own activities. Another is the essential intermediary position of the work therapist, linking staff and patients. He functions both as patient leader and as staff assistant. Still another feature is the casual attitude toward time scheduling and information distribution. This attitude pays a price in inefficiency in terms of information blind spots and duplication of effort in order to keep the system more "humanized," less mechanistic.

III   JAPANESE CHARACTER

What I write about the Japanese people will almost certainly provoke in my reader the response that Westerners, too, have these character- istics. Undoubtedly, the response is a proper one. The difference, I maintain, is one only of degree and emphasis. One of the useful results of studying other people (on a large scale, as the anthro- pologist does, or on an individual scale, as the clinical psychologist does) is that what appear to us to be exaggerations in their behavior help us to be aware of similar tendencies in our own behavior.

Many readers will know of exceptions to this generalized picture of Japanese character. Again, I recognize the validity of these excep- tions. But most Japanese (and Japanese Americans) have experienced a recognition of themselves and their people when I have spoken and written of these matters.

My discussion of Japanese character is speculative. It is the way I make sense of the personal and social milieu within which *shinkeishitsu* neurosis flourishes. The reader who demands a hard core of objective data — measured behavior units, questionnaire responses, and the like — may wish to skip this chapter. Here I intend not to convince but to provoke. If the tone of the writing implies certainty it is merely the certainty that this is the way I view Japanese character now.

SOCIAL SENSITIVITY

By social sensitivity I mean extreme concern with the evaluations and feelings of others. This concern leads Japanese people to be quick in picking up subtle social cues, to spend much time and thought considering others' evaluations of themselves, and to avoid direct interactions that would upset others. The term "sensitive" is appropriate in two senses. It means both "alert" or "receptive" to signals that intimate others' thoughts and feelings and "easily hurt," "susceptible," and "tender," that is, to take personally or to be readily influenced by others' thoughts and feelings. To be sure, some measures of these characteristics may be found in all men, but it is their degree, consistency, and extent of influence which typify the Japanese. To the extent that these characteristics become notable through exaggeration in this cultural group, they direct our attention to the possibility of documenting their existence in other groups as well.

The relationships between social sensitivity and the other values that I explore are readily drawn. The careful internal censoring of communications and the limits placed on emotional expressiveness are employed by Japanese people so as to avoid disturbing others and to preserve a nonthreatening, nonburdensome image in their eyes. Shame, shyness, polite hesitation, and the *enryo* syndrome (Kitano, 1969, pp. 103-105) are products of the extreme concern with others' evaluations of one's self. Even the achievement-oriented work ethic and the formal Buddhist and Christian practices and beliefs are strongly flavored by social sensitivity. Work and morality are defined primarily in social-situational rather than absolute terms, and the degree to which one is recognized socially as industrious or morally proper may take precedence over industriousness and religiosity per se.

Turning now to social-structural features, within the family organization we find the initial and consummate model of social sensitivity, the Japanese mother's concern with her child. It is also through this structural medium that the concern with presenting a favorable self to others is reinforced, because others' evaluations of one's self are, in addition, reflections upon one's family.

ENRYO

Enryo has both personal and social facets. By monitoring and controlling his own expression of inner feelings and desires, a person protects himself and his alter (i.e., the one with whom he is inter-acting). The alter is protected because fewer demands are put upon him to meet the speaker's needs. If I tell you clearly what I need, you may feel some pressure or obligation to respond to my need.

Clearly, if you are not informed of my wants you are likely to feel that you are under less of a moral obligation or expectation to react to them. Similarly, if I withhold negative information and criticism from you I am less likely to cause you immediate discomfort. By the same token, however, you are less likely to be angry at me for criticizing you, and you are less likely to associate me with the bad news or negative information that you received. Thus, I protect myself.

By censoring my expression of thoughts and feelings in social interaction I can control the image I present to others. Within a Japanese context others take me to be well-bred, thoughtful, courteous, humble, and unselfish. I project the proper image. My "face," my public self, is protected. The resultant social interactions, ones in which both parties practice *enryo*, are polite, civilized, thoughtful, careful, and often ritualized along safe well-worn paths.

There are problems, however, beneath the placid surface of this sea of social intercourse. As in all aspects of human experience one pays a price for one's benefits. The first and most obvious problem is that ego cannot expect to get accurate feedback concerning alter's "true" inner state. I know that you are coloring your communications to me so that they emerge as nondemanding and nonthreatening. To ask you to be frank and open with me might obligate me to reciprocate; certainly it would be placing a demand upon you, a demand that runs counter to your training in social relating. By far the simplest expedient is for me to look for indirect cues, those you do not or cannot monitor so closely. Here let me note in passing that for many interactions I do not need or want to know alter's inner feelings, opinions, and the like. We can slide through a discussion of his term paper, a conversation at a formal dinner, or some office business on these superficial but well-greased skids of civility. The obsession with baring one's inner self to others is a recent Western phenomenon with problems of its own that need not be explored here.

We have already arrived at a useful vantage point for viewing three phenomena related to Morita therapy. The inner monitoring and control process is at the heart of *taijinkyofu-sho*, or anthropophobia. The neurotic young person is so concerned with the image that he is projecting, so concerned with the signals and cues that he and alter are exchanging, that he feels fearful, overwhelmed by the interaction. The second point is that he cannot get information from other young people that they, too, feel awkward, self-conscious, and uncomfortable because they are protecting his social sensitivity just as he is protecting theirs. Thus, public announcement of symptoms is an important aspect of Morita therapy. The sense that the anthropophobic's suffering is unique and therefore abnormal is challenged by the testimonies of fellow patients. The third point is the use of therapy writing, a highly controllable channel of communication, so that the patient need not be concerned with monitoring pauses and body movements (other than those involved in writing) when communicating with his therapist.

Now let us return to the indirect cues. During a conversation it is not always easy for a Japanese to study another person while he is speaking. Japanese people ordinarily do not maintain a great deal of eye-to-face contact when listening to a speaker in a close interaction sequence. To stare at someone in any situation is considered impolite, partly because the Japanese recognize that close scrutiny by the speaker or the listener allows far too much uncontrolled communication to pass between conversants. Suspicion or aggressiveness may be signaled by an intense look.

Nevertheless, at key points in a conversation the speaker makes eye contact with the listener. Such contact may signal, "Have I made my point?" "This is important," or "How are you taking this?" The listener in a two-party conversation makes periodic head nods and frequent verbal indications that he is following along with the speaker. The listener who stops nodding or fails to continue his string of "ah's," "so's," "*naru hodo's*," "mm's," and the like indicates that he does not understand, does not agree, or, in general, has had his attention diverted away from the overt content of the conversational message.

The importance of visual clues in conversation is pointed up by the sort of anthropophobia called *shisen kyofu* (literally, "extreme fear of line of sight"). The neurotic person may worry about how long to look at another person when talking or listening. He may worry that others think he is staring. He may wonder which eye to look at when conversing. These symptoms are not at all uncommon among Japanese neurotics.

Another danger of *enryo* is that communications are subject to misinterpretation. If I must rely on ambiguous indirect clues about your true inner state, I may well project into my interpretation those feelings and needs that I want you to have. Or my guilt may lead me to perceive suffering in you which is not there. Japanese communications are notoriously vague and indirect. As we shall see, the overall strategy in social interaction in Japan is to be well thought of by alter so that his interpretations or misinterpretations of your inner state are in your favor.

In my first weeks in Japan I tried to get a Morita therapist's opinion on a sensitive but important topic. He tried to direct my attention to some other subject. I pressed him. He thought that several opinions were all right. But what did *he* think, I asked. What did *I* think, he returned the query obliquely. I replied that I wanted to know his opinion before offering mine. Finally, he stated his opinion, qualifying it and pointing out the validity of opposing positions, too. I was puzzled, then, at the difficulty I had encountered in getting him to take a stand on the issue. I came to learn that what was most important to most Japanese in most of our conversations was not some abstract goal such as arriving at a statement of truth or establishing some pronouncement of commitment; rather, the most important element was establishing or maintaining a satisfactory, harmonious social relationship.

That therapist was not concerned about being labeled "wishy-washy." After all, for him maturity means seeing problems from several perspectives. His concern was that if forced to commit himself unequivocably his position might be diametrically opposed to mine, a situation that might lead to conflict between us. In Japan one employs a large number of tactics in order to avoid direct interpersonal conflict. I do not hold that these tactics are always used with awareness. Rather they have become so useful that they are employed habitually to the degree that even on the level of the popular travelogue they have become part of the characteristic description applied to the Japanese people.

The tactics include not understanding clearly, communicating vaguely and indirectly, avoiding areas in which disquieting information might be forthcoming, ignoring conflicting information, and forgetting conflicting information. What you do not know (or pretend not to recognize) may keep social relations going smoothly, at least on one level. If alter thinks well of me, he will interpret the ambiguous stimuli that I send him favorably. If he does not think well of me, he will misinterpret even my favorable communications. Thus, it pays me to cultivate harmonious relations among those with whom I interact with some frequency.

One tactic for establishing such relations is to offer something to alter. In Japan (and, in some measure, in America) a single offer of a favor or a single, vague invitation to dinner communicates only a positive feeling. It implies no expectation that alter will act immediately on the offer. If the overture is repeated after an interval, if details as to a specific date or concrete arrangements are provided, then alter can expect that ego actually intends to carry out his offer.

Back again to *enryo*. Perhaps the least obvious but most far-reaching effect of *enryo* is the resultant strong dichotomization between a public self and an inner self which nobody else knows (see Doi, 1973). Some authors (e.g., DeVos, 1963) argue essentially that the public self is the whole of Japanese character, that a person becomes so identified with his public role that it becomes the totality of his being. Thus, one can make sense of the suicide of a schoolmaster when one of his students becomes delinquent or the self-destruction of a railroad executive after a train accident for which he feels personal responsibility. Perhaps for some Japanese the public self is so important that failure or shame is sufficient to provoke suicide. But there is much in the Japanese social-psychological world which fosters and protects a strong separation between public and private self.

In Tanizaki Junichiro's novel, *The Key*, husband and wife become privy to each other's diaries. The diary, an institutionalized form of inner-self expression in Japan, changes for this couple, becoming ultimately a vehicle for public-self communication when they realize that each is reading the other's diary. There is no need for a private diary in a culture with no public-private separation of self.

Why should a culture that is as group-oriented as Japan is be so plagued by self-consciousness in its styles of neurosis? Why should Zen Buddhism, a form of religious training aimed at destruction of a strong "self," thrive in a culture noted for self-abnegation? How can Japanese be both humble and egotistical? These paradoxes melt like shaved ice in a Tokyo summer when the public-private dichotomy of self is taken into consideration.

I argue further that the ritualized expressions of honor and formalized patterns and terms of politeness and respect used in the Japanese language allow the lower-status speaker to distance his inner self from interaction with his social superior. That is, when a whole set of prescribed behaviors govern our interaction, I need not respond to you on an individual level. I can maintain my inner self separate and "special" because I have not "touched" another self. This separation (a sort of depersonalization, if you will) allows a Japanese to carry out various situationally necessary social tasks without feeling necessarily a personal involvement in them or responsibility for them. Thus I disagree with the narcissistic self-*is*-role interpretation of Japanese personality. Rather than investing his self in his role, I believe the Japanese uses his roles to protect, shield, withdraw his self from contacting others. By this means both his inner self and the inner self of the other person(s) involved are safe from threat.

One final thought about *enryo*. The aim of *enryo* is protection or safety. The assumption is that others are not strong enough to handle negative information without a destructive response. If I perceive others as weak, inadequate, or in need of help, I perceive myself in that dimension as well, either strongly but unconvincingly denying my own weakness and inadequacy or accepting them. My point is that the scales I use to measure others are the ones I use on myself. This is not an issue of logic. I do not say "All men are weak," "I am a man," and "Therefore, I am weak." It is rather like the limitations of circuitry in a computer which make possible only a limited number of circuit paths. I am given little opportunity to develop the strength to deal with direct criticism or direct conflict. I do not find myself in situations that would prompt me to question my assumed inability to handle negative information. I am protected by others and I continue to protect them and myself.

It is here that we begin to understand the therapeutic implications of the public negative feedback that therapists offer patients (and Zen priests offer young monks). Dr. Kora may laugh at a patient. He tells the patient straightforwardly that his behavior is abnormal. The initial devastation gives way to growing ego strength in some patients. They learn that they can handle direct blows to the self. The protective oversensitivity develops into greater openness and forthrightness. The result is not the pseudo openness one finds in many Westerners, and the careful censoring of communication output does not disappear altogether. But for many patients the excessive strains of exaggerated *enryo* and control are eased, and life becomes constructive as well as protective.

INTERPERSONAL CONTROL TECHNIQUES

Interpersonal control techniques (ICT's) are a means by which an individual can influence others to behave in predictable, satisfying ways. An outstanding feature of the interactional repertoire of most Japanese is their ability to use ICT's that effectively influence the behavior of a social superior without endangering the social relationship, incurring punishment, or threatening the pride of either party. Ambiguity and avoidance of confrontation, a humble demeanor, and public expression of benign feelings toward and expectations of authority figures are common devices. Another technique is to perform a service or offer a gift, thus putting the recipient in debt to the giver.

I suspect that the degree of awareness that this motivation underlies some behavior varies considerably among persons and among situations for a particular person. Sometimes the expected influence on the other's behavior is immediate and concrete (as when a woman who did not wish to be interviewed took great pains to brush my coat carefully after I had accidentaly brushed against a pollen-projecting flower on her front porch). Sometimes the goals are vague and long-term or not conscious at all. I do not reject the element of altruism which may enter into these transactions. The theme of the ICT's, however, runs so strongly through the history of the people and through the developmental history of the individual that its influence on the behavior of others should not be ignored. I read with pleasure that Vogel (1963), too, saw the importance of this construct for understanding interactions within a Tokyo suburb, and himself yielded on occasion to such gentle pressures as I have.

Perhaps the sequence of desired influence foreseen, favor put, forth, favor accepted, and obligation incurred, resulting in the desired modification of behavior, lies outside the awareness of most Japanese most of the time when such sequences are in process. Most are aware, however, that to interrupt the sequence, once under way, the alter must somehow politely refuse the favor. If he accepts, the obligation is automatic and he faces anxiety resolving into guilt and shame over time until his share in the "bargain" has completed the sequence. Once the favor has been accepted, ego has a right to expect the desired results. If the results do not materialize, ego's reaction may be anger or withdrawal and apathy. (I suspect that which of the two reactions he selects depends upon his perception of the power situation at the time.)

Now, for this method of control by obligation to work effectively in any culture there must be strong emphasis on internalized norms. That is, there must be a strong expectation (backed up by powerful social sanctions) that the recipient will comply with the giver's request once he has accepted the gift or the service. The recipient is expected to perform, to "come through," in spite of his feelings later or the difficulties of the situation. Conflicts between incurred obligations and later circumstances with conflicting obligations and feelings are the stuff of nearly every Japanese movie and novel. But the stress is on fulfilling the responsibility, and the prime agent of success is the will. I was told that if one has sufficient will one can learn any language at any age. Mentally disturbed people are often popularly seen as lacking will. The extreme efforts of neurotics to control even their feelings by will can be viewed profitably from this perspective. That is, they feel obligated to meet the pressures and obligations of their lives by exerting their will. With single-minded purpose they seek to fulfill the demands placed upon them by the social "others" in their lives. They fail. They claim, then, that they cannot meet the obligations, instead of saying that they do not want to meet them or that they are not trying to meet them. I have heard more than one Morita therapist challenge his patient: "Rather than 'not being able to' you don't want to try."

The sick role is as effective a refuge in Japan as it is in America, but it carries a heavier burden of moral stigma in Japan. Thus, feelings of inferiority are a common accompaniment to neurotic symptomatology. Complaints about significant others, the social system, and difficult circumstances (i.e., outwardly projected loci for the cause of the problem) seem to me still to be relatively rare in Japan, but they are growing in importance.

A PERSONAL HISTORICAL INTERPRETATION

In this section we look at one understanding of the way in which an individual Japanese comes to develop and maintain the characteristics described above.

Parents in every culture have some idea of the kind of habits, goals, and cognitive structuring of reality they would like to have their children adopt, and they more or less systematically go about instilling the preferred pattern. The main goal of socialization, according to some Freudians, is to effect a workable balance between the individual's needs and the functioning of society. Certainly, if all humans indulged all their impulses, society would cease to exist. The predictability of behavior would drop so low that the web of social expectations binding a society together would burst apart. The point of this section is simply that the Japanese *shinkeishitsu* neurotic is the extreme product of a form of socialization that works too effectively on some persons. The argument holds that some Japanese are, in a sense, oversocialized; the techniques of social control involving sensitivity to others' cues and feelings work so well that the satisfaction of personal needs and the development of a strong personal identity are stifled.

The task of socializing the infant or the young child is in some ways the easiest and in some ways the most difficult of purposeful behavior change situations. The parent need not break down some already existing complex cognitive structuring of the world. The child is not a tabula rasa, but he approaches that ideal much more closely than does, say, the American prisoner of war in a Chinese Communist thought reform center. The child has no preconceptions about legitimate and illegitimate educational techniques, just and unjust ends, and so forth.

On the other hand, the parent must cope with the limitations of the child's neurological system. He must go slowly, match information input to the capacities of the child, and allow for wide latitude in the absorption of principles and their application to daily behavior. Whereas a logical explanation or a verbal threat may achieve results in the religious conversion of an adult, they are unlikely to make headway when applied in the directed behavior change of an eight-month-old infant.

The argument here presented is based on my field observations as well as those of Vogel (1963) and Lanham (1966). It is not clear whether the description applies to other than the urban middle-class family in Japan, although it is my impression that it probably does. Certainly, the most detailed information on Japanese child-rearing practices that are relevant to this argument comes from urban middle-class Japanese families. Data from rural areas and fishing villages do not, however, provide disconfirmation; indeed, they provide some support for the positing of practices and results similar to those described below (see Kerlinger, 1962, pp. 404-405; Beardsley, Hall, and Ward, 1959, pp. 293-299; Norbeck and Norbeck, as cited in Lanham, 1966).

The urban middle-class Japanese parent has developed a few impressively effective techniques in the rearing of children. Primarily, it is to the mother that the responsibility of raising the children falls, but the father, too, may use similar techniques. The key to understanding Japanese child-rearing practice is that the mother's primary concern is to establish a warm, wise, benevolent image in the eyes of her child. If she succeeds, socialization is relatively simple. Vogel (1963) writes: "The explanation of the . . . [middle-class] mother's success in training without discipline is that she teaches only when the child is in a co-operative mood. She ordinarily does not think in terms of using techniques to get the child to obey her or of punishments if the child does not obey her. Her aim is to establish a close relationship with the child so he will automatically go along with her suggestions. To the extent that she thinks of techniques for dealing with the child, they are methods for keeping the child happy and building their relationship so that he will want to do what she says" (pp. 244-245).

Many observers of Japanese enculturation practices (e.g., Norbeck, 1965; Lanham, 1966; Elzinga, 1972b) have noted the frequent use of praise and other rewards. Not only are rewards more effective than punishment from an operant-conditioning perspective, but they also strengthen the projected image of the benevolent mother. Again, the mother may go to great lengths to explain why compliance is beneficial for the child (Norbeck, 1965, p. 245; Lanham, 1966, p. 328). But in a given situation, if the explanation is unsuccessful in winning the child over to her side, the mother will often give in to the child's demands. In that event the mother's explanation to her child may be interpreted as an attempt to enhance an image of superior knowledge which is utilized in the service of the child, but if that image does not "come across" (i.e., if the child cannot understand the mother's point) she can submit to the child's demands and enhance her image of benevolence as an alternative secondary gain from the transaction.

A child who sees his mother as nurturant and wise in the sense described above is going to be somewhat dependent. In other words, the child will learn that the easy way to get a reward is simply to communicate a desire for it and/or wait for the mother to provide it. The comparative passivity of Japanese children is already noticeable in the three- to four-month-old infant (Caudill, 1969). Iga (1968), too, notes that the Japanese child develops the expectation that "others are always on the watch to satisfy his needs" (p. 243). And there are additional techniques that Japanese mothers use to promote dependent passivity. One technique is to speak of threats of danger from other persons and from ghosts and gods (Lanham, 1962, pp. 229-230; Iga, 1968, p. 239). The child learns to fear the reactions of others and so he clings more tightly to the security of his nurturant mother. The mother can periodically test the effectiveness of her image presentation by threatening to go away or simply pretending to walk away from the child. Lanham (1962) describes a child crying hysterically as its mother pretends to walk away. The description is an excellent illustration of both a control technique and a test of the success of the mother's desired image projection.

An occasional instructive occurrence in our neighborhood in Kamakura, Japan, was the pitiful wailing of a naughty child locked out of the house during the daytime; the child banged on the door, promising to be good if allowed to come in. Our children, in direct contrast, were punished by being kept inside the house and were permitted to go outside to play as a reward. Such contrasts in definitions of rewards and punishments seem to reflect fundamental national differences in the evaluation of personal freedom and independence versus nurturant belonging.

Another technique for fostering dependency is to convince the child of the delicacy and sensitivity of his psyche. A child can be taught that independent behavior may result in serious damage to his psyche through, for example, the laughter of others. As one mother reported, "I would rather give . . . [a little girl] a mild talking to than a severe scolding which might make her ashamed and *hurt her innocent mind*" (Lanham, 1966, p. 329, emphasis added).

Of course, no one suspects Japanese mothers of being calculating manipulators of their children, fully conscious of the methods and results discussed above. On the other hand, Japanese wives have been traditionally taught to study their husbands and children, to be sensitive to their needs, and to respond to the needs immediately. And there definitely is awareness that a warm, dependent relationship will smooth the socialization process for all concerned (Vogel, 1963, pp. 244-246). I believe that one reason why Japanese people in general and *shinkeishitsu* neurotics in particular fear that their thoughts and feelings show on their faces, revealing too much to others, is that their mothers could predict with some accuracy their thoughts and feelings as children. After childhood there is little opportunity for checking the reality of such fears with their peers. So the idea persists.

As indicated above, if the child sees his mother as wise and nurturant he is likely to go along with her instructions initially because obedience will pay off for him. But once her image is established, the "traditional Japanese mother's strongest weapon in disciplining her child is the very self-sacrifice with which she dedicates herself to her offspring. . . . The mother who exhausts herself on behalf of her child is a source of potential guilt that a Japanese child so brought up cannot escape" (DeVos, 1963, p. 27).

Thus the Japanese child soon finds himself in a highly circumscribed situation. He is manipulated but eager to obey, not only because of the payoff for him, but eventually because of guilt for disobedience. Rebellion is minimized. Hostility and passive resistance toward the benevolent mother might meet with the responses, "You're only hurting yourself; you don't understand the consequences of your act," and "How can you do this to me? I'm always trying to do what is best for you." "Anyone who has observed the Japanese family functioning will agree that the strength of the mother is far from fictional alone; and the diaries kept by so many Japanese during the war provide still further evidence to support this point. It is surprising to an American to see expressed, so often, nostalgia for the mother and, so rarely, nostalgia for the wife. And these were, for the most part, not only very private and personal documents, but composed by males of combat age, mostly in their thirties or younger" (Hulse, 1948, p. 54).

But the child is learning something else besides and beyond dependency, social rules, and obedience. He is learning a technique for manipulating other people. He is learning the power of a projected social image and the methods for projecting it. He is learning that what people think of him is crucial for manipulating them and achieving rewards. He is learning to be sensitive to their needs, to respond quickly to their needs, and thus to build up an "account of goodwill" upon which he can draw when necessary, just as his mother built up reserves in his account as he grew up.

In a sense, he learns to be a self-sacrificing member of society. He learns to delay his gratification until some later date. He learns to depend on the goodwill of others for the later payoff of his investments of service, courtesy, and sacrifice. He also learns to be careful about accepting favors from others because favors come with obligations attached. Thus Iga (1961) notes that the "Japanese are deeply concerned with what others think of them," and it is no wonder that

DeVos finds that the "Japanese worry about how they appear to others" (1963, p. 33) and that they "show a subtlety or degree of sensitivity to what might be considered by others a minor assault on one's social presence" (1963, p. 34). DeVos further notes that suicidal acts seem to follow circumstances that caused the victim's social image to be debased. According to my interpretation, to suffer a blow to one's social image in Japan is not only to suffer a blow to one's sense of identity (an experience understandable to all men), but it also damages the principal source of control one has over others in the eventual satisfaction of one's needs. It is something like having one's social savings lost in a social depression.

It has been argued that the technique of social control is learned by the Japanese child from his mother. But one would expect that it is maintained because it continues to be an effective tool at many levels of Japanese society. Let us look at some of the historical and social-structural features that contribute to the maintenance of this combination of dependency and image presentation.

Since before the Tokugawa regime, Japanese society has been organized hierarchically. Male-female, professor-student, husband-wife, *daimyo-samurai*, *oyabun-kobun* — traditionally the Japanese have had interlocking sets of social superior-inferior roles (Norbeck, 1965; Sansom, 1962). The superior member of the dyad has the responsibility of protecting and rewarding the inferior member and the privilege of demanding services and esteem in return. The social inferior must be sensitive to the desires, attitudes, and moods of his superior. Simultaneously, the inferior must be in control of his own behavior (and, one step further, his psychological state) so that he does not alienate his superior and thus bring down punishment or withdrawal of rewards. The inferior's alertness, plus several indirect means of communicating his needs to the superior (ICT's), usually nets him satisfactory material and self-esteem rewards. The inferior, however, has no direct control over these scarce goods (Iga, 1968).

Another feature of Japanese social structure, though undergoing changes in recent years, is that shifting from one superior to another is generally very difficult. A woman with a domineering husband, for example, finds it nearly impossible to divorce him and remarry; or a factory worker with a harsh foreman finds it extremely difficult to change jobs.

The social superior has few problems in this system. He generally finds it to his advantage to keep his demands and privileges within reasonable limits. With this strategy he maintains a self-image of benevolence and avoids guilt. Incidentally, he also minimizes the possibility that indignant subordinates might resort to subtle undercutting and passive resistance should he take a more abandoned course.

Many people face the problem of communication and control up the hierarchy without endangering their own de facto dependency status (Hulse, 1962). A simple example might be, "How do I let my boss know I want a raise without risking his anger and my possible dismissal?" It is here that the interpersonal control techniques learned from his mother prepare the middle-class Japanese for adult life.

In the first place, the inferior's problem is somewhat reduced by Japanese sensitivity to social communications of all sorts. As argued above, this social sensitivity is learned by imitation of the Japanese mother. That is, in Japan any social signal, whether it be directed toward superiors, peers, or inferiors, is likely to be detected. Superiors cannot be expected to act on an undetected problem.

The Japanese are very skillful at signal emission or signal management, for this ability is really only a part of projecting a social image. Thus, signal management is an important technique for maneuvering in Japanese society (Hulse, 1962, pp. 302-303). The Japanese language is replete with concerns about signal management. Apparently one function of the end-of-the-sentence *keredomo* ("however") or *ga* ("but"), the provisional *desho* ("probably"), and the cautious *-so desu* ("it seems") is to signal careful attention to the listener's response and soften the speaker's commitment to his communication, just in case he may have said something potentially disruptive to the social relationship. Similarly, the Japanese have a tendency to prefer indirect messages with various possible interpretations in situations where a firm stand may threaten the stability of an important social relationship (Koestler, 1961, pp. 216-226). For interesting accounts of Japanese social image projection see the delightful novel, *The Honorable Picnic* (Raucat, 1924), and Hulse's equally perceptive essay (1962, p. 303).

When the relevant recipient of a communication is the public as opposed to a familiar person or a small group and communications therefore are more likely to be misinterpreted or disruptive, some Japanese may be quite uncomfortable and *hazukashii* (the meaning of this word sometimes approximates "shy"). In such situations, as on a public conveyance or at a lecture, most Japanese (even tense, neurotic patients) have the ability to sit almost perfectly still. The slightest movement may attract attention and be interpreted as a communication by those nearby. For example, on the train a very slight movement is sufficient to signal that one is preparing to get off so that others can begin clearing the way and initiating subtle negotiations about who is to get the vacated seat. The culturally shared understandings include standardized behaviors — such as reading or sleeping or feigning sleep — signifying that a person has removed himself from communication status on buses or trains. One may assume that eye contact, a blatant kind of communication, is avoided (Kasahara and Sakamoto, 1970).

In a similar way, the culture provides standardized intermediary roles to maintain signal control in delicate situations. "Delicate" as used here defines a situation in which emotion-laden material is to be communicated, and both parties are expected to have heightened awareness of the other's signals. The *miai* marriage arranger, the interpreter, the real estate broker, and sometimes the nurse are examples of such intermediaries.

I would argue that these qualities of dependency and social sensitivity, this manipulation through image projection and self-sacrifice, mark Japanese national character. If these traits are projected to an extreme the result is a person who is so sensitive to signals from others (especially his social superiors, but peers and inferiors as well) and so concerned with his own signal management and image presentation that he is concerned with nothing else. During a casual conversation he processes so much irrelevant input from himself and his partner that he cannot keep the thread of the conversation in mind. And in a crowd there is such a flood of signal input that he becomes panicky. This extreme type is none other than the *shinkeishitsu* anthropophobic (*taijin kyofu-sho*) neurotic patient for whom Morita therapy was developed.

The introspective accounts of anthropophobic patients, though not couched in these terms, are concordant with this interpretation. Now, of course, I do not argue that this Japanese concern with image projection is the only factor in producing *shinkeishitsu*-type neurosis. It is my impression that it is a necessary but not sufficient cause for development of this kind of disorder. Others (e.g., Kim, 1967; Iga, 1961, 1968) have emphasized the suppression of outwardly expressed aggression in Japanese culture as a major factor in disrupting

Japanese personality. Whatever the causes of neurosis, I would argue that this Japanese emphasis on social relations and image projection colors the symptomatic expression of anthropophobic neurosis. This conclusion parallels that of Kora (undated) whose argument is based on linguistic and philosophic grounds.

(From a theoretical perspective it is worth mentioning in passing that Ruth Benedict, (1934), has hypothesized that the extreme development of national character is not considered abnormal in a culture since it merely displays favored characteristics to an extreme. If this analysis of *shinkeishitsu* anthropophobia is to hold, i.e., if this disorder can be seen as an extreme development of a Japanese national character trait, then Benedict's hypothesis must be reformulated.)

One of the main functions of Morita therapy may be seen as the freeing of the individual from his oversensitivity to social signals and demands, so that he no longer need be overly dependent on others for life satisfaction. He need not be so alert to social clues and he need not be so conscious of the self because there is no need to control his behavior output so carefully. And, in fact, some patients who have undergone Morita therapy pass from an extreme of sensitivity and overcontrol to an extreme of thoughtlessness and insensitivity to others' feelings in the pursuit of personal ends.

The process of freeing a man from the excessive demands of society may be called "desensitization." From an oversocialized starting point the subject moves toward complete freedom from social restraint. Whereas the Japanese is socialized to be dependent and sensitive to others' social signals and to project a socially acceptable image by carefully monitoring his own signals, in the desensitization process of Morita therapy and (as we shall see) of Zen he is trained to respond to the immediacy of a situation without complex monitoring. "If a task needs to be done — do it," becomes his maxim.

NATURALISM AND THE LOCUS OF PREFERRED ACTIVITY

The general philosophical orientation among the Japanese which might be termed "naturalism" (Yamamoto, 1964; see also Kumasaka, 1965) provides the broadest ideological foundation for Moritist theory. This naturalism comprehends the value of accepting phenomenological reality without direct resistance. It is epitomized in the oft-repeated illustration of the bamboo that bends before the wind, flexible, never breaking, springing back after the force has passed. This conception, probably of Taoist origin, was incorporated into Buddhist thinking in China before passing into Japan. One learns to accept and appreciate the natural rather than becoming obsessed with what ought to be, rather than disrupting the natural order of the external world.

"Sometimes our mind is sharp and clear, at other times dull and listless. The important thing is not to let this worry or hamper you" (Kapleau, 1965, p. 115). These could be the words of a Morita therapist, but they are not. They are the advice of a Zen master offered to his student with regard to *zazen*. A further sense of this acceptance is found in the following two excerpts:

> In summer you adapt yourself to the heat, in winter to cold. If you are rich, you live the life of a rich man; if you are poor, you live with your poverty. . . . Lived this way, life isn't a problem. Animals have this adaptability to a high degree. Human beings also have it, but because they imagine they are this or that, because they fashion notions and ideas of what they *ought* to be or how they *ought* to live, they are constantly at war with their environment and themselves. (Kapleau, 1965, p. 134)

> When we chain ourselves with notions of what we *must* have happen, we lose what *does* happen. When we free ourselves to accept what does happen, we might even allow ourselves to appreciate it and live it fully. (Huber, 1965, p. 101)

Such is the conception of freedom through acceptance of the natural. The reader will recall that it is the resistance of the neurotic patient to his condition which perpetuates his problem. A key term in Moritist thinking is relevant here: *arugamama*, meaning "the acceptance of pheonomenological reality," or, literally, "as it is." There is a general misunderstanding about this term and the broader ideology it represents. The West has been presented to many Japanese as holding to a philosophy of active struggle with nature, of accepting a rationalistic idealism in which man is the measure of all things and objective reality must be brought into line with man's needs and desires. In contrast, the Oriental peoples have been characterized as naturalistic in orientation in the sense of passively accepting their status as a part of nature.

Perhaps these caricatures hold some degree of truth, although one can find numerous circumstances in which the oversimplification simply does not hold. For example, Japanese farmers have fought insects that attacked their crops and American Midwesterners have waited passively in storm cellars for cyclones to pass. These behaviors are in direct contrast with the stereotypes, but they are manifestly appropriate to the respective situations.

Instead of an active-struggling versus passive-acceptance dichotomy, I would suggest that a more useful contrast between Oriental and Western approaches to problem solving lies in the locus of preferred activity. One's phenomenological reality is a product of one's inner state and objective reality. By manipulating either factor it is possible to change phenomenological reality. It seems that, in very general terms, the West is more accepting of activity directed toward changing objective reality and the East is (or was) more accepting of actively changing one's inner attitudes toward or attention to objective reality. Of course, this generalization is gross; exceptions are readily found, increasingly so as cross-national communications increase. But the Eastern naturalistic approach is quite clearly present in Zen, Naikan, and Morita therapy.

The difference between East and West is pointed up by Leonhard's attempts to use a modified form of Morita therapy in East Germany. He wrote (translated from Leonhard and Iwai, 1966; Iwai, personal communication):

> I was wrong to think that we should suggest to the patients that their anxiety would disappear. The important attitude is not one of enduring suffering while waiting for cure, but rather we must lead the patient to a general acceptance of his life condition (as it exists in the present). So there is no point in wondering whether or not the patient's anxieties will remain in the future. He must accept whatever his life brings to him; if it be anxiety, then his acceptance will handle it perfectly.... It is difficult to expect German patients to accept this attitude. They want to be cured of their symptoms, and they do not want to be told to accept their state as if it were eternal.

In other words, the German patients wanted to manipulate their phenomenological world by medication or withdrawal from their symptoms (conceptually, it is almost as if they desired to walk away from their symptoms, as if symptoms were external and detachable "things"), rather than changing their attitude toward something that is a part of them, part of reality.

But I must reemphasize that the Japanese value is not passive resignation. It is simply tactical. Certain sorts of problems are held to be best handled by indirection and internal change. "Thus the skilled master of life never opposes things; he never tries to change things by asserting himself against them; he yields to their full force and either pushes them slightly out of direct line or else moves them right around in the opposite direction without ever encountering their direct opposition. That is to say, he treats them positively; he changes them by acceptance, by taking them into his confidence, never by flat denial" (Watts, 1958, p. 37).

In the social sphere, too, the Japanese individual, rather closely confined by social restrictions and responsibilities, often responds to interpersonal situations and problems by trying to adjust himself rather than his circumstances. Certainly, direct opposition to the will and desires of other persons who exist as part of his external reality is to be avoided. Thus the Japanese middle-class parent, rather than opposing the will of his child, often yields. A child may be permitted to continue rowdy behavior without repeated nagging until his activity leads naturally to a slight injury, a frightening crash, or simply fretful exhaustion. Then he is consoled and shown how his uncontrolled behavior led to such consequences.

Essentially the same refusal to oppose the will and desires of another, trusting that the natural consequences of his act will surely prove the wisdom of a different (suggested) course, was observed in the relations between Japanese psychiatrists and an American anthropologist, husbands and wives, cab drivers and tourists, and, classically, between Morita therapists and their patients. For instead of ordering the patient to work immediately upon his admission to the hospital, the Morita therapist permits the patient to indulge himself in what appears to him to be a quite desirable state, complete withdrawal. He learns, naturally, the results of withdrawal during the bed-rest period. At the end of the period he is motivated to work. With a minimum of human manipulation the patient has been maneuvered into understanding the unnaturalness of withdrawal from society and the naturalness of constructive activity in the service of his society and himself.

JAPANESE CHARACTER AND DISCREPANCIES BETWEEN THEORY AND PRACTICE

Looked at in one way, Morita therapy seems to be particularly harsh and demanding. The patient comes to a respected teacher (*sensei*) for guidance and is expected to put forth great effort in following the prescribed course of treatment. But the course of treatment seems uncompromising and difficult to follow: a week of bed rest with no diversions, then increasingly demanding physical labor. The patient must compulsively attend to the task at hand. His diary must conform to rigid standards of criticism. His daily behavior must be under strict control. He must attend the *kowa* lecture and speak frankly and publicly about his personal symptoms. Rebellion and passive resistance are out of the question; even complaining is suppressed.

Several writers have commented on the severity of the method and on the authoritarianism that must exist to keep the patient conforming to the demands of the setting (Jacobsen and Berenberg, 1959; Kumasaka, 1965; Levy, 1965). These writers and others were responding to Moritist theory; possibly they were responding to Moritist practice forty years ago; certainly they were responding to the Morita therapy presented by Japanese and Western authors in articles of the 1960s. They were written of a harsh authoritarian Morita therapy, a chimera that simply does not exist in modern Japan.

The description is distorted in several senses. It characterizes Morita therapy as a single treatment method, ignoring the substantial variations or styles of the therapy. It gives a narrow, static description of Morita therapy. It portrays a method of such severity as to be probably unworkable in any culture under conditions of voluntary admission and open (unlocked) wards.

In actuality, Morita therapy is a much freer, more human endeavor than one would gather from reading the literature. It is certainly more directive and consistently authoritarian than any contemporary Western therapy, yet this aspect is not the whole, and it is to the divergence between Morita's theory as it appears in print and Moritist practice working itself out in Moritist hospitals that this section is devoted.

In contrast with the severe caricature of Morita therapy drawn above, my field notes contain the following observations from many Moritist hospitals: patients chatting, reading, and listening to the radio while on absolute bed rest; patients failing to work compulsively, idly chatting for long periods of time; patients noticing but failing to pick up scattered leaves and failing to straighten disarranged slippers, messy working areas, and public entrances; complaints and outright disagreements with doctors; patients failing to attend *kowa* lectures and failing to submit diaries; patients oversleeping; patients talking about their symptoms. I also observed doctors failing to work alongside patients; doctors using psychoanalytic terms and interpretations of neurosis; doctors encouraging patients to talk together about their symptoms. Many more discrepancies could be cited.

The responses of authority to these violations were simple reminders of the rules or, most often, no comment at all. The violations went unnoticed or were ignored. Why? What accounts for these discrepancies? One of the contributing factors is the presence of several unstated values within Japanese culture which are in direct conflict with stated Moritist values. At this time we shall take a look at some of these unstated values and suggest some of the ways they undermine (or reinforce) the theoretical means and goals of Morita therapy.

From my observation there seems to be a value in Japanese culture which fosters what may be called the "humanization of rules." From early childhood parental prohibitions are accompanied by explanations of the restriction in terms of the child's needs. Rather than simply exerting his will (with an adult's superior experience and strength to back up the order), the Japanese parent often goes to great lengths to explain the situation to his child and stress the need for obedience (Lanham, 1966). The child thus learns that a rule is to be obeyed primarily in terms of its effects on someone — on himself initially — but gradually the effects on his family and on his nation are taken into consideration, too. Obedience is nearly always viewed in terms of personal and social consequences of acts rather than, say, spiritual breaches of absolute laws (Koestler, 1961, p. 207). And, for the child, the consequences are not governed by parental rewards or punishments, but by rewards and punishments he can detect as inherent in the situation, including the social situation. For a somewhat similar analysis see Lanham (1966) and Vogel (1963).

In adult behavior, as well, it is generally assumed that rules are not being obeyed for the sake of obedience, but because personal and/or social consequences result from disobedience. The individual Japanese may not be fully conscious of these consequences at every choice point, but on questioning he can usually offer rational personal and social reasons for obedience; even if he cannot give the reasons, he generally assumes that they exist. In some instances, when a Japanese feels that he is aware of the major personal and social implications of a rule, he is free to act contrary to the rule without thereby causing himself any additional distress. Thus, if a patient is chatting with her roommate while on absolute bed rest, it is assumed that she has weighed the various possibilities and consequences and has decided to talk. Just to make sure that she had evaluated the consequences of her act, the proper and most common response of a passing nurse was to remind the patient of the importance of lying quietly in order to be cured. But the nurse realizes that she is not aware of the patient's inner needs at the moment, so the simple reminder is enough. If the patient fails to stop talking there is no serious ego involvement on the part of the nurse; there is no compulsion to force the patient to stop talking "because of the rules about that sort of thing." Both Lanham (1966) and Vogel (1963) have noted the lack of ego involvement in Japanese parents when their children resist their advice.

In Japan one sees people jaywalking in full view of the police, or entering paths marked "Entry Prohibited," or rushing untidily out of their slippers, and others seem to assume they had a good reason for doing those things. (For further examples of such rule breaking see Hulse, 1962, pp. 301-302.) Seemingly everyone assumes that the consequences have been scanned and that for that violator at that time obedience to the rule was secondary to some more pressing social or personal need. Of course, there are limits to such tolerance. When the violation is clearly harming others one may intervene forcefully, but there is a broad spectrum of rules covering essentially minor matters of a formal or personal nature which allow flexible responses in a culture where few are ego-attached to obedience per se (Koestler, 1961, p. 228).

The implication for Morita therapy is, of course, that the rules set down primarily for the personal end of curing the patient are rules the patient may choose to break with minimal social repercussions. If one is confronted with the importance of a rule for cure, and one does, in fact, see it as important, then rule breaking will result in feelings of shame and guilt, but such feelings are relative to other ends that have been achieved by breaking the rule. The result is that obedience to hospital rules can never be so rigid as the literature suggests.

On the other hand, flexibility in responding to rules keeps

patients from approaching a panic state. When the patient feels he is "up against the wall" he is tacitly permitted to dodge restrictions until the value of cure becomes primary again. This attitude toward rules applies also to standards and ideological positions. If a standard is not applicable in a given situation it need not be followed solely for consistency's sake. Such an attitude has contributed to the proliferation of styles of Morita therapy.

Returning to the illustration of the passing nurse discovering a patient talking while on absolute bed rest, there is a second reason why she does not reprimand the patient. That is the high value placed on maintaining harmonious social relations in Japan. Although this point should not be pushed too far, the Moritist hospital staff is aware that their jobs are easier and the patient's progress is more certain if the hospital runs along without interpersonal tension. Not only within the hospital setting but throughout Japanese culture there is a concern with keeping down social discord and maintaining at least superficial pleasantness. Many have noted that on a string of small islands with so large a population such concerns seem appropriate for survival.

The valuing of positive human relationships may be found in all cultures, to be sure; yet it is the degree to which it dominates Japanese life, at times taking precedence over rule breaking and honesty, which makes it noteworthy. In the hospital situation the emphasis on harmony works in contrasting ways. It serves to soften the response of staff to rule violation and so passively encourages deviance, but it also keeps the patients in line as they try to please those with whom they have a good relationship. Under these circumstances the kind of deviance is more likely to be passive sins of omission, such as failure to attend meetings, straighten slippers, and so forth, than to be active sins of commission, such as argumentation, destruction of property, and violence.

As discussed in detail later, the emphasis on humanized rules and human relations, although undermining strict obedience to therapy's rules, effectively minimizes the hostility and the rebellion that are likely to occur in any ideological reform and behavior change system. In this sense, these values are crucial in producing the desired result of curing the patient, despite their undermining of the theoretical means.

There is a simple lesson here for researchers in psychotherapy: the verbalized theory and the actual practice of psychotherapy, of any psychotherapy, are not the same. Genuine understanding of the effectiveness of any therapeutic system can come only from knowledge of both theory and practice. What psychotherapists say they do in therapy is important because it tells us what is meaningful to them. Yet there are techniques, habits, and orientations that are unnoticed or inconsequential from a particular psychiatrist's theoretical perspective. From other standpoints, in terms of other models, these acts and attitudes may be the keys to understanding changed behavior.

One must bear in mind that the results of any psychotherapy are explicable in terms of other theoretical systems. In other words, patients undergoing any psychotherapy may change their behavior, but not necessarily for the reasons put forth by their psychotherapist (London, 1964). Detailed comparisons of Morita's method with other systems of therapy are drawn in chapter 5.

A REMINDER

Perhaps I should remind the reader that I am not attempting here to present a rounded description of Japanese character. Lists of national character traits and more comprehensive discussions of Japanese personality may be found in Caudill (1973), Elzinga (1972b), Kahn (1970), and Yamamoto (1964). In this chapter I am seeking, first, to clarify some of the traits that seem to me to be relevant to an understanding of neurosis and treatment in Japan and, second, to point out some of the traits of normal Japanese character which stand out when one looks closely through the lens of neurotic pathology. The second aim is, on a smaller scale, not unlike Freud's effort to build a general theory of human psychological functioning based heavily on his understanding of neurotic patients' mental functioning. The advantages in terms of accessibility and openness and magnification are similar in both instances, as are the dangers of distortion and missing data.

IV   A CULTURAL-HISTORICAL PERSPECTIVE

Anthropologists have long held that cultures are patterned systems, so that change in one aspect of the system provokes change in other aspects. Japan is a changing culture. The economy, ideologies, values, leisure activities, the family structure, geographic mobility, population composition by age — all are changing. One would expect psychotherapy to be undergoing change, as well. The changes that are taking place in Morita therapy — a treatment form with a history of more than fifty years in Japan — have been influenced by other cultural changes.

It is useful to try to understand why changes have come about, for several reasons. My ultimate goal is to contribute to the development of a metatheory that will someday allow us to create or tailor a form of psychotherapy to fit a particular cultural setting and to fit a particular individual in that setting. One medicine is not effective for all diseases, nor is one dosage appropriate for all patients. Why should a single therapy form be maximally effective in all cultures and for all individuals in one culture? Looking at changes that have taken place in certain cultural settings suggests possible forms of relationships between culture and psychotherapy, should we desire to create others.

A second purpose is to help the Morita therapists themselves become aware of trends whose outlines they may be unable to perceive because they are too close to the subject. If they agree that such trends seem to be developing, they can choose to accelerate, reverse, retard, redirect, or ignore them on a rational, aesthetic, or stylistic basis, but at least with awareness that the trends exist.

Finally, the interrelationship of several aspects of culture — in this instance, psychotherapy, symptoms, ideology, economics, and so on – can be illustrated by this case study in understanding Morita therapy. Describing the interrelated patterns of culture and explicating how they came to be are long-standing anthropological tasks.

The evolution of a psychotherapeutic system is a fascinating process. Strictly speaking, I cannot specify with assurance the causes of the changes that have occurred in Morita therapy since its initial years in the 1920s. I can, however, provide documentation that changes have occurred and can describe concomitant changes in Japanese culture, in patient symptomatology, and in the profession of psychiatry which seem relevant to the historical development of Morita therapy. And I can provide the reader with some of the Moritist's own understandings of the changes and their causes.

THE HISTORICAL SETTING

Students of Freud will note more than a few similarities between the early development of psychoanalysis and that of Morita psychotherapy. Both the characteristics of the founders and the general psychiatric atmosphere were similar. Shōma Morita was a natural charismatic leader, surprisingly free from the restraints on individual expression imposed by the strict sociocultural milieu in which he was raised. He was born in 1874 in Kochi Prefecture. In his adolescence he suffered from neurasthenic symptoms, including palpitation, heavy-headed feelings, and a morbid fear of dying. He cured himself by his own method. Morita has been called by some a philosopher who had to go to medical school for financial reasons. He was graduated from the prestigious University of Tokyo Medical School in 1902.

Like Freud, Morita experimented with hypnosis as a therapeutic technique and abandoned it. There soon developed around him a band of loyal followers who further developed and expanded his psychotherapy, jealously defending it against criticism. His supporters cared for him through illness and advancing age. Again like Freud, he continued to read and write actively until near his death in 1938.

Morita's contribution to Japanese psychiatry is best understood in the light of psychiatric thought in Japan at the turn of the century. Much influenced by neurologically oriented German psychiatry, the Japanese considered neurasthenia to be a kind of physiological nervous exhaustion. Patients' nerves were thought to be weakened and irritable. Morita, like Freud, made the conceptual leap of explaining neurosis in mentalistic terms as opposed to neurological ones. Morita acknowledged his intellectual debt to the bed-rest therapy of Wier Mitchell, the scheduled-living therapy of Binswanger, and the persuasion therapy of Dubois, but he modified their techniques and developed a unique rationale for their use in combination.

Morita explicitly disclaimed any strong connection between his therapy and Zen Buddhism. There is no doubt, however, that Morita was strongly influenced by Zen modes of thought, both in his personal background and through the general sociocultural setting of late nineteenth- and early twentieth-century Japan.

Morita's distinctive conceptualization of neurosis and treatment was a distillation of ideas and orientations pervading the intellectual atmosphere of his time. It was essentially Buddhist in its emphasis on accepting one's experience of suffering as a means of transcending misery and losing one's self in productive effort for the good of one's fellows. Ideas similar to Morita's are readily found in the literature of his period. Several selections from a single work by Japan's most respected and representative author in the early 1900s, Natsume Sōseki, will illustrate the occurrence of such ideas in the literary world. *The Wayfarer* (or *The Living*, depending on how the Chinese characters of the title are read) is concerned with the neurotic suffering of a scholar as seen from the perspective of his wife, his family, a friend, and himself. The following passages from the book contain ideas that strongly suggest a Moritist orientation.

The advice of a friend pinpoints the neurotic's misconception that he alone suffers in some peculiar way: " 'Now what you call insecurity is the insecurity of the entire human race, and it isn't peculiar to you alone — if you realize this, that's that. Constant motion and flow is our very fate' " (p. 285).

The distinction between intellectual knowledge and experiential knowledge is apparent in the passage: " 'When you say it is frightening, it is simply because you feel it is convenient to use the word frightening. That is no genuine fright. In other words, it is nothing but the fright of the head. Mine is different. Mine is the fright of the heart' " (p. 286).

Even the specific Moritist thought concerning insomnia is echoed in *The Wayfarer:* " 'When you can't sleep you are trying very hard to get to sleep, are you not?' I asked. 'Exactly. That makes it all the more difficult for me to sleep,' he said" (p. 291).

Perfectionism, idealism, and hypersensitivity are qualities of the neurotic noted by both Sōseki and Morita: "Your brother is a sensitive person. Aesthetically, ethically, and intellectually he is in fact hypersensitive. As a result, it would seem that he was born only to torture himself. He has none of the saving dullness of intelligence which sees little difference between A and B. To him it must be either A or B. And if it is to be A, its shape, degree, and shade of color must precisely match his own conception of it; otherwise he will not accept it. Your brother, being sensitive, is all his life walking on a line he has chosen — a line as precarious as a tight rope [sic]. At the same time he impatiently demands that others also tread an equally precarious rope, without missing their footing. It would be a mistake, though, to think that this stems from his selfishness" (pp. 295-296). Here, too, are the germs of the Moritist ideas of the basic superiority of neurotic character and of the neurotic's selfish attitude.

For Morita, neurosis is fundamentally that misdirection of attention which interrupts the smooth flow of normal life with intrusive selfconsciousness. Sōseki agrees: "No matter in what frame of mind he may be, no longer is he able to go forward unless he first subjects his action to scrutiny. That's why the flow of his life is being interrupted every moment. It must be as trying as being called to the phone every other minute during mealtime. But it is his mind which interrupts, as well as his mind which is interrupted; in the last analysis he is controlled by these two minds which accuse each other from morning till night just as a wife and her mother-in-law might. As a consequence he cannot have even momentary peace" (p. 297).

Cure must come from abandoning the self, according to Buddhism, Morita, and Sōseki, as well: "Rather, clinging to it all [his own lofty standard], he yet becomes desperate for happiness. And he himself recognizes full well the very contradiction that enmeshes him. 'If you stop regarding your own self as the axis of life and fling it overboard altogether, you will feel more comfortable, believe me,' I again suggested" (p. 299). Again, "It makes me immeasurably happy to see your brother so absorbed in these trifles as to almost forget himself" (p. 311).

" 'Wouldn't it be handier to go the other way around?'

" 'The other way round?' he returned, his eyes sparkling earnestly.

" 'Yes — that is to say, to be so absorbed in the crabs, and thereby forget yourself. If you were thus perfectly one with your object, that would be the state you're talking about.'

" 'Indeed,' he responded uncertainly.

" 'Indeed? You are actually practicing it. Don't you realize that?'
" 'I see' " (p. 312).

Moritists, too, see the way to normalcy to be near at hand. As one former Moritist patient wrote in her letter to me, "I can only say that it wasn't as difficult as I thought it would be to achieve this peace of mind I have now." Moritists well understand Sōseki's thought: "What, as a friend, I am working for with him is only to have him regain the position of the average person like me. To put it somewhat differently, it means the seemingly ridiculous act of converting the extraordinary to the ordinary" (pp. 312-313). In other words, the task of cure is to convert the neurotic perception of the world to a more ordinary one, one less embellished with the artificially constructed turmoil of disturbed perception. To be sure, any perception of the world seems to be constructed (Berger and Luckman, 1966; Lilly, 1972), and all "normal" or "ordinary" perceptions of the world seem to admit some realistic suffering (e.g., the loss of loved ones, dying, sickness, aging), but the contrived suffering of the neurotic perspective seems unnecessary and, from this standpoint, amenable to change. Indeed, Freud himself saw that in dealing with his patients' suffering "much would be gained if we succeed in transforming your hysterical misery into common unhappiness" (Breuer and Freud, 1957, p. 305).

Morita therapy was fully developed by the 1920s and was being practiced at several hospitals and clinics. There was (and still is) a certain clannishness within each of the medical institutions in Japan which retards the spread of new methods and ideas. Morita therapy became associated with the small private medical school, Jikei University, where Professor Morita was assigned to teach. The therapeutic technique failed to make much headway in other institutions of higher learning, with one exception. Professor Shimoda of the large public university at Fukuoka, Kyushu University, supported Morita's theory and began training his staff in Morita's methods.

The development of Morita therapy through the 1930s and 1940s was deeply influenced by world events, particularly the Great Depression and World War II. Small hospitals and clinics struggled along; some were burned out in bombing raids.

In the immediate postwar period Morita therapy was introduced to the West by two psychoanalysts who visited at Kyushu University (Jacobsen and Berenberg, 1952). Since then numerous articles written by both Japanese and Westerners and representing a variety of theoretical perspectives have appeared in English (e.g., Caudill and

Doi, 1963; Kora, 1965; Kora and Sato, 1958; Ohara and Reynolds, 1968).

CHANGES IN THE PATIENT POPULATION

The "softest" argument for a relationship between culture and neurotic symptoms allows for a kind of "cultural possibilism." If there were no atom bomb or environmental pollution we would not find atom bomb phobia and PCB (an environmental pollutant popularized in the Japanese mass media) phobia among Japanese patients recently under treatment. The surface expression of these symptoms clearly reflects culturally meaningful phenomena.

But on a deeper level, leaving aside the expressive content of the obsessions and phobias, as I have argued above (see also Reynolds, 1969b), Japanese culture shapes the basic neurotic character in certain ways. Both in the cultural history and in the personal history of the Japanese people extreme sensitivity to interpersonal signals and cues has been strongly reinforced. In order to function smoothly in Japanese society today one must be careful to pick up small expressions of preferences and desires from significant others and to control the expressions of one's own preferences and desires. Except under certain culturally sanctioned conditions (such as social drunkenness), expressions of anger, hostility, bluntness, and sexuality are strongly controlled and suppressed. The anthropophobic (taijin kyofusho) Japanese neurotic patient clearly shows this national character trait to an extreme. He is so sensitive to detecting cues from others and processing and controlling his own emissions that he cannot function in society. Other neurotics, too, unable to express feelings of anger and sexuality with propriety seem to have settled for the more acceptable rewards of dependency, that is, being cared for (in both senses of the phrase) by others. In a sense the Japanese neurotic can express his hostility toward others through complaining of mild vague physiological and psychological symptoms, thus demanding their sympathy and time.

It seems reasonable that changes in a patient population might precipitate changes in therapy style. Here we shall examine the results of three formal studies and a composite of impressions gleaned from the clinicians themselves.

A study of over 700 neurotic patients who came to the Jikei

University outpatient clinic (published in two parts, Takeyama et al., 1966; Ohara et al. 1966) compared patient populations in 1953 and 1961. Although there are well-known dangers in using age-group data to represent changes in a population over time, I use such data here as a secondary suggestive resource to supplement the primary comparisons between the two years, 1953 and 1961.

Overall, there was no increase or decrease in the number of neurotic patients presenting themselves for treatment during this period. But there were shifts in the symptomatic expression of neurosis. Bodily complaints were the most frequent presenting symptom for both males and females, but the percentages of this type of complaint declined between 1953 and 1961. Obsessive phobics increased somewhat and frequencies of this neurotic form were inversely related to age. Ordinary *shinkeishitsu* (neurasthenic) diagnoses increased over the eight-year period (Miura and Usa, 1970.) The trend is clear: with increasing education body complaints and hysteria decrease while obsessions and phobias increase. In other words, there is a shift toward a more direct psychological locus of complaint and away from the indirect distortion of bodily functioning to express "dis-ease."

Incidentally, there was a large increase in the percentage of persons who came for treatment because of job-related problems. Patients from the smaller towns and villages were increasingly plagued both by work difficulties and by family problems. Such results are not surprising in view of the drastic revisions in Japanese village life during the past thirty years.

Turning now to a 1973-1974 random sample of Seikatsu no Hakkenkai members (sample size = 452 persons) (Hasegawa, 1974*a*), we can make a rough comparison with the 1961 outpatient population described above to extend the search for trends another decade. These sample populations seem to have been drawn from the same pool of neurotics.

The number of females seeking treatment has increased. A male to female ratio of 3:1 in 1961 has become 3:2 by 1974 for obsessives and ordinary (neurasthenic) *shinkeishitsu* diagnoses. Women have continued to have a disproportionately high frequency of anxiety neurosis; there is no change in the 1:1 male-female ratio in this diagnostic category.

Obsessive-compulsives have increased sharply compared with

ordinary and anxiety *shinkeishitsu* patients, while anxiety neurosis continues to be absent among teenagers and students.

In general, compared with the outpatient population in 1961, the Hakkenkai membership of 1973-1974 does not tail off so steeply with increasing age, especially in the obsessive-compulsive and neurasthenic categories. Both populations show a high percentage of obsessives among younger persons, along with anxiety neuroses and somatic complaints in the older age-groups. Ishii (1972) found a similar association between age and diagnosis in an analysis of replies to a newspaper article about Morita therapy.

What can we make of these data? My impression is that the increased number of women and elderly patients reflects not only greater permissiveness in seeking professional help but also a decline in the family's willingness and ability to handle disturbance in the traditional in-group way. The increased proportion of obsessive neuroses continues a trend reflecting more focused, less disguised symptoms. That is, the problem area is more likely to lie within the awareness of the patient. He is less likely to feel a generalized anxiety or a vague psychophysical reflection of his personal and interpersonal difficulties.

Moritist hospitals report changes in the inpatient population as well. A study by Ohara and Reynolds (1968) documents some of these changes. Ten representative Moritist hospital directors returned questionnaires on hospital conditions existing in 1964. In the 1920s in Morita's hospital, Shinryojo, the predominant form of *shinkeishitsu* treated was the obsessive-phobic form. In 1964 obsessive-phobics still predominated in only half of the ten reporting hospitals. Two hospitals had more anxiety hysteria, one had more anxiety hysteria and neurasthenia, and two reported no predominance of a single type, but rather many combinations.

There are other shifts in the patient population. In the 1920s the hospitalized patient was more often a male than a female and generally in his twenties or, next most frequently, in his teens. He most likely was admitted for inpatient care in April, the period in which students receive notice of their school entrance examination standings and businessmen close their fiscal year. The modern hospitals also reported more male patients than females in 1964, and the patients were most often in their twenties but next most frequently in their thirties. Thus the inpatient population is shifting toward a slightly older group. Five hospitals reported no wide seasonal varia-tion in admissions. Four hospitals reported highest admission numbers in July and August (summer vacation period), and only one reported April and May as the peak period. All hospitals, including Shinryojo in the 1920s, admitted the smallest number of patients during the Japanese New Year period.

After discussing the modern Japanese inpatient with experienced Moritist clinicians throughout Japan, I have compiled a summary of their impressions of change in this hospitalized group.

Therapists find patients these days less willing to accept authority, less conscientious and persevering in carrying out pre-scribed treatment, and less cooperative with routine. This finding is due partly to the wider range of patients (including depressed and mildly psychotic patients treated with medication) admitted to Moritist hospitals.

Within the neurotic group, mixed *shinkeishitsu* types seem to be increasing. Therapists report an overlay of strong overt dependency in many recent patients. And the characteric strong will of the *shinkeishitsu* patient has become somewhat less common.

More "acting-out" behavior seems to be encountered now then previously. Probably because of the increase in expressive acting-out behavior of students, the *shinkeishitsu* expression of the neurotic suppression of anger and sexuality has declined. In addition to the typical overly controlled patients seen increasingly by Moritists, there are childish, even explosive, patients. The positive valuation of excitement and of constant external stimulation in modern youth culture contributes to this increased activity and behavioral expres-siveness.

It appears that patients' values are changing in other areas, too. The Morita therapist can no longer expect consistent social support, feedback, and modeling in the milieu of his discharged patient. In Japan of the 1920s a person found meaning in life by contributing to his family, his community, and his nation. His self-concept was tied strongly to the proper execution of his role. Recent alternatives such as individualism and expressivity challenge these traditional values; many patients feel the conflict though they may still lean toward the traditional values. Work itself as an ultimate value is called into question by the modern emphasis on leisure activities. (See Yamamoto, 1964; Iga, 1967; Matsumoto, 1960; Plath, 1964.)

Changes in the kinds of patients admitted to Moritist hospitals force the hospitals to change. Values that were simply assumed to be shared before must be taught. For example, at Ushibuse Hospital in Numazu part of the therapy is teaching Moritist patients to sit quietly and to unite themselves with nature. Gardening, nature walks, and careful observation of animal life are an integral part of the treatment process. That such an orientation must be taught to Japanese people would probably have been unthinkable in Morita's day; it was simply assumed to be part of the psychological equipment of the patient.

Moreover, the modern Japanese patient is dissatisfied (at least initially) with instructions to accept his symptoms. He desires to be rid of them. He sees them, as Westerners do, as attached to him rather than as a part of himself. He may be aware of other therapy forms that aim at taking away symptoms. Moreover, the modern patient wants to understand intellectually why he must do what he is told to do. He wants reasons, and he is less willing than patients in earlier years simply to accept the therapist's instructions on the basis of his faith in the authority and experience of the *sensei*.

One Moritist pointed out that the larger number of female inpatients reflects not only increased freedom to enter a hospital but also, perhaps, the strain of bearing increased responsibilities in a culture moving in the direction of sex-role egalitarianism. Some of the women enter the hospital because of difficulties with an authoritarian husband (*danna-sama*); they do not respond well to an authoritarian therapist. The traditionally stern Morita therapist must adapt himself to present a softer, more reasonable image. A rational, gentler demeanor also fits well with the expectations of intellect-oriented youthful patients. But there are still elderly patients arriving for treatment who respond well to the forceful, directive, authoritarian approach. As we shall see, however, the trend is clearly toward rationalism and egalitarianism in treatment philosophy.

DEVELOPMENTS IN TECHNIQUE

It can be argued that the practice of Morita therapy has developed in the direction of less face-to-face one-to-one contact between therapist and patient and an increasing patient-therapist ratio. Morita began by treating a few patients in his home. He virtually accepted them into his family. To my knowledge only Dr. Koga and Dr. Masugi preserve such a style today. The next stage saw the establishment of Moritist hospitals by former patients and students of Morita. The hospitals have become larger over time, owing primarily to economic pressures.

In an overlapping but more recent period Morita therapy began to be practiced extensively in outpatient programs. A single therapist could handle fairly large numbers of outpatients, sometimes treating them in addition to his inpatients. Again, primarily for economic reasons, the tendency was in the direction of increased patient loads and decreased contact with individual patients.

A more recent development is a group session in which fifteen to twenty neurotic persons gather once a month for three or four hours with one or more therapists. Group members maintain contact in the interim through an organization magazine. The ultimate in non-face-to-face contact is the most recent therapy form of exchanges of letters between therapist and patients. The exception to this trend is that books and, later, magazines have long held a respectable position in this treatment form.

As noted earlier in the discussion of Sansei Hospital, national health insurance has brought mixed opportunities to Moritist hospitals. It has opened up the possibility of treatment to many persons who could not otherwise afford it. But hospitals must accept more patients who, individually, pay smaller bills. Larger staffs must be hired, and so the hospital population must be kept near capacity so that the staff can be paid. In turn, the need for more patients reduces the selectivity that the hospital can exercise in admitting applicants. Nonneurotics must be admitted, and the resulting wide range of disorders makes it difficult to maintain the therapeutic milieu that marks Moritist hospitals. Strict, impersonal rules become necessary.

As noted by Reynolds and Yamamoto (1973), it is not only economic pressures that have brought about mass treatment methods, but also the therapists' own desires for a private life. Professionalism produces fewer young psychiatrists who are willing to work alongside their patients cleaning gardens or painting buildings. Moreover, a twenty-four-hour-a-day commitment to living with one's patients seems onerous to many young therapists. Research into abbreviated forms of Morita therapy and increasing emphasis on outpatient treatment are the obvious results of these pressures.

From the client's point of view, methods offering occasional outpatient sessions or group meetings on Sunday are more convenient than hospitalization because he loses less job time. Moreover, abridged therapy forms are more easily concealed from family and friends and are less shameful and less costly. Of course, severely disturbed group members and outpatients are still referred to hospitals, but increasingly the philosophy adopted by Morita therapists is that if the patient can function in society he can work on his problems out there without the necessity for the sheltered milieu of the hospital. When therapists hold such a philosophy, one of the characteristic features of Morita therapy, absolute bed rest, cannot be utilized in the treatment program of many patients, since it is possible only for inpatients.

Let us look at several specific changes in characteristic elements of Morita therapy — such as work, absolute bed rest, and group meetings — which make visible undercurrents of ideological shift and flow.

Work. — The high valuation placed on work by the Japanese culture has been pointed out by many anthropologists (e.g., DeVos, 1965, p. 645; Caudill and DeVos, 1961; Norbeck, 1965). Yamamoto's (1964) summary of Japanese national character studies notes the regard for work as one of the common findings. The phenomenon of Japan's high economic productivity (DeVos, 1965), along with the fact that in 1968 Japan had the world's lowest unemployment rate despite its large population (*Asahi Evening News,* July 23, 1968), provides indirect evidence that work is highly valued. As Norbeck (1965, p. 20) points out, "The lazy person in Japan is more than merely lazy, he is regarded as untrustworthy and morally unsound. . . . Whatever the origin of this ideal, the modern Japanese 'naturally' values industriousness and 'naturally' wishes to succeed."

There is some apparent disagreement among writers as to the exact nature of the work ethic in Japanese culture. Kumasaka, visiting in the United States, writes, "Manual work is a path through which a patient unifies with nature" (1965, p. 641); he adds that the Japanese patient has a special attitude toward work which is not likely to be found in Anglo-Saxon patients. On the other hand, DeVos claims that "the Japanese, just as was true for the Protestant Calvinists of northern Europe, often find an existential resolution in hard work" (1965, p. 645). But the work ethic in Japan seems to me to be fundamentally different from the Protestant work ethic with its underlying individualistic emphasis. The Japanese work ethic is based on a presumption of social or societal repayment. To put it differently, in my interpretation presented above, the Japanese work ethic is not work for work's sake, or work for heaven's sake, but work for some defined person's or group's sake.

There seems to be some disagreement on the subject of work even among Morita therapists (see chap. 1). I have been told by one Morita therapist that the Japanese consider work an end in itself, that if one asks a Japanese (as he asked his patients) why he works, the person will be hard pressed or, more often, unable to give (as an American informant might) a series of personal and social ends that can be accomplished by means of work. In contrast, Dr. Kora's writings clearly and consistently make the point that work is a means toward obtaining primarily social but also personal subgoals whose successful accomplishment results in feelings of self-worth.

Perhaps such analysis of the specific nature of the Japanese work ethic is more detailed than necessary for our purposes. Whatever the deeper interpretation, it is sufficient here to point out that there is substantial agreement on the high valuation of work in Japanese culture and that stress on the work ethic supports the techniques of Zen and Morita therapy and give consensual acceptability to the goal of task accomplishment in Morita therapy.

It may be true that the value of work is undergoing change in modern Japan (Norbeck, 1965; Plath, 1964) as the competing values of leisure and personal expression become evident. One would expect, then, a trend toward broader interpretations of "work" (e.g., as described above for Kora Koseiin and Nomura hospitals) to include recreational activity.

Morita therapists take different positions on the issue of work and play. Some hold that during therapy only work should be permitted. Play is seen by such therapists as rather frivolous, as an escape employed by some patients to avoid confronting reality. Other therapists see work as preferable to play in that patients can make a social contribution through work. They hold that occasional play is acceptable and natural — a refreshment for more work. A third group points out that work and play are sometimes difficult to distinguish conceptually, that either can be an escape, and therefore that both are desirable activities in which the patient can "lose himself."

Work within Moritist hospitals takes many forms. In most hospitals it includes the traditional chores of filling an oil stove, burning trash, wiping walls and ceilings, and the like. Often it is assigned in rotation and is done by pairs or small groups. At other times the patient is encouraged to discount his own work at hand. In large psychiatric hospitals with small wards for patients undergoing Morita therapy, work is difficult to find or to create because janitorial and custodial personnel are assigned all clean-up and repair tasks. Modern conveniences have simplified and eliminated tasks in even the most conservative hospitals. When one looks at the type of work still done by patients at Kora Koseiin, for example (cleaning offices, weeding the garden, drying persimmons, caring for pets, and so forth), as opposed to the routine, commercial piecework done by patients at Sansei Hospital, one gets a picture of the changing nature of work carried out in Moritist hospitals.

The taken-for-granted value of work prominently underlies Moritist philosophy. From a couple of directions, however, this value is being undermined. Old-timers say that in Morita's day the kinds of work people did were more meaningful in the sense that the results were often immediately visible and the people for whom the work was done were known, face-to-face associates of the worker. It is more difficult for patients to find satisfaction in the mass-production tasks that society offers them in modern Japan. The basic issue, however, is whether the meaning of a task lies in the nature of the task or in the attitude of the worker or in both; modern Moritists increasingly stress the nature of the task in resolving the questions.

Related to the problem of meaningless work is the greater attention given to leisure in Japan. National polls indicate that Japanese people have growing amounts of leisure time and that they are more and more adopting a work-for-the-purpose-of-leisure attitude. Particularly among young people (in the age brackets most often encountered by Moritists), this change of attitude is rapidly taking place. Developments in Moritist theory in the direction of allowing play equal status in treatment programs can be seen in the light of changing Japanese attitudes toward leisure.

Morita's own thinking about the stages of increasing work loads changed during the 1920s. At first he established clearly defined stages and forbade contacts between patient and family until the final stage. Later, however, he supported a gradual resumption of work and allowed freer social contact. It was common at Shinryojo Hospital for patients to engage in gardening, repair work, and shopping expeditions for the hospital. There was no formal recreational therapy, but games of various sorts were played.

In this area there is a great deal of variation among the hospitals today (Ohara and Reynolds, 1968). Two hospitals observe three clearly defined stages of increasing work loads; five hospitals increase the work load gradually; and three hospitals have dropped this aspect of therapy completely. Similarly, recreation therapy shows wide variation today. Three hospitals offer conventional play opportunities; two offer golf, chorus, dance, and music therapy; and five report that they provide no recreation therapy since Morita therapy is based upon a work ethic.

Isolated bed rest. — Characteristic of Morita therapy is the initial week of isolated bed rest. In Morita's Shinryojo Hospital the patient either was alone in a small private room or shared a large double room. His doctor, following a detailed formula for the interview, visited him once each day for one minute. In modern Morita therapy the principle of contemplative isolation is still maintained, although four hospitals report that two or three patients share a medium-sized room. Two hospitals report a somewhat shorter (five days on the average) bed-rest period. And there is more flexibility in the therapist contact, ranging from no visits at all during the bed-rest period to visits twice a day. Differences in frequency and duration of visits are closely related to philosophical disputes over transference. Bedside routines employed during the initial period of therapy vary from no visits at all to visits of as much as thirty minutes, during which any one of a number of psychotherapeutic techniques is utilized. The practical effectiveness of the transference phenomenon within Morita therapy is an issue of debate, but some therapists use the bed-rest period to establish a satisfactory relationship with the patient.

Dr. M. Puuko (personal communication) has speculated that in Morita's day strong social pressures and the deep embedment of the individual in the group made isolated bed rest a useful tool to bring the patient, alone, into contact with himself. Alienation, rather than group immersion, she argues, is characteristic of modern urban societies, including Japan. To counteract alienation, then, Morita therapists pay more attention to group processes and attempt to shorten or eliminate the bed-rest period.

Group meetings. — As noted above, Shinryojo Hospital was quite familistic in its atmosphere. Patients and staff dined together and shared common living facilities and gardens. Morita considered the whole day to be training time; patients and staff gathered around him during the day and evening for informal instruction. No formal meetings were held. After some patients were discharged, contact was maintained by keeping them in Morita's home, which functioned as a dormitory. Others kept contact through the monthly magazine, *Shinkeishitsu*, with a circulation of 2,000.

In the 1960s four hospitals had no formal patient-staff meetings, one had such meetings every day, and the others had meetings from once every month or two to three times a week. The meeting content varied widely. In one hospital meetings were held to criticize patient behavior, and in another, to allow patients to talk about their experiences. In one hospital the doctor replied to the patients' questions, and in another he gave a formal lecture. Four hospitals published newsletters for ex-patients (monthly, bimonthly, or quarterly) with circulation ranging from 250 to 1,800; five did not publish newletters at all. Again the trend was toward a more professionalized formalized therapeutic setting and away from a familistic milieu.

Drugs. — Another obvious change in technique came with the introduction of drug therapy. Psychotropic medications were not used at Shinryojo Hospital. They were simply ineffective in the 1920s. Today, during the bed-rest phase of treatment, two hospitals rarely use drugs and two frequently use drugs, with the other hospitals intermediate between these extremes. After isolated bed rest two hospitals use no drugs, two use drugs in the treatment of anxiety, four use them to treat depression, and two use them for various categories of illness. It is noteworthy that the modern Japanese therapist, like his Western counterpart, often encounters patients who request only psychopharmacological therapy and fail to understand the importance of the other aspects of treatment.

Western psychiatry has contributed greatly to the development of effective psychopharmacological agents. The influence of Western psychiatry on the introduction of psychiatric drugs in Japan would be hard to overemphasize. The ideology of the West has had an equal impact on Moritist techniques, which have become more feeling-oriented, more exploratory, and more egalitarian during the therapy's fifty-year history.

The definition of cure. — The emphasis of Morita therapy was on improved behavior with the accompanying expectation that emotional distress would improve concomitantly. One would expect, then, that the standard for discharge from Shinryojo Hospital was change in behavior, as indeed it was. The modern Moritist hospitals are divided equally between those that discharge on the basis of changed behavior alone and those that discharge on the basis of changed behavior and changed feelings. No Moritist hospital discharges its patients on the basis of the patient's feelings only.

Nevertheless, within hospitals and outside them cure has increasingly come to mean "feeling better" and the clearing away of symptoms in addition to improved behavior. Either explicitly or implicitly patients are offered the hope of cure in a sense much different from that used originally by Morita. There is an intermediate rationale which holds that improved behavior usually leads naturally to improved feelings. But any concern within improved or less anxious feelings implies that an evaluation of one feeling as preferable to another has crept into the therapy. Feelings are no longer accepted as they are, without evaluation. Certainly the hopes of improved feelings, self-confidence, and the like are more easily understood by modern patients than the need for accepting life as it is. Perhaps Moritists are responding to the increased competition from other forms of therapy available in Japan today. It appears likely, also, that the Buddhist ethos, which supported Morita's view of feelings and character development, no longer carries great weight in modern Japan.

New Orientations

A kind of experimental, explorative, tentative attitude appears among modern Moritists who work on new developments of the therapy. I still sometimes hear the early and confident "Your case is easily cured." Nevertheless, as Morita therapy is used with hypnotherapy, meditation, group techniques, and public education, there is a sense of experimentation, a concern with gaining others' views of these efforts and strategies, and an interest in a descriptive, statistical evaluation of the results. The trend from dogmatism to exploration would seem to be catalyzed by increased awareness that other therapeutic options are available and useful for some patients. But it is the general movement in Japan away from the system of over-ridingly strong personal ties to one's mentor which permits rapid innovation and more impersonal evaluation of therapeutic results. A few older therapists still strive to preserve Morita therapy as they perceive it to have been. They are motivated by their belief in its effectiveness, by their ties of loyalty to Professor Morita, and per-haps, by personal hopes of public identification with the earlier forms. Since they are already convinced of the value of the therapy, their papers and conversations usually center on historical or theoretical-philosophical issues rather than empirical investigations of current treatment results or innovative possibilities.

Related to this new explorative approach is a kind of tolerance for alternate interpretations and alternate perspectives, at least behind the scenes. I have heard some young psychiatrists say that they do not believe in Moritist principles but they use them with outpatients because patients find them helpful. Therapists are some-times troubled by patients who bring out conflicting opinions of various Morita therapists in public meetings. I noticed also an increased tolerance for joking about Moritist ideas. Laughter can reflect a kind of distanced or noninvolved perspective. Recently I have begun to hear patients and therapists laughing together over spontaneous jokes like the following: A girl was beginning to sun-burn as she sat in the bright summer sunshine. As she started to move toward the shade, a fellow patient laughed and told her to accept her condition "as it is" (*arugamama ni*), purposely misusing the Moritist phrase. In another example, the leader at a party explained a new game. "Shall we practice it once?" he asked. "No, 'enter into reality,'" a patient retorted. These jokes suggest that the Moritist phrases no longer have a "sacred" quality.

I have already mentioned the trend toward less strictness and authoritarianism and toward a gentler egalitarianism. This is not to say that the *sensei* has altogether abandoned his position of respected authority based on his experience. But, generally speaking, he gives orders less and explains more these days. Partly, this trend seems to be a function of the increasing option that patients have of switching doctors. Since there are more doctors and some health insurance support is available, shopping around is more feasible. An additional cause of declining authority is probably the gradual adoption of some of the Western democratic disrespect for authority. Interest-ingly, as the hierarchical emphasis declines, Moritists dwell more and more on the establishment of rapport with the patient. Patient-therapist relations seem to be shifting toward more egalitarian levels.

In group meetings of the most recent type there is much more verbal interaction among group members than previously. Until the last two or three years the communication form in group meetings was usually either a lecture or a series of therapist-patient exchanges, with the therapist asking a single patient about his symptoms, the patient replying, the therapist giving advice, then turning to the next patient, and so forth. Today in some groups patients respond to fellow patients, sometimes at the direction of the therapist and sometimes not. Partly this development seems to be a result of the adoption of Western "democratic" (in the Japanese sense of the word) tradition by therapists and patients, but it also reflects the broader choice of therapists and therapies available to patients. They can now go elsewhere if their *sensei's* strict authoritarian demands and commands become onerous.

Verbalization seems to take a proportionately larger amount of therapy time in the 1970s than it did in the 1920s. In fact, in some current forms of Morita therapy, there is practically nothing but spoken and written communication when therapists and patients are together. Certainly the tradition of patient and therapist working silently together in the garden or cleaning the house has all but disappeared. Play between therapist and patient continues — I have already touched on the meaning of the switch from shared work to shared play. Here, however, the point is that when rational, intellectual understanding is seen as important, verbal transfer of information increases.

We have already entered the area of phiosophy, ideology, theory. What has developed in terms of Moritist theory during the past half century?

DEVELOPMENTS IN THEORY

Introduction of values. — From Morita's original position, what we call "symptoms" are neither good nor bad; they simply are. The patient's feelings of fear, anxiety, self-doubt, joy, peace of mind, and the like are to be accepted as part of the reality about himself. They *are* his self in the sense that his phenomenological world is he himself, is what he experiences. Negative valuation, for Morita, entered not into the area of feelings but into the area of behavior. Behavior has social consequences, and society ascribes values to behavior. To do one's work is preferable to avoiding it. To converse with one's superior at the office is preferable to fleeing from the conversation. Therapy was aimed at improving the patient's behavior. Feelings were to be accepted as they are. To suffer or not to suffer is part of reality, but it is worth little attention compared with behavioral accomplishment.

Of course, it is common for people to want to feel better, that is, differently, with less suffering, shyness, insecurity. But such a goal is neither possible (in the sense of being under direct conscious control as is speech, say, or as are arm muscle contractions) nor desirable (in the sense that it implies dissatisfaction with and resistance to the aspect of phenomenological reality which cannot be directly controlled, creating even more unhappiness as perfectionist desires are compared with imperfect reality).

A corollary of this position was that the origins of anxieties need not be probed in individual cases. The general source of fears and anxieties was known in the Buddhist sense of resistance to normal suffering. A brief history was all that was needed from a particular patient in order to diagnose him as *shinkeishitsu*. No detailed recounting of traumatic experiences and the like was necessary. In psychoanalysis, for example, recollection of early experiences permitted the freeing of unconscious materials, provided insight into the origins of current neurotic patterns of behavior, allowed early experiences to be relived in a more sheltered and ego-oriented setting, and so forth. Insight is necessary in Morita therapy, too, but it is different from the insight of psychoanalysis. For the Moritist patient it means seeing himself in the present in the particular way espoused by Morita therapists. In passing it is interesting to note that such a corollary also allowed the patient to avoid recollecting anxiety-provoking interpersonal difficulties within his family, a social unit that retains much of its sacredness even in modern Japanese society. At any rate, causes of anxieties and fears were, in Morita's day, located within the patient and not within the history of events that happened to him or of relationships in which he participated. The result of such an emphasis was that generalized intrapsychic processes (such as *sei no yokubo*, psychic interaction, perfectionism, and idealism), rather than detailed individual personal histories, could be the focus of attention. In sum, early Morita therapy emphasized acceptance of feelings in the phenomenological present with little interest in interpersonal interaction, past events, or individual causation of symptoms.

Even in Morita's time *shinkeishitsu* was ambiguously classified as both a learning problem and an illness. Illness is bad, something to be got rid of, negatively valued. It is legitimately treated only by physicians. Even today the therapist who does not have a medical degree is under a disadvantage; he is careful to direct persons at Moritist meetings to be diagnosed by a physician. People suffering from an illness usually have both impaired behavior and subjective complaints of one sort or another. The goal of the physician is to do away with both kinds of problems, objective and subjective.

Of course, Morita had said that the subjective "feeling" complaints are neither good nor bad; they just "are." One solution to this dilemma of evaluation was to reify the experience of being *shinkeishitsu* into a character type or personality with both positive and negative aspects. The *shinkeishitsu-sho* person is a worrier and a perfectionist; he is introspective and intense but also patient, thorough, upright, and prudent. What seems to have happened is that the unvalued experience of *shinkeishitsu* was translated into this characterological pattern with both positive and negative aspects. And just as other character disorders can be treated psychiatrically, so can *shinkeishitsu-sho*. As Davis (undated) has noted, "Often 'the illness' is treated (isolated) as if it were an entity independent of the patient, to be 'defeated' by patient and therapist," (p. 19).

An identical process developed in Morita's conceptualization of anxiety. For Morita anxiety was a personal experience, or, better put, it *was the person* when the person was experiencing it. But, over time, anxiety came to be externalized and reified so that both its unpleasantness and its adaptive value could be described and explained. These reifications of illness and anxiety are useful when therapists come to adopt a rationalistic, scientific stance. A child accepts anxiety as part of himself. It is the adult, the rational adult, who conceptualizes anxiety as outside himself, as something from which he suffers.

The early Western conceptions of neurosis as an illness to be cured by psychiatrists and the appeals of patients to be helped in escaping from their symptoms probably both contributed to bringing about the incorporation of values into Morita's scheme. The non-valuing standpoint of Zen Buddhist tradition gave way in time to the flood of value-laden philosophies such as state Shintoism, Shin-Shu Buddhism, and Christianity.

An interesting illustration shows the contrast between a non-valuing and a valuing orientation. In a group meeting, a minor disagreement arose over the purpose of meditative sitting (*seiza*). One person held that the purpose was simply "to sit," whereas another believed that the purpose was to promote good health. It is not surprising that the second person, the one who appealed to the commonly accepted value of health, was a modern Moritist.

Although modern Moritists give lip service to the position that *shinkeishitsu* patients' feelings are neither good nor bad, it has come to be accepted that feelings are both good and bad. Furthermore, as can clearly be seen in changes in technique, their promises to make the patient feel better, get rid of his symptoms, and so on reveal their basically negative valuation of the *shinkeishitsu* experience.

Arguments from rationalism and naturalism. — One of the by-products of reifying anxiety as something external to the person, something that happens to him, is that its origins and causes can be handled within a rationalistic framework. Increasingly patients and therapists have come to be dissatisfied with admonitions concerning the necessity to accept one's symptoms (I cannot write here "accept one's self," where self equals symptoms). They want to know why. Rather they want to know some acceptable why. They are still unwilling to explore the family discord, the suppressed aggression, and the repressed sexuality that, I believe, motivate many of these neurotic disorders in Japan.

Two different explanations seem relatively satisfying to all concerned. The first I call an argument from naturalism. It likens anxiety to a natural process like a fever. A fever calls our attention to some problem. It forces us to rest, thus attacking the problem. Similarly, anxiety alerts us to some difficulty in our environment. If we look for its source and deal with the source the anxiety goes away. The problems involved in recognizing that some people die from fever (thus negating its beneficial effect) and that some anxieties seem to have no recognizable stimuli in the recent past or present seem to be ignored.

A slightly more complicated but similar argument is that man must live in harmony with nature. Anxiety disrupts the harmonic rhythmic relation with life, and harmony can be restored by following Moritist practice. Even the Kierkegaardian position that "he . . . who has learned rightly to be anxious has learned the most important thing" (quoted in Davis, undated), the notion that existential anxiety is a wellspring of constructive, creative energy, appeals to the principle of separation of the person and the anxiety. Man *uses* anxiety rather than man *is* anxiety. The danger of these and other simplistic analogies found in psychotherapies around the world is that they fail to consider the complexities of reality. They must ignore much in order to be readily understood and remembered. Of course, such arguments from naturalism are most effective in cultures that have adopted a view of man as part of nature.

The influence of Western psychiatry can be seen in the current concern among Morita scholars with clarifying the theoretical foundations of their therapy. This concern is in part a reaction to criticisms directed at Morita therapy by Western analytic psychiatrists, two of whom concluded that "Suppression is the dominant theme in [Morita] therapy; conformity the goal!" The value of rational-intellectual understanding in addition to the traditional Moritist emphasis on experiential understanding is part of the attempt to establish the scientific status of this therapy. The rationale offered the patient is that understanding his symptoms intellectually is a precursor to rationally changing his behavior, which, in turn, will indirectly change his feelings. But just as the symptoms have been externalized from the patient for purposes of explanation, so the causes have been externalized from Morita's original intrapsychic processes. Situational pressures are seen to cause anxiety nowadays. For example, job changes, a new marriage, moving from one neighborhood to another, the birth of a baby, and the like are seen to precipitate neurosis. In other words, what happens to a patient is equally as important as his character in explaining the onset of his symptoms. Certainly, these external causes are more clearly specified and elaborated than in Morita's day. Even one of the most conservative Morita therapists, who sees the onset of neurosis as primarily an internal characterological experience, views cure as strongly influenced by the environment of his hospital; that is, he introduces a situational element into his explanation of cure.

A useful illustration of the way intellectualization has entered Morita therapy may be found in the interpretation afforded Morita's paraphrase of Dogen's words, "Anshin no tameni yoshin ga ari" (literally, "Anxiety is for the purpose of a peaceful heart"). Originally the phrase meant that without suffering we would not know peace, an argument that holds that opposites or contrasts define recognizable reality (Kondo, personal communication). "If there were no darkness we wouldn't recognize light" is the same kind of argument. For some Morita therapists, however, the phrase has come to mean that anxiety draws our attention to certain problem areas in our lives, as described above. If we deal with the causes of the difficulties in these problem areas the anxiety will diminish. According to this interpretation anxiety is a kind of signal alerting us to conflict that can be alleviated, with resultant peace of mind. Such, of course, was not Dogen's intent, but the phrase has a useful place these days in succinctly summarizing for patients one of the new Moritist orientations.

One hears that fear of loud noises, fear of flying, and fear of snakes are all natural. Worrying about success or cancer or sexual performance can be useful, provided the worry leads to constructive behavior. Then the feelings of worry are instrumental.

The meaning of "practice," too, has come to be seen in a new light, a more rationalistic perspective. For Morita, practice was not desirable because the patient became a "practicer"; that is, his reality became a reality of practicing, especially practicing in order to get well. Genuine tasks, natural tasks, were to be undertaken by the patient. If he feared riding on trains, for example, he was not to ride on a train for practice in order to overcome his fears. Rather, if some errand required riding on a train he was to do it in order to accomplish his errand. In a sense, the patient could change his behavioral reality while leaving his fears as they were.

Practice for practice' sake and practice for the purpose of cure are still frowned on by Morita therapists when stated in such stark form. But practice has crept into the reality of therapy. Some Moritists hold that self-confidence comes from successes, however minor, and that success can never come from avoidance of or fleeing from anxiety-provoking situations, but only by entering into them. Thus, increased facing of such situations increases the chances of success, self-development, self-confidence, and so on. Therefore, such situations can be "encouraged" to happen, if not artificially created. For example, one patient was advised to find or create errands that would require short train rides, then longer and longer ones. Others are encouraged to make detailed preparations for speeches or conversational gambits so that they can bring them off skillfully at the right moment. Instead of waiting for reality to bring the challenging situations, there is an increasing emphasis on rationally creating the situations and facing them in the patient's own time, when he feels prepared – a procedure that closely approaches what one might call "practice." At least one therapist holds that conscious practice for the purpose of cure is an intermediate, positive step between fleeing from challenge and entering into natural situations.

Another change has come about in the discussion of symptoms among patients. Originally patients were permitted only minimal sharing of their neurotic experiences with one another. The patient was to direct his attention to more useful activities aimed at constructing a new behavioral reality for himself. He was not to focus attention on his symptoms by talking about them. Discussing symptoms would serve only to aggravate them through psychic interaction. An intermediate step between silence and free sharing as found today was the view that some objective talking about symptoms should be permitted provided it did not degenerate into complaining, mutual sympathizing, and commiserating.

Today public and private discussion of symptoms is a major part of Moritist practice. In fact, listening to others' problems and telling about one's own take up at least a third of the time in most Moritist group meetings. The trend toward supplementary rational-intellectual understanding again seems to be the primary force. The patients learn that they are not unique in their neurotic suffering. They hear testimonials and learn of specific therapy-related techniques by which others have become well. Such information is considered by all to be beneficial. Thus intellectual knowledge has come to take precedence over the danger of directing attention to the patient's own symptoms.

Attempts to establish Morita therapy as a science began with Morita's own efforts and desires. He disavowed any direct connection between Morita therapy and Zen Buddhism. He appears to have held the belief that only two options faced Moritists: to consider his therapy a science or to consider it a religion. He chose science. I believe that Morita's own views were much closer to a Zen perspective than to a scientific one, but that such views are no more religious than science is. Moritists themselves are divided on this point. Clearly, choosing the scientific route offered many practical advantages in Morita's era.

Modern Moritists recognize weaknesses in Morita's theory, including his explanation of the origins of anxiety and his minimal attention to the specific ways child rearing may influence the development of neurosis. But, of course, the reason for these inadequacies is that the domain Morita selected to work in was the phenomenological reality of the present. Origins and historicity are irrelevant, in a direct sense, and enter only when one steps back from the direct experiencing of the patient and undertakes a scientific, causal explanation of his experiencing. When Morita did step back his explanations of causes were still in terms of intrapsychic processes which the patient could check against his current experiencing.

So Morita therapists have imported and adapted various ideas from other psychotherapies, personality psychology, and social psychology to fill in the gaps in their theory of causality. In addition, they use these ideas to help explain the efficacy of Morita's treatment form. The causality theories include Doi's concept of *amae* (the need to be loved and cared for) as well as some social psychological understandings of Japanese society, particularly Japanese family structure. Various Morita theorists have used behavior therapy, logotherapy, Binswanger's approach, Gestalt psychology, Horney's neo-Freudianism, and other theoretical systems to explain and legitimize Morita therapy's methods. There is also some hope that Morita therapy, looked at from these imported perspectives, will be more palatable to Western therapists. In the next chapter I make detailed comparisons between Morita therapy and other therapy forms.

In a broad sense, all psychotherapy is an educational process. Certainly Morita saw his method as educational rather than medically curative. But it was not until rationalism and intellectualism permeated his therapy that a mental health education movement could develop and grow. Not surprisingly, the movement began with a nonphysician and it continues after his death under the leadership of another lay therapist. Group therapy meetings of the sort currently sponsored by the Seikatsu no Hakken group could occur only after the public dissemination of Moritist information became a major therapeutic enterprise.

With the educational emphasis can come a de-emphasis of the therapy itself. Normal persons, too, can profit from this way toward personal growth. The philosophy of life underlying the treatment method can be taught to teachers, businessmen, police, and even ministers. The teaching has begun already.

CHANGE IDEOLOGY

When a therapeutic form is in the process of development, what attitudes, organizations, and behaviors facilitate change? Why is it that styles and techniques in Morita therapy can proliferate and evolve so rapidly?

One factor that seems to be important is the absence of a formal organization among Morita therapists. Professor Morita founded no association for his followers. He gave them individual directions and left them to pursue their own courses. No conservative governing body sprang up to criticize deviations from orthodoxy. In fact, Moritists have only recently begun to communicate with one another across geographic distance and university lines. Until quite recently one style of Morita therapy (e.g., Dr. Yokoyama's or Dr. Noda's) could develop virtually unrecognized by other Morita therapists. Today some conservative voices are raised, to be sure, but they have no organizational structure or support beyond their own individual influence.

An attitude that has recently emerged to legitimize change I shall call "fixing Morita in his time." This attitude is a recognition that Morita's approach and ideas were related to his cultural-historical milieu. The implication is that elements and ideas of his therapy are effective relative to his time. (Freud has been similarly "fixed" by some.) It has been pointed out that in Morita's day in Japan there were no safe, effective tranquilizing and antidepressive medications, no real alternative theories of neurosis based on psychological mechanisms, and few, if any, life-styles available to the patient other than the one that underlay Morita therapy. But times have changed. There is an equally firm conviction among Moritists, however, that the basic elements of Morita's theory and practice cross temporal and cultural boundaries. The discussion may become heated when the question is raised regarding what ought to be considered basic.

In Morita therapy meetings one meets a variety of understandings about Morita therapy. Particularly in the meetings of Seikatsu no Hakkenkai, innovative ideas are permitted public expression. Such permissiveness seems to be a function of the stage of development of the organization. It is in a growth period and needs numerical strength to give firm support to the numerous local groups. In particular, physicians whose approaches are similar, if not identical, to those of Moritists serve as leaders and co-leaders in these groups. Another factor seems to be the explorative, open-minded quality of the headquarters leadership. There is a willingness to move in new directions should the requisite changes prove helpful to the membership without deviating from fundamental Moritist principles. There is a genuine sensitivity to members' needs. Leaders make a conscious effort to gain membership feedback via surveys of different kinds.

An extreme relativist position was taken by one Moritist in a group meeting when he asked a patient, "What does Morita therapy mean to you?" Such a question signifies a major shift in the thinking of some modern Moritists. That a patient could hold a meaningful opinion on this subject is a novel stance, that he should express it publicly is rather surprising, and (more basically) that Morita therapy could have more than one meaning reveals a tremendous leap toward change ideology. Incidentally, after the question, "What does Morita therapy mean to you?" was posed, a senior therapist revised it to suggest that at different stages of progress a patient comes to a closer and closer understanding of the true meaning of Morita therapy, but that did not seem to be the original intent of the question.

Clearly, change is occurring in Morita psychotherapy, and it is not haphazard change. It moves along with changes in other aspects of Japanese culture.

THE ROOTS OF CHANGE

Values

One factor producing change in the nature of Morita psychotherapy is the changing value orientation of the Japanese people. In the Japan of the 1920s meaning in life was most often found by contributing to the larger whole of one's family, one's community, or one's nation through proper performance of one's role. Individual freedom and self-actualization were simply not understood in the same sense as they are in the West. Ultimately, according to the influential Zen Buddhist philosophy, the self did not exist at all; it was a social fiction. One's sense of well-being, then, was a spurious by-product of a false concept. Morita, also influenced by Zen philosophy, considered too much self-consciousness to be the cause of neurosis. He held that losing oneself in work (William James's "sciousness") was the cure. From such a perspective work had ultimate positive values, for by work one gave oneself to the group and lost oneself in the work simultaneously. These values are quite obviously still present in Japan. Recent alternatives to the supremacy of a work ethic, however, offer meaning for life in, for example, leisure activities or personal freedom from certain social mores. The current social milieu fails to provide the overwhelming social feedback that reinforced the work ethic in the early twentieth century; patients are somewhat less willing to accept the underlying value orientation of Morita therapy. Again, modern Morita therapists are being put in the position of having to treat persons who are simply not emotionally capable of being productive (or of seeing themselves as such).

Another kind of shifting value orientation is affecting the successful application of Morita's techniques. It is clear that various symbols during hospitalization support a familylike socialization theme. Bed rest precedes the "rebirth" of the patient. The doctor-patient relationship is analogous to a father-child role dyad, including moralistic training and education, personal counseling, and even shared facilities and meals. Nurses are considered much like elder sisters to the patients. Patients contribute to the upkeep and larder of the hospital. And, like a child who needs have no awareness of the process of enculturation and no particular confidence in his parents' ability to direct him adequately in order to make a social adjustment, the patients are required to exhibit neither of these qualities. Perhaps the effectiveness of the moralistic, prescriptive resocialization in Morita therapy is maximized when the patient views his doctor as a pseudo parent. Throughout much of Japan's known history, including the 1920s, the family model was applied to other role relationships, such as professor-student, factory owner-factory worker, and doctor-patient relationships (Iga, 1967). More recently, however, professionalization and specialization tend to work toward the compartmentalizing of orientations in the mind of the patient, thus minimizing the possibility of the adoption of an all-encompassing life philosophy; such a philosophy is, in a sense, the precise objective of Morita's thought. Modern hospitals report that the familial atmosphere becomes more and more difficult to maintain. The general decline of a familistic orientation in Japanese society is evidenced by the waning desire of parents to be dependent on their children in old age (see 1950-1967 surveys in Matsubara, 1969).

Is there evidence that the values I have ascribed to the Japanese do, in fact, exist? Let us examine first some evidence that traditional values still survive in Japan. Then we shall look at data reflecting recent trends in shifting value orientations.

A 1972 cross-cultural study (*Yoron Chosa*, 1973) surveying young people between the ages of eighteen and twenty-four found revealing differences in the responses of Japanese youth compared with youth in other countries. Of the eleven countries surveyed, Japan had the highest percentage of persons (28.0%, compared with 8.9% for the United States) who saw meaningful work as their main goal in life. The work ethic is not dead in Japan.

The social carefulness and hesitancy of the Japanese are reflected in the response to a question asking what the respondent would do if he saw someone who seemed to be lost. Of all the nationals the Japanese were least likely to address the lost person or even to "see" him (31.9%, compared with 50.9% of the Americans). The Japanese were most likely to assist the stranger only if he took the initiative and asked directions (64.9%, compared with 45.5% of the Americans).

Nearly one-quarter (23%) of the Japanese stated that they had no friend with whom they could talk openly on a personal topic (the highest percentage in all eleven countries, compared with 8% of United States young people). Social protectiveness and difficulty in self-disclosure seem to be evidenced here.

The idealism of Japanese youth shows clearly in that 73.5 percent were at least somewhat dissatisfied with their country's way of life. Again, this was the highest percentage in the eleven countries.

Taken as a whole, the survey documents elements of a work ethic, social hesitancy, difficulties in self-disclosure, and idealism among Japanese young people. These are all key aspects of characteristically Japanese neurotic symptoms, both from the Morita theorists' perspective and as observed by Western researchers.

Thus far I have presented evidence that traditional Japanese values and concerns still operate to some degree in modern Japan. And I have argued that these values contribute to shaping the expression of neurosis in Japan. Now I propose to document some of the changes in value orientation which I consider to be affecting symptom expression and change in therapeutic theory and practice.

Survey data documenting change are difficult to find. Despite the numerous surveys conducted each year in Japan, rarely are questions regarding values asked in precisely the same way twice or more over a twenty- or thirty-year span. Again I am forced to compare responses of different age-groups queried at the same point in time. The results are consistent but not conclusive in themselves. Those familiar with modern Japan are well aware of the trends toward individualism, interest in leisure, expressiveness, and so forth (Norbeck, 1965; Plath, 1964). In some sense, then, this documentation by survey data is intended for the reader who desires something more than a list of references and the simple assertion that such changes have taken place.

Akuto (1972) reports the results of large-scale public sampling surveys in Japan. More than 40 percent of modern Japanese consider leisure at least equal to work in giving meaning to life. Young people are more likely to be leisure oriented. Only males thirty years old and older show higher percentages of agreement with the view that they use leisure time in order to prepare for work. Both sexes and all other age-groups have higher percentages of persons who state that they work in order to enjoy leisure. Is it any wonder that play therapy is a growing aspect of Morita therapy?

Older persons report higher valuing of obligation and filial piety. Younger persons (and persons with higher education) report higher valuing of freedom and individual rights in fixed-choice questions. Increased longevity and better health have consistently gained ground as the most important things in life in interviews conducted in 1953, 1958, 1963, 1968, and 1972, rising from 12 to 47 percent in the period covered. Japanese young people's concern with social relationships is reflected in the relatively high percentages of responses of love and friendship as the most important things in life. These characteristic responses from persons in their teens and twenties have remained relatively unchanged over the nineteen-year period.

The overall self-control and repressive defenses of the Japanese people, as well as the change toward greater awareness and expressiveness in youth, show clearly in data from a magazine poll taken in 1970 (Horvat, 1971). Table 18 shows that young Japanese are more willing to report expressive impulses, but the overall suppression of even the wish to "act out" is noticeable in the low percentage of "Yes" responses (9.4%) to such questions as, "Have you ever wanted to break something?"

Iga (1967) reports on Japanese national character surveys

TABLE 18

Affirmative Responses by Two Age-Groups
in a 1970 Japanese Magazine Poll
(In percentages)

Query	Total	15-19 years	40-54 years
Have you ever wanted to			
shout at the top of your voice?	23.3	31.2	15.0
break something?	9.4	14.0	4.7
beat someone up?	7.8	13.1	2.3
live in a quiet place far away from human habitation?	39.0	36.3	39.9
run away or disappear?	9.6	14.0	5.0
see no one?	9.3	11.5	7.0
disappear from the face of the earth?	5.7	9.6	1.7

conducted by Japan's Bureau of Statistical Mathematics in 1958 and 1963. Comparing the 1958 responses of the 20-29-year age-group with the 60-year and older age-group, we observe the differing views toward individualism. Among the young people 54 percent were primarily individualistic in outlook, compared with only 22 percent of the elderly respondents. Primary concern with the family and/or nation was reported by 56 percent of the elderly and by 37 percent of the youth. A similar trend was found when Iga compared attitudes toward the relative merits of individualism and the following of custom.

A questionnaire submitted to Japanese college students in 1949 and 1964 revealed that Japanese students, as compared with American students, placed high valuations on perseverance and obedience. But, over the fifteen-year period in Japan, the relative value of a well-rounded life (encompassing action, enjoyment, and contemplation) increased, the value of enjoying oneself increased, and the value of sympathetic concern for others decreased. The trend was clearly toward hedonism and less self-sacrifice for the group, although not to the degree shown by American students.

Iga also compared the responses of young people (from a 1963 survey) and elderly people (from a 1958 survey) to point out differences in attitudes toward man's relationship to nature. Elderly persons were more likely to view man as adapting to nature (23% vs.

15%) and less likely to view man as conquering nature (19% vs. 39%). Both young and old Japanese showed high percentages in the "man using nature" category. Moritist thought, too, has shifted away from man adapting to his emotions (e.g., anxiety) and toward man using his emotions.

Economics

Another factor is the economic one. Specifically, health insurance has opened the possibility of psychotherapy to many persons who could not otherwise afford it. In six of the Moritist hospitals described in Ohara and Reynolds (1968), insurance companies helped to pay the bills of at least half of the patients. But since hospitals must agree to accept smaller fees in order to treat insurance cases, the hospitals that do so must admit more patients, hire a larger staff, and occupy more spacious facilities. Limits on existing facilities are set by room size and occupancy during absolute bed rest in the initial stage. Limits on staff time are dominated by work therapy supervision and diary evaluation during later stages. Nevertheless, six of the hospitals had only one full-time and no part-time physicians.

Another aspect of the economic factor is that nearly all Moritist hospitals must admit patients suffering from minor depressions and less severe schizophrenias as well as *shinkeishitsu*. Although Morita therapy is effective to some degree with these depressives and schizophrenics, other therapies may be used simultaneously. Moreover, it is more difficult to maintain the familistic cooperative atmosphere within the hospital with an unbalanced range of illnesses. For example, a depressive or a schizophrenic would be more likely to disrupt hospital routine by refusing to obey his doctor, thus setting a precedent for other patients.

Medical Roles

Both patient and doctor have been strongly influenced by Western trends toward professionalization and specialization. Western concepts of the doctor's role have (with notable exceptions, such as Frieda Fromm-Reichman) tended to place the psychiatrist in a more remote professional stance. Japanese psychiatrists, influenced not only by the Western model but also by their own needs for increased income, higher prestige, and a private life free of professional responsibilities, have tended to withdraw from the sustained mutual interaction recommended in Morita's theory. The therapist often commutes to the hospital or lives in a separate building on the hospital grounds. He is likely to play with the patient, but only rarely does he join the patient in manual labor, and then only in token form. This pattern of withdrawal from the intimacy of shared living has fostered the institutionalization of a new intermediary role, a staff member who actually works alongside the patient and shares his daily life but who is not the Morita therapist (see chap. 2 for a description of such a staff member). The Morita therapist working in a hospital setting has shifted to an authoritarian advisory capacity.

In my opinion, herein lies the crux of the future of Morita therapy as a medical practice conducted within a hospital setting. When the current generation of committed Moritist hospital directors passes on, few young psychiatrists may be trained or willing to assume the responsibility of running this kind of hospital. At present only a few psychiatrists under thirty-five, perhaps four or five in all, are training to become Morita therapists. The training centers of Morita therapy and theory, such as Jikei, Kyushu, and Okayama universities, now stress psychopharmacological treatment, for very practical reasons. The few openings for psychiatrists in Moritist hospitals are insignificant in comparison with the staffing needs in the numerous general psychiatric hospitals.

The future of any psychotherapy is largely determined by its effectiveness compared with other available psychotherapies. There is no question that Morita therapy offers a fit with Japanese culture which is not provided by any Western alternative. And the evidence that Morita therapy continues to develop and evolve in response to changes in values, economic pressures, and social roles offers hope that this indigenous therapeutic form will survive.

It is said that the historical pendulum seems to be swinging back toward a concern for tradition and Orientalism in modern Japan. The the degree that traditional values promote the development of *shinkeishitsu*-type neuroses and evoke appreciation and support of Moritist theory and methods, this Japanese therapy may be expected to rise in importance and influence on Japan's mental health scene.

V   COMPARISONS

Thus far I have presented the reader with an overview of Morita therapy in theory and practice; I have given a detailed description of Morita therapy operating within a single hospital setting; we have examined the psychocultural setting in which it is practiced; and we have looked at the historical development of the therapy in relation to culture change in Japan over the past fifty years.

In this chapter I am concerned with sketching the outlines of Morita therapy by comparing it with other behavior-change enterprises, some Western and some Japanese. How is Morita's method like and unlike some of the better-known Western psychotherapies, such as psychoanalysis, behavior therapy, logotherapy? How does it compare with Zen training and Japan's Naikan therapy? How is it similar to and different from brainwashing techniques? And, finally, how does it fit into a model of psychotherapy which purports to hold true for all cultures?

MORITA THERAPY AND WESTERN THERAPIES

Living in a foreign country sharpens one's awareness of taken-for-granted features of one's own culture. In much the same way, careful consideration of Moritist theory and technique can make one more aware of the assumptions underlying Western psychotherapeutic systems.

One feature that unites Western psychoanalysts, behaviorists, logotherapists, and client-centered therapists is the assumption that we can make sense of all behavior and emotion provided we have the proper information about the client's present mental state and his past history. The kinds of data necessary for understanding behavior and feeling vary from system to system. Faith in our ability to understand these phenomena is not based on any noteworthy predictive accuracy. Complex human behaviors and emotions, such as suicide, creativity, love, patience, aggression, and sleep (to name but a few), are little understood and are hardly likely to be controlled by the plethora of theories and models advanced over the years by Western science. I am not predicting ultimate failure in our efforts to understand man scientifically; I am merely pointing out that our therapeutic forms have emphasized a rational understanding of man's behavior and that, at present, this understanding is far from precise.

Contrast this view with one that considers emotion as "noise" in the system. Moods come and go. They may be related somehow to past events, but they are essentially too complex to be well understood or accurately controlled. The emphasis can shift, then, to accepting rather than understanding this aspect of human existence while attempting to control behavior. Behavior is seen to be controllable by effort of will. Understanding and control of attention may be helpful adjuncts, but the locus of control of behavior is clearly on the level of decision making by the individual.

As I have argued elsewhere (Reynolds, 1972), Western therapies tend to view man mechanistically. Man comes to be what he is as a result of social pressures, past experiences, and the like. He is acted upon. Both neurotic suffering and antisocial acts are considered in the light of traumas, conditioning, family milieu, disadvantaged social circumstances, and so forth.

For the Morita therapist the past is, in a sense, irrelevant. Moritist training begins in the present. And the aim is not to set up corrective psychosocial or conditioning experiences (a la psychoanalysis and behavior therapy, respectively). The perfectly transparent aim is to teach the patient a way of looking at his existence and to give him assistance in putting that view into concrete practice in daily living. Already I can hear the reader saying, "Ah, yes, but doesn't every psychotherapy offer the patient a view of his existence and a means by which to put the view into daily practice?" This is true, but the differences lie, I believe, in the transparency of the teaching and the specific means and goals.

The Morita therapist says essentially: "I will teach you a lifeway. It will help you handle your suffering." Western therapists teach their respective lifeways, but in the guise of the more restricted goal of curing the neurosis. Comparisons between Morita therapy and particular Western therapies reveal similarities and differences in means and ends.

Psychoanalysis

Morita therapy was introduced to the Western world by two American psychiatrists with strong psychoanalytic orientations. They criticized Moritists for ignoring the origins of neurosis, for failing to focus on conflict material, for paying scant attention to dreams, and for minimizing transference phenomena (Jacobson and Berenberg, 1952). In other words, they criticized Morita therapy for not being psychoanalysis.

A more balanced perspective is presented by Reynolds and Yamamoto (1972, pp. 190-191):

> First, it seems clear that both theorists (Freud and Morita) were building models of neurosis founded on the misdirection of psychic interest. They diverged somewhat in their specifications of the nature of the misdirection. For Freud it was tied to the service of repression. For Morita it was tied up in a sort of obsession with the self.
>
> In both cases, then, cure is to be achieved by releasing this misdirected interest. Each individual is assumed to be capable of changing and therefore coping more appropriately. In both cases, this redirection is brought about in part at least by inner adjustments, often attitudinal adjustments. Self-acceptance is sought, be it acceptance of a self with lustful ideas and impulses or acceptance of a self with anxieties and imperfections. Relations with others may be reinterpreted to permit greater flexibility and spontaneity of behavior (though the limits of spontaneity are quite differently defined in the United States and Japan).
>
> On the other hand, there are some critical contrasts that may be drawn between the two systems. There are conditions under which increased self-knowledge is to be avoided in Morita therapy. For example, group discussion of symptoms may promote self-knowledge at the risk of focusing more attention on the self and inhibiting cure.
>
> An even clearer divergence is apparent in the two systems' definitions of cure. Freudians tend to see cure in terms of being symptom free, i.e., feeling better. Moritists tend to see cure in terms of being socially productive. That is, a patient can leave a Moritist hospital with fears and anxieties and obsessions similar to those with which he entered, yet be considered by all concerned "cured." If he is able to function in the midst of his misery he is well. And he may consider himself a better man than those of us who function without the limitations that "reality" has imposed upon him. And it may well be that when reality imposes the limitations of injury, old age,

loss of loved ones, loss of a successful clinical practice, impending death, or whatever, such a man is better equipped than we are to cope with life within the new boundaries.

One final difference worth mentioning but difficult to communicate lies in the kinds of self-knowledge that the two systems emphasize. It is our impression that Freudian psychotherapies stress more rational and interpretable symbolic forms of knowledge — such knowledge can usually be transmitted verbally. On the other hand, Moritist psychotherapies stress intuitive, essentially nonrational understandings that are best realized experientially through behavior. We recognize that both systems use both approaches to self-knowledge but the difference it emphasis seems important.

Much can be said about the relative advantages and disadvantages of insight-oriented versus acceptance-oriented psychotherapies. Depending on the patient's problems and capacities, insight therapy may be impractical or even harmful. On the other hand, acceptance at a low level of function may be second best to dealing with the *sources* of unhappiness once they are made known.

Two other points should be made here. I quote two passages from Norman J. Levy's discussion of Reynolds and Yamamoto (1972, pp. 193-194, 195):

> Morita claimed that Freud's libido theory was too speculative, partial, and dubious. For him the life force was analogous to Horney's concept of the real self, "that central inner force, common to all human beings and yet unique in each which is the deep source of growth." Kondo points out that in making the unconscious conscious the Freudians stress the notion that knowledge reached by the process of free association leads to transformation. This knowledge is arrived at through detecting and exposing the pathology of the patient and bringing it to his attention in order to help him acquire insight. Kondo holds that the Freudian therapist is out to exorcise and eradicate the pathological part so that health will be restored. In contrast, Morita was critical of the split of the subject into subject and object through self-reflection because, for him, when the self was not self-conscious, it was healthy. Morita believed that the mobilizing of the spontaneous life force could never be achieved by intellectual understanding or persuasion in an analyst's office; it must be directly achieved by actual living in a limited situation. His concern was "centered on how to help the patient accomplish self liberation and live fully here and now." Morita was not so much interested in having the patient involved in finding out traumatic experiences or other causes in the past regarding his sickness. He desired to prepare the patient to experience his spontaneous desire for activity, thus enhancing his participation in the

external world, natural and human. He did not deny the value of verbal communication but stressed the importance of understanding by direct emotional experiences. These experiences enabled the patient to develop a more realistic and spontaneous attitude toward life. This direct contact with the actual reality in activity by jumping into it and experiencing the mental and emotional processes in the stream of life had for him a greater therapeutic effect than dealing with verbal images in an office.

Kondo, in writing about the doctor-patient relationship in Morita therapy, states that therapists who obtain the most effective clinical results are those who have themselves suffered from this kind of neurosis and who have had the experience of outgrowing and overcoming it. As a result they have a genuine, accepting, sympathetic attitude toward the patient. They can understand and accept him and are in the best position to enable him to develop self-acceptance and a realistic attitude toward life. This is somewhat different from the concept proposed by Freud of the therapist being impenetrable to the patient, like a mirror, reflecting nothing but what is shown to him.

Interestingly, it is the Freudian conception of transference that stimulated some young Moritists to initiate extended personal contact with patients during the isolated bed-rest stage of hospital care.

Two Japanese psychiatrists with psychoanalytical training in the West have developed Moritist theory in analytic directions. Kondo (1953, 1961) has pointed out similarities between Morita's conception and Horney's ideas, and Doi (1962) has employed the concept of *amaeru* (desire for loving dependency) to account for the origins of *shinkeishitsu* neurosis and the effectiveness of Moritist treatment.

Behavior Therapy

Behavior therapy is said to be grounded in learning theory. When one discovers how behavior therapists operate in practice, however, one finds a not inconsiderable gap between behavior and the cognitive/imaginative endeavors that are pursued during therapy. From the intake interview to the visualizing/imagining of systematic desensitization one is reminded that the behaviorist's patients are humans and not pigeons or rats. Given the behavior therapists' characteristic blindness to these anomalies in their own treatment procedures, it is not surprising that they have been adept at claiming the effects of all sorts of therapies to be the complex working out of simple learning laws. Morita therapy, too, has been discussed within a behaviorist framework (Elzinga, 1972a; Reynolds, 1969a; Marks, 1969).

Some elements of Morita therapy do resemble elements of behavior therapy. One can "translate" a good bit of what Moritists do into a behavior therapy model. I shall quote such a translation shortly. But a translation is an approximation, and it is certainly not an explanation. In chapter 6 I provide the reader with a "back-translation," that is, a view of behavior therapy as explained in Moritist terms or something like them.

These comments are designed to warn the reader of the dangers of the "nothing but" syndrome. "Oh, Morita therapy is 'nothing but' an Oriental form of behavior therapy (or 'nothing but' Zen Buddhism)." If Morita therapy were Japanese behavior therapy it could rightly claim to be the world's first systematic behavior therapy. In fact, it is not behavior therapy and so it cannot make that claim. Although some very modern-looking behaviorist techniques have been practiced for half a century in Japan, the purposes are unique and equally valid.

Some superficial resemblances and basic differences between Morita therapy and behavior therapy can be pointed up by analyzing a few pages in Beech's description of behavior therapy in *Chnnging Man's Behavior* (1969). Beech writes (p. 54) that "three specific forms of advice are often deliberately given to the patient. The first concerns the nature of the patient's illness, the second involves giving some account of how the patient came to acquire his particular set of difficulties, and the third sets out to restrain the patient from heroic but valueless attempts to confront and vanquish his fears." This procedure certainly sounds very much like what Morita therapists do. Of course, the explanations about the nature of the illness and its cause differ, but surely the advice not to fight one's fears is identical in the two therapies.

A more careful look, however, reveals some very basic differences. Beech goes on to say that the behavior therapy patient learns that the same conditioning principles that precipitated his anxiety can be used to decrease it. He learns that he is not to face his anxiety directly because "a gradual and properly planned attack on the fear is more efficient" (p. 55). In other words, the goal is anxiety reduction, not acceptance. Finally, "the behavior therapist avoids blaming the patient for allowing himself to behave in an abnormal way, nor does he blame the patient for any lack of success which may attend his most ardent therapeutic efforts" (p. 56). The behaviorist's conditioning explanation of neurosis has relieved the patient from responsibility for his actions; he is even relieved from responsibility for lack of therapeutic progress. In Morita therapy, the patient is responsible for his behavior in spite of his fears, and therapeutic progress is his responsibility alone.

What is behavior therapy? In its broadest sense, including both specific conditioning techniques and more general behavior modification through cognitive reorganization, it is usefully described by Phillips and Wiener (1966, pp. 66-68) in contrast with insight therapy:

1. There would be less interest in the presumptive origins of a patient's difficulties, that is, little effort to find the original stimuli for the problem.

2. The client would be taught to develop new responses to troublesome situations by manipulating his behavior, his environment, or both.

3. Other people would be involved where needed to aid the patient.

4. There would be less need to depend on verbal-talking-insight therapy either partially or totally, if more effective means were available.

5. Any problem-solving responses would be identified and encouraged.

6. Undesired behavior would be prevented from occurring whenever possible, rather than being allowed to occur or studied in the hope that the analysis of it would "cure" or automatically produce behavior change.

7. The general task becomes that of finding and instituting new, desired behavior in place of the problem behavior.

8. The solution to most problems would be approached step by step, and not by depending upon "insightful" bursts.

9. Corrective behavior, whether it is only a simple act or a large response system, would be considered to occur only on a very specific basis. The behavior that directly opposes the problem-bearing tendency would be identified and promoted through such methods as desensitization, operant conditioning and reconditioning, and aversive stimulation.

10. Clinical terms and descriptions, such as anxiety in most of its uses, complexes, unconscious motivational states, and most diagnostic classifications, if they are used at all, would be reduced to behavioral descriptions and discriminable responses.

It is important to note that on every point in the above list some aspect of Morita therapy can be found. It seems quite clear that in this larger sense, Morita therapy fits fairly neatly in with the therapies of George Kelley, O. H. Mowrer, E. L. Phillips, and others, as opposed to the so-called depth or insight therapies.

In its narrower sense, however, behavior therapy is restricted to a set of specific conditioning techniques derived more or less directly from learning theory. These techniques include, among others, reciprocal inhibition, negative practice, aversion therapy, and positive conditioning. Morita therapists use neither the concise terminology of learning theory nor the theory itself, but a number of Moritist concepts and techniques can be translated into the language of behaviorism without serious distortion (Reynolds, 1969a).

A detailed discussion of three theories of the etiology of neurosis and of the kind of behavior therapy which necessarily follows from these theories will reveal that Morita therapy, as a behavior therapy, fulfills the theoretical therapeutic requirements.

Mowrer's (1966, pp. 146-148, 152) provocative view is best quoted:

> Our view, in short, is that the "sick" individual's problem lies not in how he is *feeling,* but in what he has been, and perhaps still is, *doing.* And we further assume that no therapy can be ultimately successful which involves a *direct* attack (by chemical or whatever other means) upon the patient's emotions, as such. They can be effectively modified, it seems, only through systematic changes *in behavior.* As Glasser (1963) succinctly says: "No one can help another person feel better." Neurotic persons do not act irresponsibly because they are sick; instead they are sick (sick of themselves and *feel* bad) because they act badly, irresponsibly. So the strategy of choice for the therapist is to help the other person become *more responsible* (even though it temporarily "hurts"). This, of course, is in direct contradiction to the more traditional (but manifestly unsatisfactory) view that human beings become "emotionally ill" because they have been morally overtrained and are in consequence, trying to be "too good." . . .
>
> In other words, this newly emerging point of view attributes to human beings the capacity for choice: capacity, in the first place, to choose either to "behave" or not to behave; and, having chosen misbehavior, the further capacity to choose either to conceal or reveal this fact. Manifestly, we do not, cannot choose or control *our emotions,* directly or voluntarily. Given the "appropriate" ("conditioned") stimulus *they* occur automatically, reflexly. So the

question of control and choice exists only at the level of overt, voluntary behavior. And this is why "behavior therapy" opens up vistas and potentialities which are for ever closed if one thinks of the problem of psychopathology as essentially "emotional."

A rational and effective therapy must, it seems, be a behavior therapy, which involves (1) admission rather than denial, to the significant others in one's life, of who one genuinely is and (2) rectification of and restitution for past deviations and errors. Thus, one must again traverse the same path which led him "into neurosis" in the first place but now in the *reverse* direction. If it is by sinning and then trying to conceal the sinning that one progressively destroys his social relatedness (i.e., his "identity"), the only possibility of recovering it is to move back in the opposite direction toward openness, cooperation, community, and "fellowship."

To indicate how some of these themes are echoed in the writings of Morita scholars, the following excerpt from Kora (1968, pp. 316, 322) should suffice:

When we become a person needed by others there comes real significance to our living. When our existence is not useful to others we shrink into ourselves. There is a Japanese saying that the non-contributing man presents his bowl for a third helping of rice only very hesitantly. . . . Under certain stimulus conditions waves of emotion rise in us. We must realize the fact that we cannot control these waves. We cannot freely quiet them with our will. . . . We can with comparative freedom select our *behavior*, but as for *emotions*, it is difficult to direct them with our will.

Following Mowrer, then, in Japanese neurotic patients the cause of the disturbance (or at least a main contributor to its dysfunctional spiral) is the guilt they feel because of their lazy, self-centered, and otherwise socially reprehensible behavior; the broad behavior therapy of choice is one in which they can confess their faults (as they do in their intake histories, personal diaries, group *kowa*, and informal discussions and meetings) to significant others (staff and fellow patients who take on special social primary-group status in the hospital setting described as "familylike") and make restitution (by working alongside staff and fellow patients to maintain and beautify the hospital). Communal work atones for past self-centeredness and replaces habits of laziness with a more socially constructive work orientation. Morita therapy seems to fit in very nicely with the type of behavior therapy Mowrer had in mind.

A second viewpoint, that of Mandler and Watson (1966, pp. 265, 280), seeks to put the conditions for the generation of anxiety (a feature common to neuroses) on an objective, testable basis:

> [An organism whose goal-directed behavior sequence has been interrupted] will often persist in its efforts to complete the sequence. Another apparent and frequent consequence is the increased vigor with which the interrupted sequence is pursued. Either repetition or increased vigor might produce completion. If such a course is successful, the sequence is not appreciably altered. The third reaction, and frequently the more adaptive of the three, is the tendency to response substitution.
>
> Any situation which interrupts, or threatens the interruption or organized response sequences, and which does not offer alternate responses to the organism, will be anxiety-producing.

To give a concrete example typical of young Japanese patients, a student is at first absorbed in studying for his examination but then his thoughts begin to wander. His first reaction may be to study harder, perhaps to lean closer to the book. Should this effort fail, though an American is likely to define the situation as "uncontrollable" and take a temporary break, the Japanese is likely to remain in the situation trying to control his thoughts with his will and, failing, to turn his concerned attention to his own psychological state. Thus he substitutes a response, but not a constructive response ultimately leading to goal attainment. The anxiety-generating condition is called *toraware*, meaning that one is caught by or obsessed with one's own psychological state instead of completing the organized response sequence.

In one type of treatment to reduce anxiety, the patient would be taught how to complete an organized behavior sequence in spite of interruptions. In spite of sudden self-consciousness or blushing, for example, the patient would learn to continue his conversation, to avoid the impulse to flee by concentrating on achieving his immediate goal. This is precisely what Morita therapy does. For example, with regard to occupational therapy, we read (Kora, 1964, p. 16): "When a patient engages in work in occupational therapy, he should do so without any relationship to his disease; and the primary objective of work is to achieve the end the work is intended for." In diaries and in conversations with doctors, patients are reminded by slogans (e.g., *mokuteki hon'i*, "focus on your purpose") and weighty advice for specific situations (e.g., "as you enter the bath cling to your purpose as you would to a rock") to complete their organized behavior sequences. As they develop control over responses to interruption, their anxiety diminishes.

Finally, from the narrower view of behavior therapies as conditioning therapies, Wolpe (1960, pp. 90-91) provides a revealing perspective on many of Morita's methods. All reciprocal inhibition techniques involve the principle that "if a response incompatible with anxiety can be made to occur in the presence of anxiety-evoking stimuli it will weaken the bond between these stimuli and the anxiety responses."

Applying Wolpe's behaviorist interpretation of psychotherapy to Morita therapy, the following response categories seem applicable.

1) *Assertive responses.* — Timid, inhibited patients are encouraged to behave in a more assertive manner under favorable conditions. Assertive responses are rewarded and so supersede withdrawal behavior. In Morita therapy patients are encouraged to engage in activity with others under a variety of work and recreational conditions. Timid, withdrawn behavior, including retiring to one's room for long periods, is strongly discouraged.

2) *Relaxation responses.* — In the presence of anxiety-arousing stimuli the patient is trained to relax. Absolute bed rest in Morita therapy must be almost identical in effect. The patient is encouraged to mull over his symptoms while he is lying in a physically relaxed position.

3) *Conditioned avoidance.* — The emphasis on physical work in the presence of anxiety as practiced in Morita therapy can be conceptually likened to both (*a*) conditioned inhibition of anxiety through a dominating motor response (i.e., working), and (*b*) conditioning of anxiety-relief responses (when the task or subtask is finished). Furthermore, (*c*) avoidance conditioning of obsessions occurs in Morita therapy in the form of verbal punishment during the *kowa* ("therapeutic lecture") and in the diaries.

4) *Feeding responses.* — The effect of the pleasure of eating on fear response in the classic case of "Peter" need not be repeated here. In the Morita therapy hospital, except for unusual circumstances such as absolute bed rest, all patients eat together, including those with anthropophobia. Similarly, during the bed-rest period, ruminations over symptoms are in competition with feeding responses.

5) *Respiratory responses.* — Carbon dioxide inhalation has

produced good results in reducing anxiety: "Processes antagonistic to anxiety can be found both in the excitation that goes with intense respiratory stimulation and in association with the complete muscle relaxation that high concentrations of carbon dioxide produce" (Wolpe, 1960, p. 99). These processes can be produced by physical labor as well as by more mechanical means; it is not unlikely, therefore, that some of the therapeutic effects of work therapy can be attributed to this phenomenon.

6) *Interview-induced emotional responses.* — "If, in a patient, the emotional response evoked by the interview situation is (*a*) antagonistic to anxiety and (*b*) of sufficient strength, it may be supposed that it will reciprocally inhibit the anxiety responses that are almost certain to be evoked by some of the subject matter of the interview" (Wolpe, 1960, p. 100). It is clear that Morita therapy the interview (most often conducted not in the unfamiliar office of the therapist but in the patient's room or in other familiar surroundings by a respected physician-teacher-therapist) evokes a response antagonistic to anxiety in most cases. In fact, several incidents in the literature refer to patients who, while talking about their symptoms, reported feeling no anxiety in the doctor's presence.

Further examples of conditioning therapy techniques employed by Morita therapists could be offered, including negative practice during absolute bed rest, systematic desensitization during the work therapy stages, and positive conditioning in the diary and in the *kowa,* but there is no need to belabor the point. Some of the results of Morita therapy can be understood in terms of the theoretical perspective of the behavior therapies.

It must be recognized that some elements of Morita therapy, particularly those involving suggestion and cognitive reorganization of values, are somewhat more difficult to handle from a behavior theory viewpoint. Furthermore, for every interpretation offered above there is at least one Moritist explanation for the results. Occasionally the two viewpoints are similar. For example, the Morita therapist believes that the results of work therapy are due to the patient's learning to focus his attention on achieving his goal while accepting his symptoms. This sounds something like Mandler's interruption theory. More often, however, the two viewpoints are divergent. Ideally, one should be able to devise critical experiments to decide between these and among other alternate explanations. Unfortunately, certain of the explanations offered by Morita therapists probably cannot be formulated in testable hypotheses and so are incapable of disproof. In particular, those involving the terms *sei no yokubo* (the innate desire to live fully) and *arugamama* (acceptance of phenomenal reality as it is) and those dealing with absolute bed rest may be inherently untestable.

Logotherapy

Although in some aspects the Moritist technique closely resembles behavior therapy, the technical theoretical and philosophical under-pinnings or the Japanese therapy bear much stronger resemblance to those of Frankl's logotherapy. Marks (1969) and Noonan (1969) have also noted similarities between Frankl's and Morita's conceptions of neurosis and cure.

With substitutions of Buddhism-based philosophy for existentialism, the following three passages from Frankl (1967, pp. 149, 150, 151) could have been penned by Moritists in Japan:

> ... detailed treatment of symptoms in obsessional neurotics would only give encouragement to their compulsion to brood over their symptoms. . . . The logotherapist is not concerned with treating the individual symptom or the disease as such; rather, he sets out to transform the neurotic's attitude toward his neurosis. . . . It is well known that the very tension of the patient's fight against his compulsive ideas only tends to strengthen the "compulsion."

> When the patient stops fighting them, the impulses may very well cease to obsess him. . . . That is, insofar as his illness does have some constitutional core, the patient should learn to accept the character structure as fate, in order to avoid building up around the constitutional core additional psychogenic suffering.

> In correcting our patients' misguided efforts to fight desperately and tensely against their obsessions we have to make two points: that on the one hand the patient is not responsible for his obsessional ideas, and on the other hand that he certainly is responsible for his attitude toward these ideas. For it is his attitude which converts the embarrassing ideas into torments when he "gets involved" with them, when he carries them further in his thoughts or, fearing them, fights them back. . . . The patient will finally learn to ignore his obsessional neurosis and lead a meaningful life in spite of it. It is obvious that his turning toward his concrete life task facilitates his turning away from his obsessional thoughts.

German and Japanese theorists described obsessives in almost identical terms. As did Morita, Frankl noted the obsessional neurotic's intense self-scrutiny, his shattered self-confidence, the tension between what is and what ought to be, his tendency to philosophize divorced from concrete reality, his idealistic desires for "absolute certainty in cognition and in decision" (p. 153), and the absence of "that 'fluent style' in which the healthy person lives" (p. 153). As Frankl puts it, "A pedestrian will stumble as soon as he focuses his attention too much on the act of walking instead of keeping his eye on the goal."

Gerz (quoted in Frankl, 1967, pp. 184-185) reported cure or considerable improvement in 88.2 percent of forty-one patients treated over a six-year period with the use of logotherapy's para-doxical intention (see below). This percentage closely resembles corresponding success rates for Morita therapy.

Yet another similarity between the two therapies is the sugges-tion that they can be used in concord with such treatment forms as chemotherapy, hypnosis, and relaxation training (Frankl, 1967, p. 185). Frankl, like Morita therapists, has been accused of effecting cures by "massive authoritative suggestion." Yet he, again like Moritists, can cite cures of patients who tried paradoxical intention with the initial conviction that it simply could not work (p. 191).

The case reports in Frankl's *The Doctor and the Soul* could have come from the pages of Moritist journals. The young man who found himself perspiring more than usual in a stressful situation and responded with heavy perspiration in anticipation of sweating pub-licly was caught in the same vicious circle described by Morita therapists. The suggestion to try to sweat as much as possible is one kind of advice he could have received from a Moritist as well as from a logotherapist. This advice the logotherapist calls paradoxical inten-tion. It involves willing, or trying to produce, the feared action or experience. But the Moritist might also have advised the young man to attend to the conversation at hand, to leave the sweating "as it is," willing it neither to increase nor to decrease.

Nevertheless compare Frankl's paradoxical intention with the advice Dr. Kora (1968, p. 320) gave a woman who had been suffering from fear of severe dizziness:

> She had come to the point where she could only lie in bed. Any time she raised her head, even slightly, she became extremely dizzy.

She couldn't raise her body at all. She arrived for examination in an ambulance and was carried into the examination room on a stretcher. I told her, "In order to diagnose your illness I must see you in your most distressed state, so as much as possible try to produce the greatest dizziness you can." With those instructions I took her head in my hands and raised it. However, the patient didn't complain of any unpleasantness. "That's too bad; how about this?" and I lifted her into a sitting position. Still nothing happened. The patient was surprised. I explained, "Because of your fear and anxiety over your symptoms, they occurred. Now you tried to make the dizziness appear so you weren't afraid or anxious about it and nothing happened, no dizziness. From now on, while encouraging your dizziness to come forth live an active life.

There is no doubt in my mind that what in 1946 Frankl called paradoxical intention and what Morita called "plunging into reality" are quite similar therapeutic tactics discovered independently thousands of miles and thirty years apart. Both Western and Eastern therapists seem to use the method as a means toward the end of establishing a constructive task-oriented life.

"De-reflection" is the second of Frankl's logotherapeutic techniques. It is described in two passages (1967, pp. 208, 209):

> As we see, de-reflection can only be attained to the degree to which the patient's awareness is directed toward positive aspects. The patient must be de-reflected *from* his disturbance *to* the task at hand or the partner involved. He must be reoriented toward his specific vocation and mission in life. In other words, he must be confronted with the logos of his existence! It is not the neurotic's *self-concern*, whether pity or contempt, which breaks the vicious circle; the cue to cure is self-commitment.

> Through de-reflection the patient is enabled to "ignore" his neurosis by focusing his attention away from himself. This is possible, however, only to the extent to which he becomes reoriented to the unique meaning of his life. And to enable him to find that meaning is precisely the task of existential analysis.

Here we have come to one of several key differences between the two therapies. Logotherapy must help the patient find the unique meaning of his life. Only by his discovering a personal, individual reason for being can his attention be adequately directed away from his neurosis and toward the positive and the healthy. Contrast this highly individualistic perspective with the view held by Moritists that humans all share the need to live constructively for themselves and others. One need not look beyond the immediate task or purpose at hand to find something worthy of personal commitment. Clearly the differing cultural bases of these therapeutic systems are revealed by these contrasting emphases. Frankl represents a culture in which individualism is supreme and rationalism requires the discovery of personal goals. Morita represents a group-oriented culture in which tradition laid out the goals as givens.

Let the reader compare the following two excerpts from Frankl (1967, pp. 95, 146) with Moritist thought:

> As long as the creative values are in the forefront of the life task, their actualization generally coincides with a person's work. Work usually represents the area in which the individual's uniqueness stands in relation to society and thus acquires meaning and value.

> It was necessary to induce this patient to turn away from her anxiety and toward her tasks. . . . In fact, the attainment of the positive aim will in some circumstances clear up the neurotic anxiety — since the existential basis of this anxiety will have been withdrawn. As soon as life's fullness of meaning is rediscovered, the neurotic anxiety (to the extent that it is existential anxiety) no longer has anything to fasten on. There is no longer room for it and, as our patient spontaneously remarked, "no time."

The work orientation is familiar. But Frankl is speaking of some existential life "task" while Moritists speak of daily life "tasks." And Frankl sees the rediscovery of "life's fullness of meaning" as the antecedent of involvement in one's task (i.e., having "no time" for anxiety). On the other hand, Morita sees the involvement in tasks as the antecedent (or the equivalent) of rediscovery of life's fullness of meaning.

Contrasts between the two therapies raise pertinent theoretical and philosophical questions. Do the roots of neurosis lie in existential conflict or in natural psychological mechanisms? Is life meaning unique for the individual or common to all men? Is life meaning to be discovered or is it already apparent?

A final key difference lies in the integration of ideology and technique. Moritists have developed a whole set of interrelated techniques (isolated bed rest, work therapy, group methods, *Kojiki* readings, annotated diaries, etc.) which aim ultimately at redirecting the patient's attention away from his inner suffering, breaking the psychic interaction. They spring from Morita's theory in a coherent way.

Frankl (1967, p. 177) cites Ungersma's contention that logotherapy is the only school of existential psychiatry with a therapeutic technique. In actuality, logotherapy's integration of technique and existential philosophy leaves much to be desired. Certainly one can use the techniques of paradoxical intention and de-reflection without making an existential analysis of the patient's values. Frankl himself (pp. 190-192) offers various interpretations of the effectiveness of paradoxical intention.

The Morita therapist thus seems to have both a larger set of delineated tactics and a technique that is more closely woven from the thread of theory.

Summary

Several illustrations caricaturing Moritist ideological content in terms of Western forms of psychotherapy may be useful in summarizing this section.

The diving board illustration. — There is something inherently frightening about standing on a high diving board looking down into the water. Some people would handle their fear by turning around and climbing down. This response is called *akirame* ("resignation"). Others would try to conquer their fear before jumping. They would engage in an impossible inner struggle aiming at *hakarai* ("suppression"). These people are neurotic to the degree that they allow the struggle to delay their jumping straightway into the water. The Moritist ideal for handling this situation is to accept one's fear "as it is" (*arugamama*) and jump right in despite the fear (Kora, 1964).

Perhaps the Freudian solution would be to try to understand and, if possible, to deal with the source of the fear. Those waiting their turn at the diving board might become a bit impatient with this solution. Logotherapists might look at the purpose and meaning of jumping. The behavior therapist would seek various ways of eliciting the initial jump, but his emphasis would be on positively reinforcing the act after its occurrence. He might fill the pool with champagne or lovely young ladies. In psychodrama, one might practice the jumping event in more sheltered settings, for example, in a private pool from a lower diving board. Obviously, the overt strategies are quite different from that of Morita therapy.

The flowing river illustration. — To use another analogy adapted from Moritists, life energies are like a river, and symptoms are like boulders rising from the riverbed. If the river spends its force trying to destroy the boulders it flows no farther than the boulders. In the same way, if the river gives up and eddies around the obstructions it cannot flow on. But if the river flows on toward its ultimate objective, despite the rocks, it will eventually reach its goal, and in the process the rocks may be worn down. Even if they are not worn down, the goal has been reached so it matters not at all that they continue to exist unchanged. Furthermore, every river has obstructions of some sort or another (i.e., everyone has weak points), but it is the neurotic focusing of energy on the rocks in an effort to destroy them which absorbs needed strength and distracts the river from its natural flow.

The strategy for handling the boulders espoused by early psychoanalysis was to remove them through the time-consuming procedure of probing the riverbed. The strategy of the conditioning therapies is to remove the boulders one by one. Logotherapy explores the river's mouth. The strategy of Morita therapy is, in contrast, to flow around the obstructions.

ZEN TRAINING: THE BALANCE OF
FREEDOM AND RESTRAINT

Here we turn to the first of two Eastern "therapies," if you will. Like Morita therapy, these methods of behavior change represent Japan's Buddhist tradition. And, like Morita therapy, they emphasize personal growth rather than merely cure.

Despite its professed simplicity, Zen Buddhism is a complicated subject. There are theoretical, practical, and historical differences among the schools within the various sects of Zen, which itself lies within a wider Buddhist tradition. Furthermore, each *roshi*, or master, has his own preferences and emphases in theory and method. For a broad understanding of the topic the reader is refered to Kapleau (1965), Phillips (1962), and Watts (1957, 1958).

The aims of this section on Zen are limited to three: to describe the theoretical parallels between Zen and Morita therapy; to support the claim that Zen offers a kind of social desensitizing experience for the Japanese people; and to suggest that the danger to society inherent in social desensitization is counteracted by a kind of subtle resocialization which occurs simultaneously.

The Self

Simply put, Zen doctrine holds that the misconception that there exists a "self" is the source of all man's hesitation, suffering, and desire. Ultimately, according to Zen philosophy, the self, or ego, does not exist at all; it is a social fiction. Taking a Zen position, Watts (1961) has argued that the concept of self is a fiction imposed on the young child by his society in order to exert control over his behavior, and that unless we undergo special training we never outgrow our habits of thinking as if there really were a self. The symbolic interactionists of the West — sociologists such as Cooley, Meade, and Goffman — would agree that the self is socially constructed and maintained. Zen philosophers contend that one's inner suffering and conflict are by-products of this initial misunderstanding that "I" am separate from "you" and separate from this "chair" and this "pen" and so on.

The parallel with Moritist thinking is apparent. It is precisely too much self-consciousness that results in the misdirection of one's attention and energies. The cure in Morita therapy lies in losing oneself in work. One's feelings, thoughts, and moods arise naturally in the course of daily living; they become problems only when we allow ourselves to become distracted and obsessed by them. When one thinks in terms of a "self" that "has" these experiences, rather than in terms of an acceptance of these experiences as they occur, one is thinking falsely in Zen Buddhism's estimation and "neurotically" in Moritist terms. Through guided meditation as part of Zen training one can experience loss of a sense of self. This meditation, called *zazen*, is usually accomplished by sitting in a cross-legged posture with back held straight and breathing controlled. The key to meditation (and, ultimately, to freedom) is attention.

Attention

When the Zen master Ikkyu was asked to write some words of wisdom, he wrote the single word "Attention," and upon being asked to add something he wrote the same word a second time, and again a third time (Kapleau, 1965, p. 10). In his advice to a young Western student who came to learn of Zen, Yasutani Roshi said, "When I told you to put your mind in the palm of your hand, what I meant was to focus your *attention* at that point. You must not constantly change the focal point of your concentration" (Dapleau, 1965, p. 143). Daie similarly advised his monks to hold their *koan* (a puzzle with no rational solution) in the very center of attention (Phillips, 1962, p. 312). Morita therapy has the same insistence on centering attention, on the task at hand or on accomplishing one's goals.

Obsession

In contrast with concentrating one's attention, the uncontrolled stoppage of one's natural flow of thoughts is undesirable in both Zen and Moritist systems. This stoppage can come about through obsessions, blocking, rationalizing, or trying to oppose one's thoughts. Yasutani Roshi, in his lectures on meditation, advises that "various thought forms will dart about in your mind. Now, they will not hamper or diminish the effectiveness of *zazen* unless, evaluating them as 'good,' you cling to them or, deciding they are 'bad,' you try to check or eliminate them. You must not regard any perceptions or sensations as an obstruction to *zazen,* nor should you pursue any of them" (Kapleau, 1965, p. 33). Just as the student while studying must not struggle with stray thoughts, says the Moritist, so the student of *zazen* must accept the natural flow of his thoughts.

Intellectualization

Rational understanding from the Moritist perspective as well as in Zen thought is considered to be sometimes helpful, but often disruptive, and never sufficient for obtaining life goals or facing life's problems. Intellectualizing is at best only a crutch. "You must advance beyond the stage where your reason is of any avail," writes a Zen monk (quoted in Kapleau, 1965, p. 165).

A Zen master stated that he dealt with neurotics by trapping them: "I get them where they can't ask any more questions!" (quoted in Watts, 1961, p. 29). In other words, he forces them beyond an intellectual approach to their problem. For both Zen and Morita therapy systems of thought, personal experience must validate knowledge.

Daily Practice

The Zen ideology, like the Moritist way of thought, is not to be confined to meditation alone; it must be put into daily practice. "For the soundness of ideas must be tested finally by their practical application. If they fail in this — that is, if they cannot be carried out in everyday life producing lasting harmony and satisfaction, giving benefit to all concerned — to oneself as well as to others — no ideas can be said to be sound and practical . . . the truth must be the product of one's living experiences" (Phillips, 1962, p. 254). "The basic principle of the *zendo* [temple] life is 'learning by doing'" (Phillips, 1962, p. 264). In particular, the principles of Zen must find their expression in work.

After the morning meal at most Zen temples there is a period of physical work: raking leaves, gathering fuel, sweeping, scrubbing, weeding, and other kinds of labor. The principle, "No work, no eating," is fundamental to Zen temples in Japan. The Zen master himself (like Professor Morita) shares in the common labor. And while working together with his novices he takes the opportunity to lecture on Zen principles as they apply to the immediate task. As Suzuki puts it, "The events of daily life, manifestly trivial on the surface, thus handled by the masters, grow full of signification" (Phillips, 1962, p. 263). When the Zen masters become old and unable to contribute to the life of the temple, it is said, they simply refuse to eat until they die. Work is seen as a learning situation but also as the expression of the monk's need to love and serve others.

Additional Parallels

Two other parallels between Zen and Morita therapy may be drawn here. One is the student's seeking of cure or decreased anxiety or greatness only to be redirected toward other goals, other criteria for measuring success in life. Another is the ecstasy that follows a burst of insight, ecstasy that must be eliminated before one has achieved the deepest levels of understanding. The overlap in theoretical and methodological orientation between Morita therapy and Zen Buddhism is sufficiently striking and consistent to warrant acknowledgment of Morita therapy's intellectual debt to the historically prior Zen.

Desensitization

The Japanese character has been described above as sensitive to the feelings and needs of others, yet at the same time concerned with controlling the expression of personal feelings and needs through behavior. It is one's social responsibility plus one's personal sensitivity which inhibits the Japanese person. The normal Japanese is oversocialized. The aim of Zen seems to be to promote spontaneity of behavior, that is, to break down the social controls in the mind, the psychological processes that analyze and screen impulses before they crystallize in behavior. These screening mechanisms are the root of hesitancy, doubt, and suffering. They are responsible for a careful appraisal of a given situation in terms of socially defined evaluative criteria before action can take place. "Spontaneity is not an ego action at all; on the contrary, it is action which the social control mechanism of the ego does not block. If anyone says, 'With all my heart I love you,' it is not the ego that speaks. He means that it is delightful to love spontaneously without blocking from and conflict with socially implanted notions of one's role, identity, and duty" (Watts, 1961, p. 124).

In Zen the monk is constantly admonished not to get entangled in social relations and obligations. "Don't get involved with anyone, whoever he happens to be; rather by ridding yourself of the need for others (which really is a form of self-love) remain in the Buddha-mind" (Stryk and Ikemoto, 1965, p. 81). The same admonition is found in Rinza's command: "When you meet the Buddha, kill Buddha; when you meet your master, kill your master; when you meet your father and mother, kill your father and mother" (Sato, 1958, p. 213).

Traditionally it was precisely those persons in ancient India with minimal social commitments who were free to enter the path of Buddhist liberation. It was the privilege of one who had already raised his family and passed on his occupation to his sons (Watts, 1961, p. 72). In Japan it was traditionally the younger sons and it is now the college students who have the time and freedom from responsibility to enter this behavior-change setting.

When one thinks in terms of the preservation of society these ideologies appear quite dangerous. If one can call the Buddha a "dried-up dirt-cleaner," if one can slap one's own Zen teacher, or throw things at him, what chaos faces society? (Koestler, 1961, p. 234). Why should the enlightened monk, owing nothing to any man, return to society to teach others the way to enlightenment? And why should modern Japanese companies send their workers to study Zen and expect them to return better workers? If the experience that is the climax of training enables the student to see through social fictions, dissolves his social inhibitions, and frees him to act spontaneously, why does he choose to live within reasonable social bounds? It is at this point that many analyses of Zen begin breaking down into logical paradoxes. Aside from some personal idiosyncrasy the modern Zen *roshi* is not destructive. Although he appears "freer" than many Japanese, he generally walks within the boundaries of the law. And he has chosen to return from his withdrawal from society to guide others into Zen insights. Why?

Just as we found it necessary to look at Morita therapy in practice as well as in theory, it will perhaps be useful to examine Zen practice as well as Zen theory in order to clarify these paradoxes. I submit that part of the solution lies in the subtle resocialization that is going on within the temple milieu while the monk is formally severing his ties with the larger society.

The essential point may well be that the learning of the Zen world view does not take place in a social vacuum. The directed behavior change setting is a social setting. Even the highly personal enlightenment experience of Zen must have official (i.e., social) confirmation from the *roshi*.

One important relationship within the Zen setting is that between master and pupil. It is a complex, emotionally charged dyad:

> Hakuin grew desperate and thought of leaving the old master altogether. When one day he was going about begging in the village, a certain incident made him all of a sudden open his mind's eye to the truth of Zen, hitherto completely shut off from him. His joy knew no bounds and he came back in an exalted state of mind. Even before he crossed the front gate, the master recognized him and

beckoned to him, saying, "What good news have you brought back today? Come right in, quick, quick!" Hakuin told him of his experience. The master tenderly stroked him on the back and said, "You have it now, you have it now." After this, Hakuin was never called names.

Such was the training the father of modern Japanese Zen had to go through. How terrible the old Shoju [a Zen master] seems when pushing Hakuin off the stone wall! But how motherly when the disciple, after so much ill-treatment, finally came out triumphantly! (Phillips, 1962, p. 273)

Other monks echo the note of gratitude to their master. "I owe a great deal to Gyodo-Roshi, for without his guidance I might have ended up a mere adherent of koans, a man without insight into his true nature," remarks a modern Zen master (Stryk and Ikemoto, 1965, p. 159). Again, a monk grateful to the assistant abbot of a temple in Kyoto said, " 'If it hadn't been for your wisdom, I would never had had so transfiguring an experience' " (Stryk and Ikemoto, 1965, p. 105). One readily picks up the sense of admiration and love the Zen monk has for the master who guided him to enlightenment, even though nearly all the writers on Zen seem so caught up in the philosophy of Zen that they deal only superficially with the topic of temple life.

The Zen temple social setting has more than just the master-pupil relationship; the comradeship of the fellow monks is well known. The monks are, as Suzuki writes, "common mortals engaged in menial work, but they are cheerful, cracking jokes, willing to help one another, and despising no work which is usually considered low and not worthy of an educated hand" (Phillips, 1962, p. 262). Suzuki's little book, *The Training of the Zen Buddhist Monk,* offers insight into the esprit de corps of the temple monks through the text and the illustrations of monkish life drawn by a Zen priest. The sharing of work as well as well as the sharing of successes and discouragements on the path to *satori* draws the monks into a common brotherhood.

So it seems that just as the monk is breaking ties and severing obligations to the outside social world he is establishing ties and building obligations to the agents of change and fellow subjects within the temple setting. Part of the world view he is adopting in this setting places limits on his behavior and directs him back into society to teach the world view to others. In fact, twelve times daily he recites the vow, "Sentient beings are countless — I vow to save them all" (Kapleau, 1965, p. 201). There is resocialization in the midst of the desensitization process.

There are spontaneity and openness in the Zen master. Like the Morita therapist, he seems to have accepted himself with his good and bad points, living fully regardless of them. Yet he is not a libertine. He has shifted his allegiance to a smaller reference group and has adopted a different, somewhat freer world view with slightly different values and restrictions on behavior. At this level of analysis there is much overlap between Zen training and Morita therapy.

NAIKAN THERAPY

Naikan (literally, *nai*, "inside," *kan*, "looking" or "observation") is a guided introspective form of directed behavior change with methods (but not aims) in some ways similar to those of Zen. It grew most rapidly during the 1950s and 1960s. Although it has been used successfully in the treatment of neurosis, particularly the neurosis of young people, it has achieved prominence mainly in the reformation of prisoners and juvenile delinquents.

In outline, the method is simply this: The volunteer subject is given a short indoctrination lecture and then asked to sit in any comfortable position in a divided room (or cell) facing the wall. From five o'clock in the morning until nine o'clock in the evening he is required to think about his past relationships, particularly about those with his mother. He is to think about his attitude or behavior toward her as it was at a particular period of time. The instructor visits the subject every hour or so for a few minutes asking what he has been reflecting upon, giving advice for gaining deeper insight, or suggesting a change of topic. Except for bathing and natural functions such as eating and sleeping, the subject does not vary from this regimen for the entire six-to-ten-day period of treatment. At the end of this period there may be a short ceremony during which the subject is admonished to continue Naikan an hour or so each day.

Taking a second, more detailed look, we find that the volunteer is often a young person with some prior knowledge of Naikan. He has probably read pamphlets and books on the subject, and he is likely to have heard lectures and testimonies. He enters the situation with some personal problem that he expects to clear up through

Naikan. In prisons during the orientation ceremony various important figures such as the warden give their support and encouragement to the subjects. There are no obvious rewards (e.g., parole) to motivate the decision to engage in this discipline. Motivation is considered a personal matter; one's presence and diligent introspection are sufficient. It has been suggested that volunteers are likely to be persons with introspective tendencies (Takeuchi, 1965), but that this kind of self-reflective endeavor has a comfortable place within tradition and has merit is recognized by most of the Japanese people.

The teacher, called *sensei*, has undergone the Naikan experience himself. This experience, along with the ability to communicate his experience to others, is the only prerequisite for his position. The reader will recall that the experiential prerequisite was necessary both in Morita therapy and in Zen. In Morita therapy, the top therapists had experienced cure of their neuroses along Moritist lines, and in Zen, the priest's own enlightenment must be validated before he can validate *satori* in someone else. It is noteworthy that the eminent psychologist Sato (1965a), in his introduction to Kitsuse's paper (1965) on Naikan, found it worthwhile to comment that since Kitsuse had never actually undergone Naikan treatment his observations and evaluations were necessarily limited. That Sato makes this point further attests to the value Japanese culture places on personal experience.

As in Morita therapy, the subject-agent relationship in Naikan is both a personal exchange and a kind of contract regarding responsibilities and obligations. The subject is obligated to listen and diligently to follow the guidance that the *sensei* wisely and responsibly offers. The emotions exchanged are primarily gratitude from the subject and concerned benevolence from the change agent. There is, however, a key difference between the subject-agent relationship in Naikan on the one hand and in Morita therapy and Zen on the other. The *sensei* is more humble and gentle in the former (one might say almost maternal) and more authoritarian and distant (fatherlike) in the latter. For example, the *sensei* in prison greets his subject with a bow, touching his forehead to the floor in a gesture of respect. I never observed such an act in a Moritist hospital, nor does it seem likely in the Zen setting where, in fact, it is the rule for the trainee to greet the *roshi* with a deep bow. There seems to be a corresponding difference between the subjects in Naikan and Morita therapy, too. Criminals in Japan may describe themselves as "weak-willed";

shinkeishitsu patients are said to be "strong-willed." The weak-willed subject possibly relates better to a more maternal change agent, and the strong-willed subject, to a more authoritarian figure. It is true, however, that Moritist hospitals generally contain less authoritarian change agents as well as the more characteristic authoritarian ones.

Now let us take yet a third look at the Naikan experience. Takeuchi (1965) writes that for the first couple of days the subject is directed to reflect on his close family, particularly his parents or his mother or mother surrogate during selected early periods of his life. At first his thoughts are random, but they gradually yield to direction. The *naikansha* (subject) begins to recall grievances against her for what his mother had done to him, her lack of attention, and so on. When these criticisms of his mother's behavior come out during the brief discussions with his guide, the *sensei* points out that this is *gaikan* (*gai*, "outer," *kan*, "looking"), not Naikan. The subject is to think about what he did to his mother at that time, what difficulties he caused her, how he failed to return her benevolence, not vice versa (Murase and Reynolds, 1974).

By the third day (Takeuchi writes), the subject has begun to realize how little he has done for his parents and how much he has hurt them. He feels a deep sense of having wronged them and others. Tears well up; he may even contemplate suicide. He feels a sense of worthlessness. He begins confessing his wrongs to the *sensei.*

By the final stage of treatment the subject has come to realize that suicide would be the ultimate betrayal of all the love and care his parents and others have invested in him. He recognizes that despite his misdeeds these others still loved him, befriended him, met his needs. He was worth something in their eyes. He decides to live as though one dead (Naikan therapists have borrowed this Zen phrase), devoting himself to loving service to repay the debt he owes, first to his mother, then to his family, and, finally, to his society. He feels cleansed; the world seems fresh and new. One subject was able not only to forgive but to be grateful to the co-worker who cost him the sight of his physical eyes in an industrial accident because the accident led to the opening of his spiritual eyes (Takeuchi, 1965).

This set of predictable periods of treatment progress, of subjects one after another producing almost identical complaints and questions and receiving the same replies, can be found in the bed-rest period progress reports and in the diary exchanges of Morita therapy and also, one suspects, in the Zen student's interviews with the *roshi*. It is as if the subject and change agent were acting out their parts in an oft-repeated play, whose script the subject has likely read or heard beforehand, and of whose performance the agent never seems to tire.

It is unclear whether or not the fellow prisoners can assemble for posttreatment meetings, although they apparently can recognize one another by the badges they have been awarded. In Naikan treatment outside prisons, there are various ex-subject groups.

The technique of Naikan, like that of Morita therapy, owes much to Buddhism. The sitting, the isolation, the looking within — these are derived from the training of one small subsect of Jodo Shin-Shu Buddhist priests. Originally the training was quite severe, requiring various forms of self-deprivation including prohibitions on sleep and food (Reynolds, 1974*b*). Yoshimoto Ishin modified the procedures somewhat so that they could be carried out by laymen.

The Naikan theorists talk about a real moral self which has always existed even in the most hardened of criminals. The moral self is capable of loving, of accepting obligations, and of feeling gratitude. It is also capable of feeling shame and of evaluating right and wrong. This moral self is liberated by Naikan, which seems to be a variation on the Confucian theme that man is essentially good, needing only education to bring out his goodness. However, both elements — the inherent goodness and the necessary education — must be stressed. Both of these elements show up clearly in Moritist ideology which holds that all neurotic persons are capable of living fruitfully if they follow the proper guidance. Their neuroticism is energized by their desire to live fully, a fundamentally positive impulse that has been misdirected. Similarly, the neurotic's fears and his concern for others' opinions of him are basically adaptive concerns that have been carried to extremes.

Lifton (1961) ran into some difficulties of analysis when he failed to recognize the education requisite of the Confucian premise. He noted that a premise of Chinese and Russian communism seems to be a trust in man's natural goodness, "although the extent to which both [Chinese and Russians] seek to control human bahavior makes one wonder whether their advocates really believe this" (Lifton, 1961, pp. 392-393). This pseudo paradox is resolved when it is recognized that the Chinese system of thought places a high value on education for bringing man's innate goodness to the surface.

Brainwashing, like Morita therapy, is generally viewed by change agents as an educative (better still, a reeducative) process.

According to Naikan theorists, the moral self develops in childhood. It begins as one establishes a relationship with one's mother, then with other family members, then with representatives of the broader society. Progress in the development of a moral self also seems to be a concept borrowed from Confucianism. It is no wonder that, since morality is based on obligations and feelings of gratitude, there can be none but the broadest of absolute moral standards in Japan and that these are couched primarily in social terms (Koestler, 1961, p. 207). Moral error in such a system is based on ignorance (not innate, willful, evil tendencies) and is defined in terms of the implications of acts for others, such as causing trouble or shame for them (not as transgression of some absolute moral law).

An instructive contrast can be drawn between the early Freudian and Naikan theories. Although both see childhood as a crucial period for developing a social personality, the Freudian tends to see the objective events that happened to the child as determinants of his future (e.g., a boy stumbles on his father and mother having sexual intercourse or a girl is raped by an uncle), whereas the Naikan therapist takes a more phenomenological stance in considering the child's attitude toward his life events as the key to his later personality. One might note in passing that, since the events in one's life history are not subject to manipulation (i.e., they are "frozen" in the past) but one's attitudes toward them are subject to change, all therapies must aim to change attitudes and not events of the past. The Naikan view of childhood causation of later personality therefore seems the more consistent with its interpretation of the causation of personality change in adolescence and adulthood through Naikan therapy; that is, both are based on attitudes, not on events.

An interesting parallel between Naikan and Morita therapy is that, although Morita sees all neuroses as obsessions and Yoshimoto sees all neuroses as character disorders, both break through the patient's self-centeredness with increased self-focus. Naikan uses guided meditation; Morita therapy uses the unguided meditation of isolated bed rest. Both systems then refocus the patient's attention outside himself to repayment and immediate tasks, respectively

Kitsuse (1965, 1966) has implied that Naikan's effectiveness is dependent on the Japanese sociocultural system, including values and child-rearing techniques. In this light it is interesting that Mowrer's

(1966) analysis of neurosis presented earlier has many points of similarity with Naikan's and is based on observations of American neurotics. As described above, Mowrer held that neurosis originates from misdeeds that cause feelings of alienation from others as one attempts to conceal the acts. Symptoms can be removed, then, only by confession and reparation through service, thus restoring sound social relationships. Perhaps Mowrer would not agree with all Naikan methods, but the analysis of the origins of neurosis and the aims of treatment are not dissimilar.

Historically, Naikan has followed a path well trodden by Japanese behavior change systems. The life history of its founder, Yoshimoti Ishin, is fairly well known today; his autobiographical book has been published (Sato, 1965*b*). As in Zen and Morita therapy, the historical changes in Naikan seem to have resulted in an easing of physiological and psychological hardships for the subject. Today, the scope of Naikan has broadened; there are several respected Naikan therapists, each with his own preferred variations in interpretation and technique. And Yoshimoto, like Morita, stresses the rational, scientific base of the process, denying any classification of Naikan in its current form as a religious endeavor.

SCHEIN'S MODEL OF BRAINWASHING

We have noted that, from the literature, Morita therapy seems particularly harsh and restrictive. It is appropriate, then, to examine the fit of Morita therapy to a model of brainwashing or thought reform as practiced by the Chinese Communists. (For a more detailed comparison of Morita therapy and thought reform see Reynolds, 1969*b*.)

Certainly one might expect to find some overlap in method between thought reform and Morita psychotherapy, as, I would argue, one finds overlap on some levels of generalization among all forms of directed behavior change. The model of thought reform provided by Schein (1961), however, is much less applicable to Morita therapy than is Leighton's (1968) model of cross-cultural psychiatry, partly because of the specificity of Schein's formulation. Yet there are fundamental differences in purpose and technique between these two forms of directed behavior change. In this section I attempt to point out some of the parallels and divergences between Schein's thought-reform model and Morita therapy.

Schein writes of three phases or stages in the process of the coercive influencing of American civilians imprisoned by the Chinese Communists between 1950 and 1956. The "unfreezing" stage upsets the existing psychological equilibrium of the subject affecting his needs, motives, and, above all, his self-image; the "changing" stage is one of indoctrination and is primarily a cognitive process of identification and imitation; finally, the "refreezing" stage facilitates reintegration of the new world view (including the new self-image as its central feature) through social support and other reinforcement. Thus, Schein focuses on the self as central to an individual's world view, considering brainwashing, in essence, to consist of undermining the existing self-image, providing models for identification and construction of a new self, and providing social support for the new identity.

The Unfreezing Phase

Schein sees five principal tasks facing the change agent in the initial phase of thought reform: (1) enlist the prisoner's cooperation; (2) attack his physical self; (3) undermine social support of competing world views while offering social support for adopting the Communist ideology; (4) attack the existing self-image; and (5) attack the emotional integration of the prisoner's personality.

Enlisting cooperation. – In the thought-reform prison, the change agent usually encounters an attitude of resistance on the part of his subject. Part of the change agent's efforts are directed toward enlisting the subject's cooperation in the thought-reform process.

In Morita therapy, the cooperation of the patient is simply assumed. Great efforts are not needed to enlist his cooperation. It is understood that the patient, motivated by his desire to escape his neurotic distress, will cooperate as a willing subject. On the other hand, there is individual variation among patients in degree of motivation on admission, personal acceptability of some Moritist ideas and practices, likes and dislikes regarding staff and fellow patients. Thus the task of enlisting (and maintaining) cooperation is not irrelevant within the Moritist setting, only less demanding.

Schein's model also notes the manipulation of fear and hope in the subject as a means of enlisting his cooperation. Both fear (induced by threats) and hope (of lenience) are excellent motivators and can be effectively utilized in tandem to produce maximum effort on the part of the subject in many forms of directed behavior change. Hope of cure, hope of release from prison, and hope of salvation are common motivations that draw the subject into cooperation with the change agent. The subject's expectations of relief are built in large part on the reassurances of the change agent. This is certainly true in Morita therapy.

On the other hand, should the subject take the attitude that success in the directed behavior-change system is certain, he is less likely to put forth maximum effort. It is an option of the agent to communicate that failure is possible, that it does occur, and that its consequences are best avoided. Fear is built up in the subject to stimulate active participation in the change process. In Morita therapy, one doctor was observed reminding some patients that unless they maintained the regimen or unless they "stuck it out" (*gaman shinakereba*) they would not be cured. The fear of continuing in neurotic suffering was an excellent motivator for patients in the Moritist setting. Excessive fear, however, may result in resignation, apathy, withdrawal, or panic. In every effective directed behavior-change program there seems to be some sort of escape valve, some sort of temporary relief from pressure when the subject begins to exhibit signs of panic, severe thought disturbance, and other precursors of breakdown. Such escape valves are often most noticeable during the preparation phase of directed behavior change. The humanization of rules and the valuing of smooth interpersonal relationships work as effective escape valves in the Moritist setting.

Attacking the physical self. — Schein emphasizes not only that physical discomfort undermines the subject's psychophysiological reserves, breaking down resistance, but also that torture and disease affect the self-image of the subject (1961, p. 128). He notes (p. 125) such specific methods employed by the Chinese Communist Party as "Strangeness and general inadequacy of diet in prison," "Loss of sleep due to intermittent and continuous interrogation or cellmate pressure," "Diseases like dysentery resulting from diet," "Lack of exercise," "Excessive cold in combination with inadequate clothing," "Physical pain induced by prolonged standing or squatting in cell or during interrogation," and so on. The psychophysiological aspects of early phases of thought reform and other forms of directed behavior change have also been emphasized by writers such as Sargant (1957), Meerloo (1956), and Kiev (1964).

In Morita therapy, however, aside from the psychophysiological disturbances brought about by absolute bed rest, one finds no emphasis on this aspect of initiating motivation for behavior change. Even during the bed-rest period the patient's physical comforts — adequate food, warmth, cleanliness, opportunities for defecation, and the like — are provided for. In fact, throughout the hospitalization period, efforts are made to keep the patients in prime physical health.

Group pressures brought to bear. — Schein includes several sorts of tasks in this section. One sort encompasses various methods by which the Chinese Communist Party undermines social support of any ideology other than communism. A common feature of many forms of directed behavior change is the curtailing of social contact outside the change setting. It occurs during many forms of initiation ceremony, in monasteries, in boot camps, and, increasingly, in dormitory living patterns of college students. The result of relative isolation is that the subject's dependence on social support within the change setting is increased and he becomes more vulnerable to group influence directed toward adoption of the change ideology.

Morita therapy, too, seeks to isolate the subject from his former social milieu. During bed rest, of course, the isolation is (in theory) complete. After bed rest there is a period of restriction in which visitors and visits outside the hospital are forbidden. Within the hospital, too, an effort is made to restrict social support of other ideologies. For example, religious proselyting is forbidden in Moritist hospitals.

A variety of reading materials, however, are available to patients in most hospitals. Although there is usually assigned and recommended reading in Moritist books, patients can read fiction and nonfiction from bookshelves that are readily accessible. Through this channel vicarious social support for points of view other than Morita's is admitted into the milieu. Similarly, since the patients are given free choice in their selection of television programs (at Kora Koseiin and Nomura Hospital, for example), they are exposed to shows with themes lauding such anti-Moritist values as leisure and rebellion.

Failure to remove resisting and doubting patients from a Moritist hospital through discharge or transfer similarly marks a laxity in milieu control of social support for competing ideologies. Some effort is made to limit the verbalization of complaints and doubts, but economic considerations preclude the removal of too many patients.

There is some parallel between Morita therapy and brainwashing in terms of general task accomplishment, and wide discrepancies in terms of the specific methods employed.

Another task falling within Schein's general category of "group pressures" is complementary to the task of undermining social support of competing ideologies. It is the positive utilization of the situation to enhance group pressure which supports the change ideology. For example, "No close relationships [are] permitted with anyone except in the context of reform; even clandestine communication with cellmates [is] prohibited in some circumstances"; and "testimonials by others [are introduced] in the form of confessions, etc., lauding the virtues of reform and the Chinese Communist Party" (Schein, 1961, p. 126).

Morita therapy hospitals exert some effort to direct the patients' communications and promote social ties that support Moritist ideology. But in many Moritist hospitals patients are encouraged to establish informal social ties with other patients on almost any basis, since socialization per se is seen as a positive end in itself.

Testimonials occur in Moritist settings in both formal (e.g., meetings of ex-patients) and informal (e.g., conversations between patient and ex-patient situations. Confession occurs in written communications such as the diary and autobiographies as well as during the *kowa* lectures at Kora Koseiin. Although testimonials appear to be interpreted as such by those engaging in them, the interpretation that places the public or semipublic enumeration and discussion of one's symptoms (including one's inadequacies, failures, etc.) within the scope of the term "confession" is mine and seems not to reflect the view of doctors and patients who publicly construe the event as an aspect of the gathering of a patient's medical history.

Finally, Schein's section on group pressures contains two elements that seem antithetical to the tasks mentioned above: "Creation of mutual distrust among cellmates by presence of informers" and "Solitary confinement." Not only is the former absent in Moritist hospitals (although some "informing" on other patients' laziness, poor dispositions, etc., does occur in the diaries), but it seems antithetical to the development of strong intragroup ties with associated strong group pressures toward adopting the change ideology. The latter, solitary confinement, can effectively eliminate overt social support of competing ideologies, but it simultaneously precludes maximal utilization of group pressures that support the ideology.

In Morita therapy, absolute bed rest is technically a form of solitary confinement. Yet, the shared meaning of the experience and the atmosphere in which it is conducted are in contrast with solitary confinement. Furthermore, in Morita therapy, the patient is free to adapt to or leave the situation, as best suits his own perceived needs.

Attacking the self-concept. — Within this section of the model Schein (1961, p. 127) lists a series of brutalizations, restrictions, and forced role playing aimed at undercutting the prisoner's feelings of self-worth and competence. The specific techniques include "humiliation," "identification of prisoner by number only," "prohibitions of any decision making," and the like.

This section is central to Schein's analysis of the thought-reform process. He argues that since the self-concept lies at the center of one's world view, any attempt to reform a world view must necessarily begin with reform of the self-concept. Social scientists are in general agreement that man's self-concept is socially constructed, and it must be rather consistently confirmed by others if it is to be maintained. Schein suggests that in thought-reform prisons one's cellmates and others will respond to and reward only a "self" that is acceptable within the Communist ideological perspective. This section of Schein's model emphasizes the social destruction of the existing self-image.

In Morita therapy, however, the attack on the existing self-concept is neither so brutal nor so consistent. There is some humiliation during the *kowa* at Kora Koseiin, as noted above; there is some prescription of daily routine and work assignments; some activities (such as leaving the hospital grounds) require permission from the staff; and there is some social perception of the patient as "patient" (but without complete denial of his professional role; e.g., physicians who are patients may still be called *sensei*, and older patients are unlikely to be addressed in the less respectful form of *kun*). To summarize, again we find limited parallels in task accomplishment — here, undermining the existing self-concept of the subject — but major discrepancies in the techniques by which the task is carried out.

Attacking the emotional integration of personality. — Within this section of Schein's model, a number of techniques are aimed at the task of inducing in the prisoner various negative and self-deprecatory emotions, primarily guilt, despair, and anxiety. They include "Threats of death, of non-repatriation, of endless isolation and interrogation, of torture and physical injury, of injury to family and loved ones — induction of anxiety and despair." (See also Meerloo, 1956; Lifton, 1961; Sargant, 1957.)

Although there are superficial similarities between Morita therapy and brainwashing in technique (e.g., enforced dependency, enforced self-analysis by means of autobiographies, diaries, etc.), I would argue that the differences between the two are much more prominent and important. Some techniques used by the Chinese Communist Party (e.g., threats of torture, "Constant accusation," and "Continual criticism") are simply absent in Morita therapy.

In general, one can summarize the comparative analysis of the "unfreezing" phase of Schein's model by stating that, despite some minor overlap between Morita therapy and thought reform in functions (or tasks) and techniques for accomplishing them, the differences between the two, especially in techniques, far outweigh the similarities.

The Changing Phase

Schein (1961, pp. 134-136) conceptually divides the second phase of thought reform into four sections reflecting four sources of indoctrination: mass media, cellmates, interrogator and/or judge, and self-analysis. He writes (1961, p. 136):

> ... the process of *changing* can be thought of as the mental operations which the prisoner went through in arriving at new beliefs, attitudes, values, and behavior patterns. These mental operations can be thought of as the adoption of a new frame of reference, of new standards for evaluating behavior, and of new semantic rules. The whole process was given its direction by the information which the influence agent provided to the prisoner. Before acceptable changes could occur, however, the prisoner had to learn to pay attention to the information. He usually learned to pay attention when he began to identify with his cellmates in the process of trying to re-establish a sense of identity in the hostile prison environment.

Mass Media. — Schein found "no clear evidence" that Chinese Communists made special use of mass media within the prison setting.

Morita therapists have appeared on radio and television broadcasts in Japan, and, as mentioned above, have written a number of popular books about Morita therapy. But, certainly, the thrust of the Japanese mass media is toward better-known (and, I believe, more Western-oriented) philosophies than the Moritist one, and only at points do these alternative ideologies parallel Morita's view of the world.

Cellmates. — Schein (1961, pp. 134-135) points out that the cellmate group provides an emotion-laden social setting for learning through imitation and identification, concentrated instruction, rapid feedback, and exposure of defensive evasions.

Identification and modeling also take place in Moritist hospitals (see below, p. 206). Advanced patients are put forth as models (e.g., the work therapist at Kora Koseiin) and similarities between their cases and those of newly arrived patients are emphasized. There is feedback on the patient's progress and exposure of defensive maneuvers aimed at avoiding adoption and application of Moritist principles. And there are expressions of strong feelings of comradeship, hostility, and guilt. This section of Schein's model describes the Morita therapy situation rather well.

The effectiveness of small groups of subjects in indoctrinating (in a sense, resocializing) their members should not be overlooked despite the usual research emphasis on the change agent's activities in various directed behavior-change settings.

Interrogator and/or judge. — Schein focuses on the prisoner's identification with the change agent in this section of his model. According to Schein (1961, p. 135), identification in the Chinese Communist Party thought-reform prison may follow from similar levels of intellectual functioning between change agent and subject, similar cultural backgrounds, subject recognition of the change agent's power over the subject's fate, and prolonged interaction between subject and change agent. Not only was the change agent an object of identification, but he was also the "primary audience" to which the subject directed his behavior and the subject's primary source of ideological information and of cues about the reinforcement contingencies in the prison situation (1961, pp. 135-136).

With such an analysis Schein suggests that similarities between the subject and the change agent promote identification but that differences (such as the power of the change agent and the powerlessness of the subject) do, too. From my analysis of Morita therapy (see above, pp. 65-67), it appears that there is a kind of division of role function which taps both these sources of influence. The doctor in Morita therapy, though to some degree an object of identification, maintains social distance from the patient with the result that his authority works to increase his potential for suggestion as primary audience and controller of resources. On the other hand, at Kora Koseiin, for example, the work therapist is ranked much lower in authority but provides a ready model for identification through his overall similarity to the patients.

Selecting two items from this section of Schein's model for more detailed analysis, we find that Morita therapy contrasts with one item and conforms to the other. "For some prisoners the amount of contact with the interrogator was far greater than with anyone else, including cellmates" (1961, p. 135). In contrast, from my observations, no patient in a Morita therapy hospital had more contact with the therapist than with other patients except during the period of absolute bed rest (and not always then). In fact, an outstanding (and, for me, unexpected) research finding was the prolonged period of time the patients spent each day in unsupervised activity (or inactivity) with no therapist contact.

Schein writes further (1961, p. 135): "The interrogator, by virtue of being an official member of the government and by virtue of being in charge of S's case, was the primary audience for S's behavior and hence the one most closely attended to for cues as to what was expected of S." The same is true of Morita therapy hospitals. To elaborate, it is to the therapists that the diary is submitted, to the therapists that negotiations for release from the hospital, overnight passes, and progression to more advanced stages of treatment are directed. And, as in thought reform, Morita therapists seem to provide the major indoctrination activity, including cues regarding the proper expected behavior from patients.

Self-analysis. — Since this section of Schein's model contains only two items, I shall quote them and comment on them separately.

"Discovery by S of beliefs, attitudes, values, or past behavior which, even by his old standards of evaluation justified his treatment — guilt regarding own past" (1961, p. 135). This is indeed true of Morita therapy. The diaries and autobiographies of the patients are replete with self-denigration, feelings of inadequacy, and guilt for having mistreated family and friends. These attitudes and feelings add justification to the isolation and the self-sacrificing efforts of the patient.

"Discovery by S of identity components within himself which he wished to strengthen and which fitted in broadly with the ethical generalizations depicted in the 'people's standpoint'; increased motivation to reform self further, might then result from S's recognition that cellmate pressure had allowed this 'therapeutic' discovery to occur" (p. 136). Again, this element of Schein's model seems closely applicable to Morita therapy. The patient does seem to find within himself Moritist-valued identify components that he wishes to cultivate. This recognition, along with limited success in development of the identity components, fosters feelings of gratitude, accomplishment, and increased motivation to continue further reforms.

A common feature of communism, Freudianism, Christianity, Morita therapy, Zen, and so forth is that all provide meaning in every act. That is, no behavior, however trivial from a commonsense perspective, is meaningless. Each moment is suffused with understandable yet deep and worthy purpose, be it through self-analysis, serving God, application of political knowledge, or flowing acceptance.

These systems of meaning are readily contrasted with the folk cultures in which peak, meaningful experiences are interspersed with long periods of routine and meaningless preparatory living. One puts in his hours at work to be able to enjoy evenings and weekends. One washes clothes and dishes in order to enjoy a date or a meal later.

In general, Schein's analysis of the "changing" or indoctrination phase of thought reform shows much more commonality with Morita therapy than does his analysis of the "unfreezing" phase, partly because Schein rises to a higher level of abstraction in his analysis of the changing phase. Specific techniques (which one might expect to be in contrast with those used in Morita therapy) are omitted on this level of generality.

On the other hand, I would argue that there is wider divergence between thought-reform and Morita therapy "tasks" during the initial motivating stage than in the indoctrination stage. That is, Morita therapists, in comparison with the agents of thought reform, seem to have a much easier and qualitatively different task in attacking the world view and enlisting the cooperation of a patient who enters the hospital already dissatisfied with his existence. Once the motivation is elicited, indoctrination or information input can proceed with much the same function and technique in both Morita therapy and thought reform (and, for that matter, in any form of directed behavior change).

The Refreezing Phase

Following the indoctrination phase of thought reform, Schein's model (1961, pp. 137-138) postulates a phase of reinforcement and integration of the new cognitions and behavior. This phase begins within the prison and continues after release. In the prison setting, the model holds, there are four general sources of reinforcement and integration: (1) propaganda, (2) the small group, (3) the change agent, and (4) the subject's own sense of organization and mastery. The organization of these four sources parallels that of the information sources of the preceding changing phase (mass media, cellmates, interrogator and/or judge, and self-analysis).

Propaganda. — The first source, "Communist propaganda as reinforcement of and justification for confession and attitude change" (Schein, 1961, p. 137), needs little further comment. We have already noted that, in Morita therapy, books, lectures, and so forth provide justification for confession and attitude change.

The small group. — Schein says that "reading of materials" (p. 137) is an element of the small-group study in thought-reform prisons. As noted above, in Moritist hospitals books and articles about Morita therapy are assigned and recommended to patients, and, on occasion, group reading is conducted.

Schein notes further that "analysis of materials in the presence of others" and "implicit and explicit competition among prisoners in analyzing theory and deriving practical implications" (p. 137) are elements of group study. In Moritist hospitals group analysis of materials is carried out informally, and it seems to be an element of the *kowa* in some hospitals, although not in others. However, explicit competition among patients in analysis and application of Morita's theory was not observed.

Schein describes the element, "mutual criticism for incorrect analysis or incorrect attitude toward material" (p. 138). As noted in chapter 1, the patients at Mr. Mizutani's hospital read their diaries aloud by turns and the therapist and other patients comment on the diaries and on the behavior of patients. This practice seems to be unique to this hospital. Nowhere else was it observed in institutionalized form in Moritist hospitals.

Schein indicates that there exists a "requirement to analyze material in reference to own case, show how theory applied to S's own daily behavior" (p. 138). As emphasized above, Moritist thought underscores the behavioral application of Moritist principles. The diary assignment, as well as daily talks with the therapists about the day's activities, forces the patients to apply the Moritist world view to their daily actions.

Schein found "rationalization and justification of conclusions presented in materials; generally the conclusions could not be questioned, only justified, e.g., *'Why* are the Americans imperialistic warmongering?'" (p. 138). Although it is my impression that this element probably plays a less prominent part in Morita therapy than in thought reform, it is not absent in the former. The rigid ideological stance of many Morita therapists stands out sharply in my mind. Taking a specific example from the Moritist literature (Kora, 1968, p. 25).

> One young girl in my hospital, when it came to her turn to care for chickens, wrote, "I hate to take care of chickens. When I enter the cage the chickens attack me." However, forty or fifty days later, as the time for discharge approached, she wrote, "The time is nearing to return home. It is sad to have to say good-bye to the chickens. As I enter their cage they approach me in a friendly fashion." The chickens' attitude must have been unchanged during this period, but on the girl's side love had already grown.

Of course, an alternative interpretation is that the chickens actually did behave differently toward the girl, who had become associated with feeding responses. This conclusion, however, is simply brushed away. The acceptable question is, "Why did the girl's attitude change?" There exists only one acceptable answer in the context of the paper: "because she had cared for the chickens" her love for them had developed.

Schein notes that the small-group members came to be concerned with "showing how all activities, no matter how trivial, have political implications" (p. 138). In Morita therapy all activities are held to have psychological rather than political implications. The principle of ideological interpretation of even trivial activities still holds, however.

"Further public self-analysis in reference to materials, often as part of elaborating and deepening the confession, referred to sometimes as 'thought conclusions'" (Schein, 1961, p. 138), was still another element of small-group activities during the refreezing phase of brainwashing. Within this category seems to fall some of Morita therapy's *kowa* behavior as well as testimonies in both formal and informal group settings. There seems, however, to be no summarizing event or document in Morita therapy (as there is in brainwashing) at the conclusion of the patient's hospitalization. This feature is in keeping with the Moritist principle that the habits and ideology learned within the hospital must be applied for years in order to bring substantial results.

Finally, the small group functioned during the refreezing phase in another way. The reestablishment of adequate communications and comfortable relationships with cellmates was a positive reinforcement for conforming behavior and thought in the prison setting. Similarly, in the Moritist hospital a few passively rebellious patients were observed to reestablish comfortable relations with other patients through conforming behavior. In a larger sense, however, this element of thought reform contrasts with Morita therapy. In the thought-reform prison cellmates and interrogator restricted communication and established harsh social relations in response to the recalcitrance of the subject. Relations are softened, then, in response to the subject's conformity. But in Morita therapy many patients enter the hospital because of their pervasive discomfort in interpersonal situations. For them the establishment (not the reestablishment) of comfortable social relations with fellow patients is viewed as a stage of (though not necessarily a goal of) cure.

The change agent. — In the thought-reform prison the interrogator eases the emotional relationship with his prisoner only as the latter responds to indoctrination in an acceptable manner. The differentiation between establishing versus reestablishing comfortable social relationships applies equally here.

The subject's sense of organization and mastery. — As the thought-reform prisoner reestablishes communications and satisfying social contact by adopting, however tentatively, the prescribed cognitive organization of reality, he comes to recognize the usefulness of organizing his perception of the world according to Communist principles. He gains some sense of mastery over his fate. According to Frank (1961), ideology provides the patient in psychotherapy with a conceptual framework for organizing his distress, a plan of action for dealing with it, and a sense of mastery over formerly uncontrollable forces. This sounds very much like the situation in the thought-reform prison as described by Schein.

Moritist principles, too, seem to provide the patient with an organized, rewarding framework for viewing the world. They also provide a sense of control over his symptoms through acceptance and "working around" them. A more detailed look at the techniques of reinforcement in the two situations (not to mention the content of the ideology), however, reveals major differences between thought reform and Morita therapy. For example, although certain privileges obtain with advanced patient status in Moritist hospitals, there is nothing comparable to the removal of the extreme psychophysical pressures found in the brainwashing situation.

Schein's model categorizes three kinds of experiences that influence the thought-reform repatriate to further accept and integrate the Communist ideology into his perception of the world. The first experience is the "confirmation of predictions made by cellmates and authorities" (p. 138). This element of confirmed predictions is a key technique used throughout Morita therapy hospitalization, and, from reports of some ex-patients, the therapists' predictions are confirmed during the posthospital period as well.

The second experience is to establish relations with individuals or small groups outside the prison who share the Communist ideology. The element of social support of ex-patients in Morita therapy is discussed in chapter 1. In general, Morita therapy hospitals seem to have an effective posthospitalization contact system.

The third experience discussed by Schein, "sense of personal integration, in the absence of prison supports and pressures" (p. 138), I take to mean the effectiveness of the Communist world view in providing an organized, rewarding perspective outside the prison. How effective it is probably depends in large part on the values of the broader social milieu in which the ex-prisoner operates. That is, the Communist ideology is likely to be more satisfying where there is broad social support for it as in, say, Communist China as opposed to Taiwan or the United States. The supporting contribution of Japanese values in Morita therapy has been considered in some detail in chapters 3 and 4.

Summary

Schein's model of thought reform postulates a phase of ideological indoctrination (through instruction, modeling, rapid feedback, etc.) following a phase of discomfort and undermining the subject's existing world view (including, centrally, his self-concept) and preceding a phase of short- and long-term reinforcement of behavioral and cognitive integration of the Communist ideology. On this general level of description the functioning of Morita therapy can be described in much the same terms. As one looks at the specific techniques by which these functions or tasks are accomplished, and as one looks in more detail at the subunits of which these functions or tasks are composed, however, the inapplicability of Schein's model to Morita therapy shows forth clearly at a number of points, most notably during the initial unfreezing phase.

Aside from the ideological content, perhaps the crucial features that distinguish brainwashing from Morita therapy are the initial lack of motivation on the part of the thought-reform prisoner and the confinement that was therefore necessary. Through the use of force and punishment, the thought-reform prisoner is coerced into learning about and putting into action a new world view. The motivating factor of personal neurotic distress prods the patient of psychotherapy into a very different change situation in which the change agent very likely espouses an ideology based upon and concordant with the world view of the society in which the patient was enculturated.

LEIGHTON'S MODEL OF PSYCHOTHERAPY

Morita therapy purports to be a kind of psychotherapy. How well does it fit a generalized model of psychotherapy? Leighton's model, abstracted from psychotherapies in a number of cultures, contains seven categories. I have somewhat expanded the scope of these categories and have labeled them: (1) characteristics of the patient; (2) characteristics of the therapist; (3) period of preparation; (4) suggestion and social modeling; (5) period of indoctrination; (6) group factors; and (7) posttreatment period. In the following analysis Leighton is quoted, parallels with other forms of directed behavior change are drawn, and specific relevance to Morita psychotherapy is pointed out.

Characteristics of the Patient

"Every individual is prepared during the course of his life by a set of expectancies regarding illness and treatment which are part of his culture. These are inculcated long before his own condition as a patient comes about. They are heightened, however, as he approaches being a patient and increase the suggestive power of many of the experiences he undergoes" (Leighton, 1968, p. 1177).

In a narrow sense, Leighton writes here of culturally shared conceptions of illness and treatment brought by the subject as he enters the therapy situation. In a broader sense, however, this is only one example of a broad spectrum of subject characteristics that influence the efficacy of directed behavior change.

An important question from Leighton's perspective, then, is the degree to which the patient brings the concepts, values, and strategies of Morita therapy with him as part of his mental makeup when he enters the hospital. It would seem to be more difficult to bring about cognitive change when the existing structure differs widely from the desired orientation. Some of the values of the Japanese people as they support or undermine Morita therapy have been described above. Here I touch briefly upon specific patient expectancies toward treatment; in particular, the focus is on expectancies regarding cure, the doctor-patient relationship, and Morita therapy as a whole.

Nearly all patients come to the Moritist hospital with the stated desire of alleviating their symptoms, not of accepting them. Acceptance is viewed, generally, as second best. But the fact that acceptance is viewed as a possible solution is significant in itself, for it seems to be a peculiarly Eastern (fundamentally Buddhist) conception. This attitude toward the relative preferred ordering of solutions for dealing with neurotic distress must undergo reversal during treatment.

On the other hand, the Japanese patient is likely to enter the hospital with reasonable expectations concerning the patient role. He accepts learning, obedience, and exertion of personal effort as the proper means for achieving his ends. He also accepts the therapist's status as one of authority, meriting respect, attention, and cooperation (Koestler, 1961). The patient is expected to be humble and dedicated and to become absorbed in the disciplines and tasks to which he is assigned. The burden of cognitive and behavior change is on the student, not on the *sensei*. If failure occurs it is because the student has followed directions imperfectly (in Naikan therapy, for example, only those who reflect deeply are helped; in Dr. Suzuki's hospital only those who keep the Moritist hospital rules are cured; and so forth), and both the *sensei* and his change ideology are unassailable owing to this assessment of the locus of responsibility for change. These assumptions about the key dyadic relationship between *sensei* and student seem to be common to Morita therapy, Zen, Naikan, and many other instructional settings in Japan. Caudill (1959), too, has remarked on ways in which these shared role expectations underlie the psychotherapy contract between patient and doctor, facilitating the therapeutic process. Since both therapist and patient at Kora Koseiin, for example, share these basic assumptions about appropriate role behavior and role relationships, the process of directed behavior change is facilitated.

What knowledge of Moritist conceptions of illness and treatment do patients have as they enter the hospital? Approximately half of the neurotic patients at Kora Koseiin come because they have read one or more of Dr. Kora's books about neurosis (these books, oriented toward the general reading public, contain the address and phone number of the hospital). Most of the other patients are referred from the outpatient clinics connected with Jikei University (in these clinics Morita therapy is customarily practiced on an outpatient basis). So it is no surprise that many of those admitted to Kora Koseiin, and to other Moritist hospitals as well, come with at least some rudimentary knowledge of Morita therapy. By virtue of their seeking admission and accepting hospitalization (voluntarily, but with varying degrees of informal family pressure) in a hospital that explicitly and publicly defines itself as a Moritist hospital (as, for example, nurses explain to inquirers over the phone), they are already implicitly committed in some degree to the treatment objectives and methods (at least to the extent of their understanding of them).

In sum, then, the patient entering a Moritist hospital brings attitudes and expectancies that both facilitate and hinder directed behavior change. He is likely to have some knowledge of Moritist principles before hospitalization, and he already shares to some degree some of the fundamental values that underlie Morita therapy. On the other hand, he brings expectations and habits that impede the changes that are to be brought about. Thus, in Morita therapy, the attitudes, expectations, and behavior patterns of the patient do not work consistently to facilitate the directed behavior change process.

Characteristics of the Therapist

"There is always at least one healer who has prestige and mystique. The patient achieves some measure of the healer's distinction when he emerges as one who has been successfully treated. In many places, becoming a healer involves first being a patient" (Leighton, 1968, p. 1177).

With regard to the "prestige and mystique" of the therapist, the strong tendency for him to be a physician has already been pointed out, although strictly speaking one need not be a physician in order to practice Morita therapy. A physician carries the authority and respect attached to the term *sensei* within Japanese culture (Koestler, 1961, p. 229). He is a benevolent, though strict, authority figure. Dr. Kora, for example, is a famous emeritus professor, the husband of a well-known ex-member of the Japanese Diet, an author of numerous books and scholarly articles, and an aged gentleman. One is unlikely to find a more powerful combination of qualifications to carry potential for suggestive influence over young Japanese neurotic patients.

One indication of the prestigious position the doctor's role holds in the eyes of the patients was the absolute lack of any possibility of sustained group therapy (in the Western sense) when a doctor was present. At Kora Koseiin, for example, two doctors tried unsuccessfully to institute a group therapy meeting in 1968. As in the *kowa* lectures, however, the interaction invariably reverted to the patient-therapist, therapist-patient form of communication which precluded any significant direct patient-patient communication. Usually, the meetings rapidly resolved into short questions from patients which were answered by long lectures from the therapist. In fact, so widespread was the feeling among the patients that this group meeting was simply another *kowa* (with another therapist-teacher) that they called it "Dr. Kim's *kowa*" and repeatedly had to be told to call it "group therapy," though without much success.

Of course, the attitudes that dictated against the establishment of group therapy in the Western sense were not held only by the patients. The doctor who refuses to lecture, who directs patients to reply to other patients, who stimulates free questioning and discussion, can produce something much nearer to a true group therapy. But the therapists, too, were caught in their own role-defined habits of interaction; they behaved in accordance with their own self-concepts.

Turning to another issue, it seems that in Morita therapy "the patient achieves some measure of the healer's distinction when he emerges as one who has been successfully treated." Visits by discharged patients are not infrequent at Moritist hospitals. At Kora Koseiin the visits are either informal (renewing old acquaintances, giving gifts, maintaining contacts with former fellow patients, etc.) or formal (attending the ex-patients' meeting, the outpatient clinic, the English conversation class, etc.) or a mixture of the two. These returning patients hold a rather special status in the eyes of inpatients. They are looked upon with respect, as ones who have cleared their neurotic hurdles. With some restraint engendered by politeness, the inpatients are eager to learn of the experiences of ex-patients. The latter are often asked about their prior symptoms, their length of hospitalization, their condition at the time of discharge, and their current condition. Almost without exception their replies are congruent with the advice that had previously been given by the Morita therapists. They reply that they still have some feelings of shyness, overconcern with what others are thinking about them, anxiety, and so forth; but they have learned gradually through the hospital and posthospital periods to live active lives in spite of their symptoms, and therefore they are not seriously bothered by them.

In a somewhat similar way patients who are much improved over their condition when they entered the hospital are asked to offer advice to the other patients present at formal and informal meetings. The changes in their appearance (e.g., "When you first came you looked so stiff and unhappy"), their attitude (e.g., "You didn't want to do anything"), and their behavior (e.g., "You sat back in the corner and hardly spoke a word, remember?") are called to everyone's attention, and those who remember confirm the changes while the honored patient appears shy and happy. The improved patient begins to take on some of the respect that grows with discharge and increasing age until it reaches its zenith as a guest of honor at the *keiyakikai* or attainment of the status of therapist.

The *keiyakikai* at Kora Koseiin is a semiannual meeting for discharged patients hold on Sunday afternoons. The number in attendance varies but approximates fifty. The two main features of the *keiyakikai* are the lecture by Dr. Kora and the testimonies of ex-patients. The former patients stand one by one, each giving his name, telling what he is engaged in occupationally or personally, describing his symptoms past and present, and, perhaps, delivering a short speech of gratitude, encouragement, and exhortation. The inpatients at Kora Koseiin have helped in the preparations for this event. They sit together in the back of the room listening to their symbolic elder brothers and sisters speak.

One of the fascinating points of correspondence among various directed behavior-change systems is that the agent is quite often an ex-subject. The analyst has had a training psychoanalysis; the Zen *roshi* was once a novice; the cadre and the progressive in the Chinese Communist movement were subjects of thought reform (Walker, 1956; Lifton, 1961); and the boot-camp drill instructor was once a recruit. Not only does this experience provide the agent with some of the basic knowledge of his ideology and some understanding and empathy for his subject, but it also provides the subject with a social model of one who has moved up through the system to a position of authority and privilege. Thus the change agent is likely to become an object of identification — attractive because of his present role of agent and attainable because of his former role as subject.

The three largest, most famous Moritist hospitals in Tokyo in 1968 all had directors who had suffered in the past from neurosis. Two of them, Dr. Suzuki and Mr. Mizutani, were treated in Professor Morita's hospital, and the third, Dr. Kora, studied under Morita after being self-cured. Morita therapy conforms closely to Leighton's model on this point.

The Period of Preparation

"At some point, usually early, the patient experiences a profound emotional shakeup [*sic*]. This is obtained in one or more of the following ways:

  a) By the application of external and internal medications;
  b) By physical pain or psychological discomfort, e.g., in being made to confess his iniquities or inadequacies;
  c) By having to perform in front of other people;
  d) By the drama of a ritual that builds to a climax; or
  e) By esthetic appeal through poetry, song, music (especially rhythm), and color.

"There is often a period of heightened fear, followed by a release from fear, and there is generally a terminal period of euphoria or ecstatic state. It is as if the whole procedure brought about a situation in which the structure of the patient's personality becomes soft, and then, after the emotional crisis, resets in a new form" (Leighton, 1968, pp. 1177-1178).

The main preparation period of Morita therapy as considered from the point of view of Leighton's model is clearly the period of absolute bed rest. Whether or not this experience can be termed a "profound emotional shake-up" is a matter of definition. Of course, one need not postulate a profound emotional shake-up during the bed-rest period to account for its effectiveness in preparing the patient for the indoctrination that follows. Alternatively, isolated bed rest can be interpreted as the symbolization of the therapist's power, just as the power of the older males in some preliterate societies is communicated to young initiates during initiation ceremonies. It can be interpreted as an image-building ceremony in which the therapist's abilities to predict and understand the reactions of his patient are dramatized. From the Moritist perspective, bed rest can be interpreted as a demonstration to the patient through his own experience of the natural decline of emotions and the understanding that withdrawal and boredom are unnatural and unpleasant. In a Jungian sense, bed rest may be a kind of symbolic death and rebirth into the Moritist "family." Again, it can be interpreted as a kind of shared initiation experience admitting the initiate into the patient subculture.

One thing bed rest is not; it is not severe sensory deprivation. Whatever emotional upheaval occurs does not stem from this source. Several excellent summaries of sensory deprivation experiments (Goldberger, 1966; Inglis, 1966) are in general agreement that the degree of sensory deprivation varies considerably from experiment to experiment so that comparison of results is often hazardous.

Nevertheless, the deprivation in absolute bed rest does not approach that of the weakest of experimental conditions. To be sure, there is a reduction of sensory stimuli and a reduction in social contact, but the reduction cannot be termed severe.

Following the Moritist maxim that one cannot understand fully unless one experiences for himself, I underwent a one-week period of absolute bed rest at Dr. Suzuki's hospital in the fall of 1968. There follows an English translation of my published report of this experience (Reynolds, 1969c):

> I didn't find such great distress in bedrest (as was expected from my reading of patients' accounts). Something else I didn't find was severe stimulus deprivation. There have been many experiments in America and Canada recently involving stimulus deprivation. People are blindfolded and immersed in lukewarm water for hours, or they lie in a bed with blindfold, earplugs, and thick cotton gloves in order to drastically cut down on stimulation. The effects are very strong. Only a few people can stay in such conditions for more than a few waking hours. When I read about absolute bedrest I thought that some of its effects are due to stimulus deprivation. And it is true that stimuli are reduced in absolute bedrest, but not severely.
>
> I could see any time I wanted to open my eyes and turn on the light. I even had some beautiful roses to look at for the first few days. And I could hear voices and the hospital dog's bark and radio exercises. And I could feel the rough *tatami* mat, my beard, the soft blanket, the cool sheet, etc. And the smell of the roses and of my soap, and the smell and taste of delicious food and pleasant toothpaste were stimuli that accompanied bedrest. So I cannot explain the effects of absolute bedrest simply as due to severe stimulus deprivation.
>
> *Two themes: human kindness and responsibility.* There are two themes, however, that I did find running through Japanese culture, the Morita therapy hospital, and absolute bedrest that are worth noting. One may be called the theme of human kindness or human thoughtfulness. Many social relationships in Japan tend to take on a warm personal quality even if they begin as formal professional relationships. The shopkeeper, the waitress, the doctor and nurse become almost like friends. A grateful patient may bring the doctor a gift, for example. Perhaps Japanese people feel it is "natural" to be kind and polite, but this is an attitude that we are not born with. It is an attitude toward other people that is learned just as we learn our attitudes toward flowers or snakes.
>
> In my case, the thoughtfulness of Dr. Suzuki in giving me some roses, the kindness of some patients who swept my room as I went to the toilet, the thoughtfulness of bread (instead of rice) for

breakfast, and the nurses' cheerfulness and their remembering that the shoe horn at the entrance was a gift from me — these kindnesses stand out in my mind. Such kindness is a kind of natural therapy. The new patients compare their own selfishness and self-centeredness with the "giving" attitude of these other people.

Another theme might be called self-responsibility. It is said that people become what we expect them to become. In the Morita therapy hospital patients are expected to be responsible contributing members to the little hospital society.

When I began bedrest I expected to find holes in the walls or windows through which people could check to see if I was keeping the rules about no reading, no writing, etc. At the least, I expected hourly checks by the nurses on my behavior. But that was not the case. In the morning the doctor asked if I was keeping quiet; I replied that I was. That was all. I was expected to be responsibly keeping bedrest and I was expected to report honestly — and I did.

It is immediately after arising from bed rest that the patient at Kora Koseiin is required to write a history of his neurosis and a description of his bed-rest experience. One of the functions of these tasks seems to be to force the patient to organize, and thus to cognitively "set" or "fix," the experience he has just undergone. The results of the softening process must not be allowed to fade quickly from his memory, but are placed on permanent record.

There are other means besides absolute bed rest by which psychological discomfort and "softening" are induced during the early stages of Morita therapy. In describing his symptoms to the doctor both verbally and in the written history of his neurosis, the patient is engaged in a kind of confession of "iniquities and inadequacies." Furthermore, the confession is made publicly before staff and patients during the kowa lectures.

During the kowa another useful method of softening the existing personality structure and preparing for cognitive reorganization is laughter and ridicule. As unusual feature of the kowa (noted particularly at Kora Koseiin, and apparently absent at some other Moritist hospitals), but one that seems to fit into the philosophical framework of Morita's theory, is relative inattention to the patients' sensibilities. This means that, in comparison with the extreme efforts made by many Japanese to avoid hurting others' feelings or to avoid evoking unpleasant memories or causing mental anguish of any kind, in the kowa at Kora Koseiin Dr. Kora ignores the patients' oversensitivity to the point of apparent cruelty.

For example, Dr. Kora carries beliefs and tendencies offered by the patients to extremes, making ridiculous comparisons and demonstrating the absurdity of the patients' positions. The group laughs, and soon the patient, too, may be laughing at his own fears (or, at least, smiling politely). In this group laughter one can see most clearly a second reason for the group to gather for the *kowa*. Not only is lecturing to the group a timesaving method of instruction, but also the director is using the group to demonstrate to the patient that he is wrong. In general, the director instructs the group to respond to a patient when he asks the group questions that are certain to be answered in contradiction to a patient's statement, or to show that a patient's statements are unclear, or to promote group laughter ridiculing the patient's delusions. The group provides data for cognitive reorganization by communicating disagreement with the patient's existing cognitive formulations. All this group work is carried out with particular focus on the newly admitted patient who is made to confess and perform publicly, as emphasized in Leighton's model.

On the other hand, the drama of ritual building to a climax and the appeal to aesthetics seems much less conspicuous than the use of psychological discomfort (and the occasional use of medication) to prepare the patient for indoctrination in Morita therapy.

Suggestion and Social Modeling

"Concomitant with all of the above, there is, as the treatment progresses, an increasing dependency on the healer by the patient, and with this goes an increasing susceptibility to suggestion" (Leighton, 1968, p. 1178).

The influence of suggestion in any psychotherapeutic procedure is extremely difficult to assess. Morita therapists are given to saying that the patient need not believe in the therapy to be cured by it. A more accurate statement would be that the patient need not verbalize his faith in Morita therapy or that he may appropriately maintain some coexisting doubts, but by entering the hospital and by following the therapist's instructions the patient certainly implies faith in the outcome.

As noted above, the status of *sensei* carries much benign authority in Japan. It would be wrong to describe the therapists at Kora Koseiin as warm and egalitarian. They are dedicated, interested in the patient and his problems, willing to offer help, and gratified at his improvement, but there remains a careful social distance between doctor and patient and an unwillingness on the part of the doctor to accept anything less than the expression of the patient's commitment and effort in the therapeutic endeavor.

In practice, Morita therapists use suggestion in both direct and indirect forms. Moreover, they engage in communications that in effect enhance their position as knowledgeable predictors, thus increasing their power of suggestion.

The agent of behavior change can improve his suggestive influence by building up a history of having been right before. The doctors at Kora Koseiin make use of their broad experience to let the patient know that they understand his case even before he tells them about himself in detail. They call to the patient's attention general principles of human experience (e.g., human emotions decline with time unless restimulated, boredom produces a desire for activity), and they apply these principles to the individual case to predict the patient's future condition. Before he undergoes bed rest the patient is told what to expect psychologically — and the doctors are usually right. When the patient begins to talk about his symptoms the doctor asks if it is not also true that such and such a symptom is present. And the reply, "Why, yes it is," is very likely to follow. When the patient searches for words to express the complicated feelings and attitudes that are part of his neurosis, the doctors can supply acceptable ones immediately. It is made very clear that the doctors understand and can categorize the problem for they have treated many similar problems before.

The patient undergoing Morita therapy may rebel against the doctor's categorization. His case is not exactly like other people's, he may claim, although similar, perhaps. The doctor handles such a plea for uniqueness, however, by eliciting reports from other patients which indicate congruency between their symptoms and those of the patient in question. Furthermore, he continues to make accurate predictions about the symptom complex. How could he understand it so well if it were unique? Finally, the doctor defines the desire to be "special" or different from other people as part of the neurosis itself, something to be eventually overcome by treatment.

By these tactics the doctor gradually convinces the patient of his expertise in treating a particular case. The doctor has predicted so accurately in the past, he has understood the condition of the patient so well, and he carries an attitude of such confidence, that when he communicates to the patient (and he does, both directly and indirectly) that if the patient follows the treatment plan he will be cured as others have been cured, the patient begins to turn away from skepticism.

Thus certainty and successful prediction may produce a kind of "halo effect" in which doctors are seen as "good at everything," as one patient remarked in his diary concerning Dr. Abe. The doctor is often idealized to the point that he is asked advice on all sorts of subjects. His expertise is seen by some patients as extending over the whole range of human living.

It may be added that the neurotic patient comes to the doctor with all sorts of mistaken ideas about his body, concerns about the presence of a serious illness, and so on. The doctors can cite studies, conduct examinations that rule out possible illnesses, and quote percentage probabilities of future malfunctioning. At least on a rational level, this procedure reassures the patient. Indirectly, it makes confidence in the doctor a very rewarding attitude. For if confidence fails, a good part of the supportive conceptual structure may fail as well. The reassurance was not based on the patient's having read reports or on his own knowledge of physical examinations and tests, but on the doctor's reassurance, his memory, and his evaluations of laboratory results.

Direct suggestion occurs in the interviews, during the *kowa*, and in the diaries. Some examples of direct suggestion from the diary comments are: ("Soon after I begin reading a book the words become blurred. Will this be cured?") "It's all right. It will be cured." "If you are active in sports and work the unsteadiness in your legs will disappear." "Withoutout being impatient let's wait for you to gradually improve." "Gradually you will become skillful." ("Moreover, I cannot write well; will this be cured?") "It will be cured."

Indirect suggestion occurs when citing cases that have been cured by Morita therapy, when pointing out patients who have progressed in their handling of symptoms, and when encouraging the presence of functioning ex-patients within the hospital setting.

Much has been made here of the suggestive influence of Moritists in the therapeutic process. It would be inaccurate, however, to portray Morita therapists as consciously utilizing techniques to increase the persuasability of patients. They do not use a bag of tricks to build up their suggestive influence. On the other hand, they are not completely unaware of these effects. For example, among younger therapists there is some cynicism concerning a few of the postulates of the Moritist system, but they continue to use them because they are easily understood by the patients and they seem to be effective in answering patients' questions and doubts. Rather than being expressly manipulative, Morita therapists are aware of the importance of the patient-therapist relationship in some vague sense, and they do try to influence this relationship in a general way to keep it on a positive basis. They are also aware of some effect that corresponds to the term "identification" or "social modeling" as used by Bandura and Walters (1963).

One can offer only indirect evidence that identification and social modeling occur in Moritist hospitals. On a very simple level, during a game of miniature golf, Dr. Kora exclaimed, "Nice! Nice!" after a patient's accurate putt. This English expression was subsequently copied by several patients using similar pronunciation and tone. Verbal imitation of this simple sort was repeated elsewhere, as well. Other indirect evidence of social modeling is the statement of one male patient that becoming a psychiatrist like Dr. Abe was among the most important things in the world for him.

The doctor's role fluctuates between distance from and closeness to the patient. The doctor may engage in activities that symbolize his similarity to the patients, such as working and playing alongside them, eating the same food, and helping with crafts. But always he is set apart: he is likely to be invited to play the next game of table tennis instead of waiting his turn; he may have a few extra condiments when eating; he is much more likely to be found playing than working with the patients. As mentioned above, there are reasons for viewing the work therapist as the primary model for imitation at Kora Koseiin.

In a sense, the model for both doctors and patients is Professor Morita himself. Though the attitude toward the originator of Morita therapy varies somewhat among students and patients, a substantial number hold him in veneration of a sort that is reminiscent of the respect Freud evoked in some of his followers. I was jokingly told that one Moritist hospital director thinks Morita is God. A foreign observer described the 1974 meetings in honor of the hundredth anniversary of Morita's birth as almost religious in tone. Tales of Professor Morita's life, sometimes accompanied by slides, are presented by the older professors at Jikei University psychiatric conferences; his picture graces the walls of the psychiatric department, and he looks down from the walls of Moritist hospitals. Excerpts from his personal diary and vignettes from his life appear as scholarly articles in hospital magazines and are used at ex-patient meetings. Some therapists have even made pilgrimages to his birth-place and to his tomb.

Yet for all this veneration Morita is a man whose image can be the model for almost anyone. Everyone with a fair amount of contact with Morita therapy knows that he was neurotic as a young man and cured himself. Many know that he had various idio-syncrasies, that he enjoyed drinking, that he was not much given to smiling, that he was more concerned with realistic living than with social appearances and niceties (in his later years he traveled via perambulator), that he lived with his patients. And it is common knowledge within the Moritist settings that he became the chairman of the Department of Psychiatry and Neurology at Jikei University in spite of (or, perhaps, because of) his personal limitations.

Again we find that Morita therapy fits Leighton's model fairly closely.

The Period of Indoctrination

"Underlying the treatment procedure is a dramatic myth with the following functions and characteristics:

"*a*. It provides a general orientation with regard to the phe-nomena of life, the characteristics of illness, and the rationale of treatment.

"*b*. It is worked over during the course of the treatment, pro-ducing an increased acquaintance on the part of the patient with this explanatory framework.

"*c*. The ceremonial itself, or some parts of it, constitutes a symbolic re-enactment of something which went wrong in the past and which is now being set right, and which is comprehensible in the setting of the myth. The 'what went wrong' is revealed in some part of the ceremonial and then must be corrected. There is usually a battle of anthropomorphic entities which may take place inside or outside the patient's psyche. The ritual of the ceremonial or other therapeutic activity is concerned with making this battle come out on the side of the patient. The patient does it over again symbolically without the mistake, and so through the mediation of the healer comes into harmony with great and mysterious forces within and without himself. Profound belief in the myth by both healer and patient heightens the force of suggestion and the influence of the matrix of subtle cues which are only partly realized by either" (Leighton, 1968, p. 1178).

In its broadest interpretation Leighton's model here, too, applies in large part to Morita therapy. Let us consider the Moritist philosophy as taught to the patients as the Morita myth. It is truly a myth in the sense that it is based on essentially untestable premises that are held as beliefs by some group as part of its world view. In this sense science, with its believers' faith in the order and predictability of the natural world and their confidence in the scientific method as the means of getting at that order, is a myth also. In contrast with Leighton's model, the anthropomorphized symbols are at a minimum in Morita therapy, and the essential form of the myth is consciously naturalistic, rationalistic, and scientific as opposed to supernatural and narrative.

As noted above, the Moritist myth provides a way of cognitively ordering many experiences in life, both on concrete and on abstract levels; it explains the characteristics of the neurotic difficulty and provides the theoretical rationale for treatment. (It would be useful to remind the reader that the treatment as actually practiced in any given situation may vary more or less from that theoretically provided for in the myth.)

A number of elements are involved in the content of the myth that is presented to the Morita therapy patient. He learns (1) new definitions for familiar terms, (2) new terms and phrases, (3) new values for various concepts, (4) new strategies for handling personal problems, and (5) an overall ideological framework that organizes the four preceding items.

1) Examples of redefinitions include:

"Cure," once defined as "removal of symptoms," is redefined as "living actively with symptoms."

"Hospitalization," once defined as "a period devoted to the removal of symptoms," becomes "a period devoted to the learning of how to live fully every day with symptoms."

"Neurosis," once defined as "having symptoms," is redefined as "being trapped (ensnared, obsessed) by symptoms."

"Living fully," once defined as "symptom-free living," is redefined as "purposeful living for others."

"Doctor," once defined as "one who brings about symptom removal," is redefined in this situation as "a teacher of symptom acceptance."

Finally, the problem, once defined as "having a neurosis," is redefined in terms of "self-centeredness."

2) New terms such as "psychic interaction," "defensive over-simplification," and "the desire to live fully," along with new phrases and slogans (often of Buddhist origin), are learned. Not only are the terms and phrases learned, but accompanying them are fairly elaborate interpretations of their meaning. These terms serve as mnemonic devices for coding large sets of information about the Moritist world view.

3) The value of achieving one's life purposes increases relative to the value of removing one's symptoms. Having symptoms may change from a negatively to a positively evaluated concept. Such statements as the following are commonly encountered: "Because I have these symptoms I've been able to deepen my personality. It's good that I have them"; and "Only people who have suffered from neurosis can really understand Morita therapy." It must be remembered that, according to one interpretation of theory, neurotic persons have an unusually large amount of *sei no yokubo* at their disposal. Energy and desire, when properly directed, can be utilized in the development of a superior style of living.

4) The strategies for handling emotions and the like have been described above, but to rephrase them, the patient is taught to "distance" his rational, socially constructive, goal-oriented, controllable, "initiator of action," on the one hand, from his emotions, sensations, impulses, moods, and all other uncontrollable elements of experience on the other. He is taught to recognize the uncontrollable elements, fix them in objective time and circumstance, and accept them as phenomenological reality, but then to continue with the behavior that is relevant to accomplishing his goals. It must be reemphasized that such acceptance implies no yielding, only recognition and the understanding that energy or attention must not be wasted in struggling with or fleeing from the uncontrollable element. The strategy for handling emotions is simply to allow them to pass without giving them undue restimulating attention. One can, however, indirectly influence attitudes and moods through changed behavior.

5) These new concepts, values, and strategies are not learned

piecemeal; they are learned as part of a unified ideology, a kind of life philosophy. The organizing world view can in part be summarized by the following set of postulates:

a. Each man is born with the desire to live fully; this desire is the ultimate source of his energy.

b. This energy may be directed toward healthy or neurotic pursuits.

c. Neurotic persons have an excess of this energy.

d. Man finds a sense of meaning in life and self-value by directing his energy toward serving others and by contributing to his group, particularly his family.

e. Contributing consists of setting up both immediate and long-term goals and accomplishing them. Accomplished goals are concrete and enduring and valuable in the ultimate existential sense of postulate *d.*

f. In order to accomplish one's goals one must work.

g. Behavior is controllable in the broadest sense.

h. Feelings, moods, impulses, and some behavior (like stuttering) are uncontrollable, changeable, and unenduring.

i. Feelings, moods, and so forth sometimes distract man from his goals.

Given these postulates it is possible to draw a number of further inferences. For example, from *d, e,* and *i* it follows that a man's feelings may distract him from accomplishing his goals with a negative effect on his feelings of self-worth. Again, it follows from *a, b, c,* and *d* that the neurotic person has a larger potential for service and for developing a sense of meaning in life than does his normal counterpart.

The means by which the Moritist myth "is worked over during the course of the treatment" merits a special section. At Kora Koseiin a direct assault is made on the existing cognitive apparatus and habit patterns of the newly admitted patient. From the first day the patient is compelled to deal with a new lifeway. The methods for teaching patients about Morita therapy have grown from the experience of three generations of Morita therapists, although at the outset Morita drew some elements from centuries-old Buddhist techniques. These methods are used today because they seem to be effective, but they can be and are modified, added to, and dropped according to the needs of particular patients and the predilections of individual therapists.

For example, a female patient with recurring headaches was

placed on half-day bed rest during the second phase of her treatment by her therapist. Every afternoon she was to lie down for a few hours. The term, "half-day bed rest," as well as the method, was newly adopted for this single case, It turned out not to be particularly effective, and I never encountered it again.

The myth is worked over by means of both verbal and written instructions. It is difficult to separate verbal from written instruction in terms of content because the same Moritist stories and theory that may be told to the patients informally or during the meetings may also be found in Moritist books and magazines.

Several stories of actual cases are particularly noteworthy both because of the frequency with which they turn up and because of the further understanding of the Moritist world view which they may provide the reader. One is the case of a teacher who came to Kora Koseiin because of his worry that he could not realize his high ideal of wanting to love all his students equally. He was told that his inability to love all students equally was perfectly natural, since some students are more lovable than others. His responsibility was not to love them all but to watch over all of them and instruct them. If he performed this function conscientiously he might find that a love for all of them would grow spontaneously without any efforts on his part to control his emotions.

In addition to the true stories related by the therapists, there are also illustrations and parables that not only serve to conveniently fix abstract ideas in the patients' minds but also seem to carry some of the emotional satisfaction of a point proved. One of the finest illustrations is that used by Dr. Takeyama and others. He tells the new outpatient something like this: "Every day your nose is perfectly visible, but you don't notice it. Since I just now pointed it out to you perhaps you have become very much aware of it. But, now, while you are so conscious of your visible nose, you haven't been paying any attention to the headache you came complaining of, have you? So you see, it is the overattention to your symptoms that has been the real seat of your distress."

As noted above, the directors of the most famous Moritist hospitals have written nontechnical books on the subject of neurosis and its treatment. In a spot survey of seven patients and ex-patients at Kora Koseiin only one had never read a book about Morita therapy and four had read four or more books each.

Slogans and proverbs are extensively used in Moritist hospitals.

The work therapist at Kora Koseiin was able to recollect spontaneously seven slogans in a few minutes, and almost any neurotic patient can recite several from memory. There are scrolls, framed calligraphy, plaques, and signs of various sorts containing these slogans hanging conspicuously on the walls of Moritist hospitals. Part of the patients' craftwork may be to carve the slogans into flat boards.

Favorite or key slogans differ somewhat from hospital to hospital. Among the ones most used at Kora Koseiin are *arugamama* (accepting phenomenological reality as it is), *jijitsu yuishin* (implying that one should behave as best he can within the reality he faces), *mokuteki hon'i* (meaning that one must focus on or cling to one's purpose), and *kensetsuteki taido* (literally, "a constructive attitude"). These slogans carry much more meaning than the mere content of the words that compose them. They represent attitudes and whole chains of related ideas in a convenient form that is easy to remember. This device is apparently related to Buddhist methods of instruction in which similar slogans in the form of Chinese ideographs (*kanji*) are memorized by the student while the master teaches the long chains of meaning of which the characters form the nexus.

In a similar way, but in lengthier form, Japanese proverbs are used by therapists to underline the tenets of Morita therapy. "When the outer appearance is in good order, the inner state will ripen," "Strike while the iron is hot," and "The noncontributing man presents his bowl for a third helping of rice only very hesitatingly" are examples of such proverbs. They may already be known to the patients, but they take on fresh meaning as they are clarified and repeated in the Moritist setting. Dr. Kora (1968, p. 315) gives his opinion of such instruction:

> The psychotherapy of neurosis needs to be done synthetically, not emphasizing verbal discussion, but with more emphasis on practical matters. But, since through verbal explanation the patients come to proper behavior, we should not consider our speaking lightly in the treatment of neurosis, either. Moreover, our talks should come directly from everyday experience, and, as far as possible, should contain understandable, concrete examples that appeal to the minds of the patients.

It is noteworthy that although all those patients listening might be expected to benefit from a given story, slogan, or illustration, the verbal communication is in fact most often directed toward specific patients, and the application to their condition is made explicit. This method may be contrasted with the shotgun technique in which the stories are told for the edification of any and all, as is generally true of Protestant sermons and Sunday school classes. Dr. Kora (1968, pp. 319-320) writes:

> When thus communicating with patients I am aware of their symptoms and can select examples that touch them deeply producing the desired effects. I offer this information and guidance to patients individually during consultation hours and also via their diaries; and again, when many are gathered in a room talking together I have another opportunity. For example, I might speak as follows:
>
> "In the writings of the famous blind musician, Miyagi Michio, we read that once when his neighbor was repairing his house the noise was very disturbing to the musician, but later when his own house was being repaired, he thought about how the repairs were progressing and found the sounds delightful. Identical stimuli became annoying or enjoyable depending on the way in which they were accepted."
>
> "One man couldn't stand the sound of rain on the roof, so he woke up his servants in the middle of the night ordering them to put mattresses on the roof to reduce the noise; but there are more poetically minded people who enjoy the sound of rain on the roof."
>
> Then I ask the patients, "Now, can you hear the clock ticking? In a moment they reply that they can hear it. "Until just now did you hear it?" "No, we didn't," they answer.
>
> "Well, here is Patient X. He is suffering from insomnia. In the middle of the night he became so conscious of the ticking of the clock that he stopped it. Because he struggles against it his attention is fixed upon it and he cannot escape from the sound. If he would accept the ticking as it is in a little while his attention would move on to something else and he wouldn't notice the sound. This is because human attention in its natural functioning doesn't fix itself on any particular item."

There is one further means by which the myth is worked over in Morita therapy — through the behavioral application of Moritist principles to daily life. Again and again Morita therapists emphasize that the intellectual understanding of Moritist thought is not sufficient for cure. They can support this statement by citing numerous patients who came to the hospital after having read the books and absorbed the theory, but who were unable to put the principles into practice at their homes. The Moritist hospital provides a setting for the development of habits that reflect the Moritist ideology in daily practice.

According to Peterson (1968, p. 41), " 'More people,' it is said, 'behave themselves into new ways of thinking than think themselves into new ways of behaving.' " Morita therapists make it clear to the patients that from their behavioral experience confidence in Morita therapy will develop naturally. From the beginning, however, patients make frequent slips in their diaries and speech indicating gaps in their understanding of Moritist principles and their daily application. The doctor promptly and repeatedly corrects these inconsistencies. For example, the patient may indicate that going to the store for bread has changed from a dreaded painful experience to one of real joy. The doctor then informs him that he is not well yet because going to the store should be a purposeful activity. Getting the bread should be uppermost in his mind, not enjoyment. The doctor continues that sometimes the patient will feel depressed. Would he get the bread under that condition? No, not if his acts are based on feelings. An analogous example in terms of cognitive restructuring is that of a language learner who has memorized the fundamental grammatical structure of a language but is still proceeding slowly and making mistakes in his application of the grammar to everyday speech.

Behavior application of principles also holds a special place among the methods of instruction of Morita therapy because behavior is a strategy by which one can indirectly control one's feelings and attitudes (Kora, 1968, p. 323):

> There is an old saying that when the outer appearance is in good order the inner state will ripen. We say that when we bow our heads and clasp our hands before Buddha, then our reverent feelings well forth. This means that whatever our original feelings, if we first adjust our outer state, our feelings will align themselves with it. I inject this discussion into the treatment of neurosis because it takes a long time to build a constructive attitude toward life if one waits for the inner condition to ripen. But we can work more easily from the outer appearance and produce quicker actual results.
>
> If we simply put on an athletic outfit and athletic shoes our "set" for sports comes out, but if we wear a bathrobe with our hands in our pockets it's not likely to appear. If you are frowning, your jaws and fists clenched, no matter how hard you try, it's difficult to feel relaxed. James Lange's theory has some truth in it.
>
> We may include behavior in the term "outer appearance."

Although it is difficult to change feelings with *ideas*, by *activity* we can change feelings secondarily. Even if I feel lazy, should I take my coat off and climb that tall garden tree and trim its branches, there is no doubt that this activity would elicit a more energetic mood.

It's disagreeable to get out of bed on a cold morning. If we try to force ourselves to wholeheartedly *want* to get up we would never do it — it is too pleasant just lying there. However, once we get up our attitude toward the bed changes. No one wants to return to bed once he is up. If we intend to study when our desire to study has fully matured it is difficult to ever get around to studying un-interesting subjects. But if we think, "I must study," and sit down at the desk and open a book and begin to read it anyway, in that behavior the rhythm of studying is called forth. I tell the patients that they should first regulate their outer appearance, leaving their feelings as they are, and actively pursue their course then their feelings will change.

Thus the "working through" takes many forms in Morita therapy. Written and verbal techniques are used, as are various mnemonic devices. And, of equal interest, the myth is worked out behaviorally in daily life.

On the surface, Leighton's subcategory concerning the symbolic nature of the ceremony simply does not seem to apply to Morita therapy as well as does the rest of his scheme. The "what went wrong" was a vicious cycle of self-consciousness, self-struggling, symptoms, further selfconsciousness, and so on. The patient presumably repairs this mistake not through symbolic ritual activity but through daily activity and new patterns of thought and habit. There are "great and mysterious forces" which he taps, namely, *arugamama* (in this sense, the strength that lies in accepting phenomenological reality "as it is"), but they lie only within the patient who needs not the mediation of the therapist, but rather the instruction in how to go about tapping these forces.

On the other hand (here I must thank Walter Goldschmidt for calling these possibilities to my attention), the entire hospitalization period from death and rebirth into a quasi-family setting through the reeducative process of therapy to discharge can be seen as symbolic ritual activity aimed at redoing socialization without the mistakes of self-centeredness, perfectionism, and so on. This interpretation places Morita therapy much more closely in line with Leighton's formulation.

A noteworthy feature of Morita therapy is similar to Leighton's "profound belief in the myth by both healer and patient." The Morita therapist's attitude toward Morita's ideology is one of complete acceptance and assurance, in contradistinction to the tentativeness with which Western scholars are trained to regard scientific theories. It is more akin to the attitude of some of the old-guard psychoanalysts. The Morita therapist's primary aim is not to provide himself and others with increasing evidence to support confidence in his hypotheses. He knows the effectiveness of Morita therapy, and his goal is to enlighten other people, such as patients, visiting scholars, and Western psychiatrists. Questions of scientific proof, of hypothesis testing with controls, double-blind evaluations, and so forth, are looked on as necessary to persuade a reluctant West to take Morita therapy's claims more seriously. The tests are not seen as challenges to the foundations of Morita therapy itself. I encountered this attitude particularly among older Moritist scholars, but it appeared to a somewhat lesser degree in all those with whom I spoke at length.

Specific questions about the proof of various points of theory were most likely to be met with further assertions that they are true, repeated explanations or descriptions, analogies, and examples. Further probing about the evidence for didactic assertions elicited either the response that basic differences in thinking between East and West result in an inability among Westerners to understand (see also Koestler, 1961, p. 268) or the response that the concepts or hypotheses in question are postulates. Or I got further illustrations, reexplanations, and the like with rather unfortunate effects on rapport. In general, during such discussions many Morita therapists seemed to have difficulty distinguishing explanation and description, reality and analogy, scientific proof and philosophical explanation.

It must be remembered that Morita physicians are not trained specifically for scientific research. They mix the conservative pragmatism common to all physicians who take their human responsibility seriously with doses of a desire to conduct Western-style statistical research, and they show some discomfort when Westerners refuse to swallow Eastern assumptions *p.r.n.*

The attitude of assurance is not confined to doctor-patient or doctor-researcher situations alone. Moralistic, normative Moritist reports in scholarly journals, Moritist popular books, and Moritist radio speeches are filled with *should*'s, *ought*'s, and *must*'s which imply a firm moral certainty. Moritists have continuously faced their sociomoral responsibilities, the same responsibilities that Western psychotherapists are only beginning to acknowledge and to deal with consciously (London, 1964), with the confidence that only a sincere faith in some value-defining, self-maintaining life philosophy can instill.

Group Factors

"In many ceremonials, typified by the Navaho, there is strong enhancement by the expectation of group members. Thus, family members and sometimes whole communities are involved, sharing in the sense of benefit, contributing material, work, and prayers to the outcome. Group forces are thus linked on the side of the patient's treatment, and the people with whom he has most of his interactions become committed to accepting a state of change. Hence if the patient's personality does get set in a new pattern, the group in which he is enmeshed are [sic] prepared for it emotionally as well as cognitively" (Leighton, 1968, p. 1178).

Leighton's model here seems particularly applicable to smaller preliterate societies with relatively stronger homogeneity and more face-to-face contact among all members. In dealing with outpatients, the Morita therapist may utilize the patient's family, co-workers, friends, and others as resources in helping the patient to live according to Moritist principles. In more complex societies, however, this procedure may be cumbersome and time-consuming. An alternative is to hospitalize the patient in a setting which provides fairly consistent group support for living according to Moritist ideology, or in other words, to immerse him in a smaller, more homogeneous subsociety or subculture set off from the larger society.

As in many forms of directed behavior change, the patient in Morita therapy severs his ties with family and friends during the first few weeks of treatment. Since communication outside the hospital is restricted, the patient is increasingly attracted to the patient group for understanding and support.

In the larger society some of the most effective social sanctions — What will people think of me? How will people act toward me? — are somewhat mitigated by the "sick role" and the prepatient status. The patient soon discovers, however, that he is in a small hospital society whose members also evaluate his performance (albeit by standards different from, and sometimes stricter than, those of the larger society). His stated motivations for avoiding crowds, work, trains, and so forth are understandable in this setting, but they are no longer acceptable reasons for failure to behave normally (Mills, 1940).

As a patient accepts the Moritist world view and applies it to his daily life he does seem to improve. Improvement was noted by fellow patients, the therapists, and myself. Of course, the patient's inner state is not directly observable, and, from the Moritist standpoint, it is largely irrelevant anyway. His status rises as he becomes a model for patients who have not yet progressed as far as he has. But his esteem is dependent upon his commitment to the principles and perspectives of Morita therapy. According to the principles of cognitive dissonance, as he increasingly represents Morita therapy and tells of his successful experience with it, his belief structure increasingly conforms to his representation. He is caught up in a spiral of growing commitment, status, and belief. And at the apex of the spiral is the Morita therapist. No one believes in Morita therapy with the same fervor as the therapist. In a sense, his very social existence depends on it. In other words, it becomes increasingly costly to view the world any other way than the Moritist way when one is within the Moritist hospital and is rewarded for espousing its viewpoint. The rewards and the costs are most extreme for the therapists themselves. Thus it is argued that the Morita therapist, in addition to drawing family members and others into the treatment process, removes his patient to a social setting in which he is symbolically reborn into a community that espouses Moritist ideology.

Posttreatment Period

"The culture generally prescribes post-treatment sentiments for patient, healer, and persons in the community. This cultural set constitutes strong motivation to play the role of the successfully treated patient" (Leighton, 1968, p. 1178).

Directed behavior-change gains may be sustained by reinforcement from the society in general, from other ex-patients, and from the change agent. Leighton points out that in a small society it is possible for the whole community to participate in the ceremonials of cure. Such participation prepares the community for the patient's return. Subsequent periodic ceremonies may sustain the group sentiments and expectations.

Alternatively, ex-patients may form small groups for mutual support. Joining a cult seems to help prevent psychiatric relapse among the Yoruba (Prince, 1964). Similarly, Wesley's follow-up methods for religious revival included organizing groups of not more than twelve persons to meet periodically and share their experiences (Sargant, 1957). In more complex societies, just as patients can be segregated into smaller subsocieties (such as hospitals) to provide a more homogeneous milieu for indoctrination, so they can form ex-patient subgroups after their hospitalization ends in order to preserve social support even while living in the larger society. In other words, they take elements from the therapeutic community with them when they return to society.

In the Moritist system, the ex-patient's social support for maintaining his new cognitive orientation is provided primarily by other ex-patients and by therapists. Moritist hospitals maintain effective posthospital communication through magazines, meetings, outpatient contact, and informal visits by ex-patients. The decision to maintain ties with the hospital is, however, solely the ex-patient's. He is free to sever contact simply by failing to sustain it; generally, no positive act of notification is necessary. Of course, some ex-patients elect to stay on at the hospital as staff members and some elect to go on to medical school in order to become therapists, but these are few in comparison with the total number of patients treated.

Summary

Leighton's model of psychotherapy is broad enough to provide some applicability to the relatively "advanced" Morita therapy functioning in a literate culture. Looked at from Leighton's perspective, Morita therapy shows a number of features in common with other forms of psychotherapy practiced around the world. It shares certain subject characteristics, change agent characteristics, periods of preparation, indoctrination, and postindoctrination, and characteristic relationships between therapist and patient and between the patient and other members of his society, and, like other forms of psychiatric treatment, it contains a myth that organizes and instructs and offers hope.

VI   SOME BROADER ISSUES

In this chapter I want to go beyond the description of an Oriental psychotherapy and the revisions it is undergoing. I have tried to present to Western psychotherapists a viable non-Western form of treatment which, I feel, merits more than a cursory glance.

To say that Morita therapy is "culture-bound" and that it is obviously inapplicable to Westerners allows the clinician to readily dismiss the implications of Moritist thought for his own practice. He can avoid the pointed questions and issues that Professor Morita raised some fifty years ago. I do not mean to imply that Morita therapy offers final, or even better, solutions to these questions and issues. Rather, I wish to make a small contribution toward creation of a metaprocess for the rational development of psychotherapies, including theories and techniques designed to be applicable to certain kinds of patients in certain kinds of environments. I want psychotherapists to be aware of their psychotherapy-related assumptions about man, society, neurosis, and cure, and, through their awareness, to have the choice of retaining or rejecting those assumptions.

For this purpose, it matters not at all whether Moritist claims of a 90 percent rate of improvement or cure are objectively verifiable. The contrasts, both apparent and real, between "their" thinking and "our" thinking point to uncharted rivers, bypassed backwaters, and deep pools of profitable contemplation. The question becomes, "What have we to learn from the juxtaposition of Moritist ways of looking at the world of personal suffering?"

THE ISSUE OF CURE: SYMPTOM CONTROL OR
SELF-CONTROL

"The ability to suffer is a measure of an individual's faith in God, and the *curandero* sees his major task as helping his patient accept this suffering as his share of the burden of the world's sin and ignorance and as his part in God's world. Thus it is that the validity of a *curandero*'s claims rest in large part on the extent of his basic devoutness and piety. The more religious he is and the more he can help others to accept their suffering and accept the will of God, the better healer he is thought to be. The prevention of human suffering is not an end in itself" (Kiev, 1968, p. 34). And, in the words of Albert Camus, "The important thing . . . is not to be cured but to live with one's ailments." When the sympathetic reader smiles and agrees that teaching a patient to live with his symptoms is fine but that it is better still to help him get rid of them, two different responses might come from a Morita therapist. First, there is some doubt regarding any therapist's ability to successfully erase the range of symptoms presented in therapy. How effective are we at getting rid of symptoms? Second, and more basic, is the idea that we might profitably consider what symptoms are, whether they are at all separable or removable, and whether the effort of trying to eliminate them might be better spent in building a constructive acceptance of self.

When a Westerner begins feeling depressed or anxious he first labels his mood and then he begins to search his memories of recent events for a cause, a reason why he feels the way he does. If he is well educated he has, potentially, a wide variety of past events that could serve as an explanation for his mood. For example, he may have learned that the cause of the anxiety may lie in the distant past, perhaps in his infancy or in his early childhood. He may have learned that a part of his mind is adept at camouflaging and distorting and even suppressing memories altogether, so that what seems unlikely to be a cause of the anxiety may be the cause after all.

There is some satisfaction in having located the reason for the mood. There is the vague impression that by doing so one has gained some control over the mood through the capacities of reason and recollection. One may believe that if one can avoid the situation that caused the mood, at least to some degree, the mood itself can be avoided in the future.

In every psychotherapeutic system the patient can find a sense of understanding and control over his upsetting experience, as Frank (1961) has emphasized. The psychoanalyzed person finds "bearableness" in a symptom (e.g., anxiety) because he knows its origins, he knows a method by which he can learn more about specific origins of specific symptoms, and with this knowledge he believes he can ultimately free himself from the occurrence of that symptom. In other words, he has confidence that he can understand and control his symptoms through psychoanalysis. And the attitudes and skills for understanding and controlling his symptoms can be developed and refined. This is a rationalistic approach to symptom control.

The Moritist patient finds bearableness in suffering because he knows the suffering will decline with time. Meanwhile, he can accomplish his aims anyway. His skills and attitudes can be developed and refined, too, but understanding is subordinate to acceptance, and symptom control is subordinate to self-control.

As noted above, the Japanese patient most often comes to the Moritist hospital seeking symptom removal, but, in the end, self-control and acceptance may preempt first place as the patient comes to realize that everyone has troublesome characteristics, unhappy experiences, and pain of some sort or another. He discovers that the quality of accepting and persevering can protect one to some degree in these inevitable situations, even though alleviation of specific symptoms cannot.

In this sense, Moritists offer a very effective coping mechanism. Certainly we cannot control all that happens to us. A traumatic event can occur unexpectedly and set any psychiatric patient back months or even years. But if the patient can be trained to keep in mind his purposes and to see his attitude toward (i.e., his acceptance of) the event and not the event itself as crucial to his well-being, any personal disaster can become simply another example in a long string of experiences displaying how effective his acceptance of reality is and how wise was the guidance of his Morita therapist. This is an acceptance approach to self-control.

I must reemphasize here that in the West acceptance has the implication of passivity and positive valuation of the status quo. That is not true in Japan. As Morita put it, "If it's raining and you have an umbrella — use it!" Changes can and should be made, but only in the realm of the realistically controllable, that is, in the realm of behavior.

Another strategy for handling suffering, which is increasingly popular in the West, requires recognition and exploration of the upsetting feeling. It focuses not on past causes but on present effects. The aim is to develop a highly differentiated coding apparatus for describing one's current phenomenal state. It is necessary to probe sensitively, to be in tune with oneself, to compare the "now" experience with other experiences one has had. Although this strategy, which I call "the artistic approach" to symptom control and self-control, is costly in terms of time and seems self-centered in a way that would be unacceptable to Morita therapists, it has much in common with Morita therapy.

Gestalt therapy aims at helping the client to live in the present, to increase his self-acceptance, and to accept responsibility for his behavior. It does not have a vision of what behavior is more desirable for any particular person at any particular time. The only moral accepted by the Gestalt therapist is that the patient should be aware (Perls et al., 1965, p. 15). "The relevant past is present here and now, if not in words, then in some bodily tension and attention that can hopefully be brought into awareness" (Enright, 1970, p. 20). Thus, in practice, the therapist watches for splits of attention and awareness and for evidence that attention is developing outside awareness.

One important technique is to encourage the client to "stay with" his feelings rather than to avoid or escape from them. Perls, the founder of Gestalt therapy, emphasized the role of phobic avoidance in all neurotic behavior. The therapist encourages the patient to assimilate the emotional dimensions of life which have been unpleasant. In this way the patient gains in self-confidence and develops a far greater capacity for autonomy. He is better able to deal with the inevitable frustrations of everyday living. Perls and other Gestalt therapists suggest that the only way to validate the workability of their technique is for the individual to experience it himself. Proceeding now to further examination of the issue of experiential knowledge, we shall shortly return for a final look at the topic of "attention."

EXPERIENTIAL KNOWLEDGE

My research required that I attain some understanding of Moritist theory and practice; I would not be satisfied with description and acceptance.

Why should isolated bed rest almost inevitably produce a peak emotional experience by the fourth or fifth day? How is it that physical activity in the midst of neurotic suffering eventually seems to bring relief? What is the source of the strength and confidence born as one gives up his inner struggle and adopts the ethic of self-sacrificing labor? Questions such as these are asked by patients, too. Ultimately, the therapist's response is most often some variant of the following: "It is human nature. It is the way we are. It's not necessary for you to understand how the treatment works. Apply yourself wholeheartedly to your regimen and you will be cured."

The importance of experiential knowledge has been emphasized by Reynolds and Yamamoto (1973, pp. 224-225):

> As we have seen, Moritists have developed theories about the etiology of neurosis. And they do, on occasion, offer the patients interpretations about neurosis and the rationale behind their therapeutic procedures. But, like Zen masters, they have a deeply ingrained disrespect for rational understanding as anything but a temporary sedative for a feverish intellect. We interpret this disaffection with rational understanding to be based on the Moritist's practice of operating on the level of *experiential* understanding. We think that the Moritists sense the lacunae between *the experience of* neurosis and *talking about it* as well as the critical difference between *explaining a treatment* and *undergoing* it. Experience is emphasized in Morita therapy as it is in psychoanalysis. And both systems recognize the importance of having undergone the treatment experience prior to practicing it as therapist.
>
> Recently, in our culture, too, we have been called upon to come to grips with the special qualities of experiential knowledge. How can one "really understand" what it is like to be Black, to be a drug addict, or to be on an LSD trip unless he has experienced it? We are beginning to realize the inadequacy of words in translating these intensely personal and private experiences into public and communicable discourse.
>
> It may be that the Moritists, recognizing the lack of meaningful communication in this sphere, have elected to follow (or have adopted by default) the use of experiential guidance, arranging within a narrow range of settings the environment that will produce in a patient a relatively predictable (though personal) sort of experience. We note a parallel here to Franz Alexander's concept of the "corrective emotional experience." This role of an experiential guide, as opposed to that of an interpretive analyst, emphasizes the essential uniqueness of experiential knowledge on the one hand and the common human reactions to specific situational pressures on the other.

SOME BROADER ISSUES • 225

Absolute bedrest is a classic example of a teaching technique that provides the preferred sort of experiential/behavioral insight (as opposed to intellectual/motivational insight). In a sense, absolute bedrest sets an experiential limit, a bench mark the patient can use to evaluate his tendencies toward isolating himself socially and behaving nonproductively. He "knows," with a fundamental gut-level knowledge, that extreme isolation and inactivity are unnatural for him — such a life would be unsatisfying.

By my conception of "satisfying knowledge" I mean an understanding that is acceptable to an individual. It fits into or expands his overall view of the world, and, most important, its acquisition prompts him to stop seeking more information about a piece of knowledge. By this last definitional component I wish to imply neither that the individual is no longer curious about associated topics, nor that he ceases to seek information in closely related areas. But "satisfying knowledge" provides a sense of closure, of "givenness," from which one sallies forth on other data-gathering expeditions. An element of knowledge may lose its "satisfying" quality when its "givenness" is called into question by the "givenness" of another piece of knowledge. In other words, "satisfying" knowledge retains its satisfying quality only until challenged by other knowledge.

Here let me emphasize that I am not talking at all about the criteria for acceptance of knowledge. I am not saying that knowledge acquired through scientific investigation, for example, is or ought to be more satisfying than knowledge acquired, say, through a vision. The satisfactoriness of a piece of knowledge is completely relative to the individual. It is a subjective determination. Unsatisfactory knowledge is often signaled by such phrases as "I don't get it," "Perhaps so, but . . .," "What do you mean?"

The issue is not the public verifiability of phenomena and the methodology by which scientific understanding is made possible. The issue is what is psychologically or aesthetically satisfying as an end point to one's questioning. It is the problem of how one decides he need not probe further into a query at a particular time. At the one theoretical extreme is the person who accepts his reality as it is with little need to ask questions about it. At the other extreme is the person who remains constantly dissatisfied with his understanding of everything. All of us have developed canons of acceptable explanation. Such canons may include the spoken word of an authority, the authority of the printed word in a newspaper, a journal, or a book, the word of a trustworthy layman or informant, our own observation or insight, the meaning locked in a parable or illustration or example, the evidence provided by a scientific experiment, or a divine revelation. None of these is an inherently acceptable source of explanation. One must agree within himself or with others (explicitly or implicitly) to accept them. Furthermore, the type of explanation that appears reasonable and satisfying may vary from situation to situation and from problem to problem.

Let us reflect for a moment about the sources of satisfying knowledge. Across cultures and throughout human history personal experience has been a prime source of satisfying knowledge. Personal experience includes knowledge gained through everyday perceptions, hallucinations, visions, and other normal and paranormal states of consciousness.

With the ability to communicate in complex verbal patterns came the extended possibilities of attaining satisfying knowledge from the experiences of other individuals. (Although I do not rule out the possibility of acquiring satisfactory knowledge from others on a nonverbal, behavioral level, it is a complex issue I choose to avoid for now.) When other persons provide information with potential for becoming satisfying knowledge we must add a dimension of evaluation of source which was not necessary before. But, at first (both phylogenetically and historically), the transmitter of knowledge was a grown person and the satisfactoriness of his knowledge could be evaluated on the basis both of who he was and of how the knowledge fitted into the subject's view of the world. In fact, earlier on, the transmitting person and the receiving person shared similar world views, and so the way a new piece of knowledge could "fit in" was comparatively easily passed along.

Magicians, illusionists, perceptual psychologists repeatedly remind us that our sensory input systems can fool us and thus distort our experiential basis for satisfying knowledge. Psychologists of many persuasions, sociologists, brainwashing experts, hypnotists, and the like argue that our cognitive organizations are distorted, culture-bound, and even "wrong." But again, I am not concerned here with objective or intersubjective reality, but rather with the subject's own experiencing of what he thinks he knows. So if Mr. X is fooled into believing that the magician actually sawed his assistant in half, I am not concerned with whether the magician did in fact saw her in half, but whether Mr. X is satisfied that he did.

We live now in an era in which printed communication permits transfer of information from all sorts of unknown sources. Science or, more accurately, scientists offer and accept a large amount of information without explicit awareness of the audience for the information or its source. To be sure, scientific principles require replicability and public verifiability, but, in practice, many research findings are taken to provide satisfying knowledge by other scientists without personally replicating the study. Within the community of scientific scholarship the veracity and completeness of reports are, on the whole, taken for granted. Outside the scientific community, however, the satisfactoriness of many research findings as knowledge may be in question because of the layman's inability to grasp the conclusions and/or the methods, his inability to fit the findings into his existing world view, various ad hominem critiques, and so forth.

Again, I am not arguing for a relativity of explanation rather like the concept of cultural relativity. I believe that for many problems scientific knowledge and the methods by which we arrive at such knowledge make sense to many humans despite their culture, just as the values of good health and long life and the opportunities for eating, resting, exploring, and so forth make sense to most people in most situations whatever their culture. What I am suggesting, however, is that in some areas of human existence the scientific accumulation of knowledge is impossible within the currently understood boundaries of scientific methodology. In such areas I believe that the explanations offered by personal experience, religion, or pseudoscience are themselves worthy of scientific study and that they provide their adherents with the same sort of relief from explanation seeking which is available at the conclusion of a well-conducted experiment. We scientists need to remember that.

In a sense we have been drawn into the area of the satisfactoriness or acceptability of an explanation throughout this book. The cultural, social, and economic variables I have offered seem to me to account for a great deal of the variation in Morita therapy over the years. Some of these variables also seem satisfactory to Moritists. The changes in Morita therapy that have occurred are clear and undeniable on the level of the specificity with which they were presented. The causes of the changes are less clear and more open to question.

We have also encountered the parallel problem of "making sense of" Moritist cure and the cause for it. In the latter instance even the issue of objectively determined cure or lack of it is in question. Moreover, the type of explanation for the therapeutic results achieved through Morita therapy varies considerably in acceptability from professional to professional. Finally, in an extreme case, the subjective changes that occur in a patient and the reasonable and satisfying understanding of the roots of these changes vary even more widely from patient to patient.

Among the first difficulties I encountered in studying Morita therapy was that the sort of explanation I was seeking (the sort that satisfied me) frequently was not forthcoming from those I interviewed. From the therapists I sought a systematic theory of how and why Morita therapy worked. And I wanted objective evidence that it did work (fully realizing the difficulty of getting any kind of objective evidence on the efficacy of psychotherapy); I had in mind some type of double-blind controlled study as an ideal. What I got were illustrations, case histories, and an apparently ill-sorted array of assumptions and untestable hypotheses strung together to provide an explanation for the development and cure of neurosis. When pressed, some therapists could show me statistical tabulations of their clinical impressions, pre- and posttreatment psychological test results of selected single patients, and analysis of questionnaires and diaries in studies conducted by and for Morita therapists. When I revealed that I considered such evidence interesting but unsatisfactory they seemed either hurt or angry or puzzled by my obtuseness. Then they presented me with further case histories of successes. Clearly, they were satisfied with the evidence and with the explanation. And they could dismiss my difficulties with the issues as my own problem (except that I "represented" American academia, and if they wanted to discover how to convince American psychiatry of the effectiveness and reasonableness of Morita therapy they would do well to begin with this already somewhat "Japanized" anthropologist). Some, to be sure, took the convenient course: "You Westerners can never understand the Japanese [Oriental] mind." A very few accepted the challenge to make Morita therapy acceptable in an objectively verifiable sense to Western minds and began quasi-experimental manipulations of the various elements of treatment to determine which are necessary, which modifiable, and so forth.

My difficulties with patients were exaggerated versions of the troubles I had with their therapeutic guides. Morita therapy worked, many would tell me. That was enough for them.

Recognition of the value of experiential knowledge has led me to incorporate experiential tactics in the study of suicide (Reynolds and Farberow, 1973a, b), aftercare facilities (Reynolds and Farberow, 1974), and psychotherapy (Reynolds, 1974b). Experiential research requires the investigator to adopt an alternate identity, to immerse himself in a social system by occupying an already existing social role, and to make oscillating observations of his inner functioning and his outer environment. Refinements of this technique allow for checks on the reliability and validity of these phenomenological reports (Reynolds, 1974a).

THE ISSUE OF ATTENTION

When I first came to Japan to study Morita therapy I naively expected that it was understandable as an Oriental version of behavior therapy. I expected to find operant conditioning and desensitization applied without awareness by Morita therapists.

My first major problem came when I learned that some patients (including the famous Moritist, T. Suzuki, himself) had been cured by absolute isolated bed rest alone. The cure was the result of desensitization, perhaps, but certainly the cognitive — the imagining, remembering, awareness — aspect of human existence entered strongly into cure by absolute bed rest. Certainly, no simple operant conditioning was acting to result in cure. And if bed rest were some form of desensitization combining relaxation and rest with imaginings and recollections, then to call this procedure behavior therapy seemed somewhat strange; the cure was through cognition, self-generated and self-adapting.

As my understanding of Morita therapy progressed I began to have doubts that there was some single therapy that could appropriately be labeled Morita therapy. Some therapists emphasized work while others permitted play; some insisted on a family or familylike environment; others argued that Morita therapy could be practiced even on an outpatient basis or through letters; some stressed the links of Morita therapy to Zen Buddhism, whereas others minimized them;

there were disagreements on what types of patients could be effectively treated, and so forth. There seemed to be as many Morita therapies as there were Morita therapists, a condition not unlike that found in psychoanalysis and behavior therapy when one looks carefully at the actual practice of the therapists.

Since there was disagreement among Morita therapists themselves on what was essential to Morita therapy, and since many claimed to be practicing *junsui* ("pure") Morita therapy, it became something of a challenge to me to see if I could find the thread or threads that ran through Morita therapies, some "essence," if you will, which characterized Morita therapy. The essential theme that I hit upon seemed to tie together absolute bed rest, work therapy, Morita's theory of neurosis and cure, and virtually every other aspect of Morita therapy in theory and practice. It led me to consider Morita therapy to be something beyond a behavior therapy. And, more important, it led me to the recognition of a gap in Western psychology's understanding of human mental functioning.

The theme was "directed attention." For Morita, neurosis was misdirected attention, and cure was redirecting attention. The whole of Morita therapy may be viewed as efforts to guide patients by setting up situations in which they learn to refocus their attention on more productive and constructive topics.

Laying aside the issue of the mechanism of absolute bed rest for the moment, I should like to consider the usefulness of looking at Morita therapy as a behavior therapy. Suppose, for the moment, researchers can find behaviors that appear to conform to behavior therapy models — ignoring (extinguishing) complaints, physical labor producing weariness thus reducing anxiety, stepwise assignment of tasks, increasingly difficult modeling, reinforcements in diaries, verbal positive reinforcement of acceptable behavior, and so forth. I have no doubt that we can find such behavioral contingencies in the large number of interactions that occur in Morita therapy settings each day. But what if we do? There is a tendency to conclude that these contingencies then explain the cures obtained through Morita therapy. I think not. In the first place, there are a large number of inconsistent models and reinforcements in the hospitals. In the second place, I am skeptical of "satisfying" explanations. Too often we look at a problem just long enough to feel that it can be explained by our system of understanding, and then we turn away and go on to some other problem.

Suppose, for the sake of argument, that Professor Morita was right. Suppose that an effective treatment mode for neurosis must provide a philosophy and a strategy for redirecting a patient's attention away from himself. Suddenly, then, psychoanalysis and behavior therapy are seen in a new light. Both offer purposeful redirection of the patient's attention. In behavior therapy the patient learns a set of tactics for relaxing or controlling the behavior of others or for charting his own behavior. He is drawn out into the objective world of behavior. His inner focus of attention is broken into again and again as he interacts with the therapist, follows the behavior regimen, and so on. One can imagine Professor Morita considering behavior modification as a crude form of attention training.

Now, let us consider for a moment what Western psychology and psychiatry have to tell us about attention in this sense. The fact is that they can tell us very little about attention. We have some data on eye movements reflecting attention (when viewing a painting, for example); we have some data on attention span, some on distractions and distractibility, and the like. But we have virtually nothing on "the spotlight of consciousness," as I call it, meaning what we attend to every moment of our lives. The primary reason, of course, is that for some fifty years Western psychological science has frowned on the research tactic of naturalistic, introspective observation. But current interest in the drug experience, meditation, and biofeedback literally demands accounts of the focus and play of attention. We need a psychology of attention.

Why is it that I am thinking now about the next words to write and not about what I will eat for lunch? What causes the tiredness in my legs to fade in and out of awareness? Why does the phobic patient disregard his phobia at times? Why did you notice that your nose lies within your visual field when I mentioned that fact? Why does a child allow himself to be "distracted" at some times and not at others? Are these simply questions of motivation? What do we really know about attention? Very little; and I submit that the paucity of knowledge is in large part the reason that some dismiss Morita therapy and others try conceptually to squeeze it into the mold of some other therapeutic system.

As I have said, Western psychological science has long held introspection (and, to a lesser extent, naturalistic observation) in disrepute. Morita therapists have not. They have called on their own experience and listened to their patients' verbal accounts of neurotic existence. Some Morita therapists can predict with great accuracy what will happen to their patients' attention while the patients are undergoing absolute bed rest, are engaging in hard work, are sitting in *zazen,* are conversing, and so forth. Interestingly, they can predict but they cannot explain; they recognize and codify a repeated sequence of internal and external events, but they have only a sketchy, piecemeal theory to explain the connection between situation and attention. In other words, their explanations do not provide "satisfactory knowledge" to the Western positivistic scientist.

In sum, I am arguing that Western psychology provides no clear understanding of why ideas fade in and out of consciousness, why we are aware of inner states at some times and not at others, why we notice what we notice, how attention operates. Gestalt psychology, Ornstein's (1972) psychology of consciousness, and various theories of motivation offer the beginnings of understanding, but no more than that. Morita's theory, though it fails to answer these questions, does recognize their importance (in human existence in general and in neurosis in particular). Even without understanding the phenomena, Morita therapy in practice provides techniques for redirecting patients' attention away from the circuitous, looping attention paths that are dysfunctional and evocative of distress.

BEYOND BEHAVIOR CHANGE

In the end, Morita psychotherapy is more than a technique for changing behavior through redirecting attention. It is a life philosophy, a world view, and an ideology that makes change in behavior meaningful.

BIBLIOGRAPHY

Abe, T. Supplementary study of nervosity, with special reference to personality tests. *Shinkeishitsu*, 1960, *1*(2), 27-46.

Akuto, Hiroshi, et al. *Hendoki no Nihonshakai*. Tokyo: Nippon Hoso, 1972.

Alexander, F. *Psychoanalysis and Psychotherapy*. New York: Norton, 1956.

Asahi Evening News. Japan has lowest unemployment rate. July 23, 1968.

Bandura, A., and Walters, R. H. *Social Learning and Personality Development*. New York: Holt, Rinehart and Winston, 1963.

Barker, R. G., ed. *The Stream of Behavior*. New York: Appleton-Century-Crofts, 1963.

Beardsley, R. K., Hall, J. W., and Ward, R. E. *Village Japan*. Chicago: University of Chicago Press, 1959.

Beech, H. R. *Changing Man's Behavior*. Middlesex: Penguin, 1969.

Benedict, R. Anthropology and the abnormal. *Journal of Genetic Psychology*, 1934, *10*(2), 59-82.

———. *The Chrysanthemum and the Sword*. New York: Houghton Mifflin, 1946.

Berger, Peter L., and Luckmann, Thomas. *The Social Construction of Reality*. New York: Doubleday, 1966.

Blake, R. R., and Mouton, J. S. The experimental investigation of interpersonal influence. *In* A. D. Biderman and H. Zimmer, eds. *The Manipulation of Human Behavior*. New York: Wiley, 1966.

Breuer, Josef, and Freud, Sigmund. *Studies on Hysteria*. New York: Basic Books, 1957.

Burton, A. The use of written productions in psychotherapy. *In* Leonard Pearson, ed. *The Use of Written Communication in Psychotherapy*. Springfield, Ill.: Charles C. Thomas, 1965.

Buss, A. H. *Psychopathology*. New York: Wiley, 1966.

Caudill, W. *The Psychiatric Hospital as a Small Society*. Cambridge, Mass.: Harvard University Press, 1958.

———. The cultural context of Japanese psychiatry. *In* Marvin K. Opler, ed. *Culture and Mental Health*. New York: Macmillan, 1959.

————. Around the clock patient care in Japanese psychiatric hospitals: The role of *tsukisoi. American Sociological Review,* 1961, *26*(2), 204-214.

————. The psychological study of Japan. Paper prepared for conference on "The Study of Japan in the Behavioral Sciences." Rice University, April 11-12, 1969.

————. The influence of social structure and culture on human behavior in Japan. *Journal of Nervous and Mental Disease,* 1973, *157*(4), 240-257.

Caudill, W., and DeVos, G. Achievement, culture and personality: The case of the Japanese American. *In* Yehudi A. Cohen, ed. *Social Structure and Personality: A Casebook.* New York: Holt, Rinehart and Winston, 1961.

Caudill, W., and Doi, T. L. Interrelations in psychiatry, culture and emotion in Japan. *In* Iago Galdston, ed. *Man's Image in Medicine and Anthropology.* New York: International Universities Press, 1963.

Caudill, W., and Schooler, C. Symptom patterns and background characteristics of Japanes psychiatric patients. *In* W. Caudill and Tsung-yi Lin, eds. *Mental Health Research in Asia and the Pacific.* Honolulu: East-West Center Press, 1969.

Caudill, W., and Weinstein, H. Maternal care and infant behavior in Japan and America. *Psychiatry,* 1969, *32*(1), 12-43.

Clark, D. H. *Administrative Therapy.* London: Tavistock, 1964.

Cooley, C. H. *Human Nature and the Social Order.* New York: Scribners, 1902. Republished by Free Press, 1956.

Cotton, H. A., and Ebaugh, F. G. Japanese neuropsychiatry. *American Journal of Psychiatry,* 1946-47, *103,* 342-348.

Czerny, J. Zu den psychopathologischen und philosophischen Fragen der japanischen Neurosen-Psychotherapie nach der Morita-Konzeption, (System Zen). *Akt. Fragen Psychiat. Neurol.* Basel and New York: Karger, 1967, *6,* 66-81.

Davis, Jeffrey. Morita therapy. Undated, mimeographed.

DeVos, G. A. Role narcissism and the etiology of Japanese suicide. Paper read at International Conference of Social Psychiatry, London, 1963.

————. Discussion. *International Journal of Psychiatry,* 1965, *1*(4), 643-645.

Dogs, W. Morita ryōhō Zen saimin (Morita therapy Zen hypnosis). *Ima ni Ikiru,* 1968, no. 28, 2-5.

Doi, L. T. Morita therapy and psychoanalysis. *Psychologia,* 1962, *5,* 117-123.

————. *Omote* and *Ura. Journal of Nervous and Mental Disease,* 1973, *157*(4), 258-261.

Elzinga, R. H. A unique form of psychotherapy: Morita therapy. M.S. thesis, Amsterdam, 1972*a.*

————. Some aspects of phobias in Japan. M.S. thesis, Amsterdam, 1972*b.*

Enright, J. An introduction to Gestalt technique. *In* Fagan, J., and Shepherd, I. L., eds. *Gestalt Therapy Now.* New York: Harper and Row, 1970.

Erikson, E. H. Growth and crisis of the "healthy personality." *In* Clyde Kluckhohn et al., eds. *Personality in Nature, Society, and Culture.* New York: Knopf, 1961.

————. Identity Youth and Crisis. New York: Norton, 1968.

Eysenck, H. J. The effects of psychotherapy: An evaluation. *Journal of Consulting Psychology*, 1952, *6*, 319-324.

Eysenck, H. J., ed. *Behavior Therapy and the Neuroses.* New York: Macmillan, 1960.

Farber, G. The student as nigger. *UCLA Daily Bruin*, April 4, 1967.

Festinger, L. *Conflict, Decision, and Dissonance.* Stanford: Stanford University Press, 1964.

Frank, J. D. *Persuasion and Healing.* Baltimore: Johns Hopkins University Press, 1961.

Frankl, Victor E. *The Doctor and the Soul.* 2d ed. New York: Bantam, 1967.

Fujita, C. A. A guide for understanding Morita therapy. Unpublished manuscript, 1968.

Goffman, E. *Asylums.* New York: Doubleday, 1961.

Goldberger, Leo. Experimental isolation: An overview. *American Journal of Psychiatry*, 1966, *122*(7), 774-781.

Grossberg, John M. Behavior therapy: A review. *Psychology Bulletin*, 1964, *62*(2), 73-88.

Harrower, Molly. Therapeutic communications by letter-notebooks and record transcriptions. *In* Leonard Pearson, ed. *Use of Written Communications in Psychotherapy.* Springfield, Ill. Charles C. Thomas, 1965.

Hasegawa, Yozo. Personal communication, April 22, 1974*a*.

_____. *Moritashiki Seishin Kenkoho* (*Moritist Mental Health Method*). Tokyo: Business, 1974*b*.

Henry, Jules. *Culture against Man.* New York: Vintage, 1963.

Hinkle, Lawrence E., Jr. The physiological state of the interrogation subject as it affects brain function. *In* Albert D. Biderman and Herbert Zimmer, eds. *The Manipulation of Human Behavior.* New York: Wiley, 1961.

Hinkle, Lawrence E., Jr., and Wolff, H. G. Communist interrogation and indoctrination of "enemies of the state." *AMA Archives of Neurology and Psychiatry*, 1956, *76*, 115-174.

Horvat, Andrew, trans. *Shukan Asahi* polls. *Japan Interpreter*, 1971, *7*(2), 150-158.

Hoskovec, J. Psychoterapeuticke aspekty systemu Zen. *Cs. Psychiat.*, 1963, *69*, 406.

Huber, Jack. *Through an Eastern Window.* Bantam Books ed. New York: Houghton Mifflin, 1965.

Hulse, Frederick S. Convention and reality in Japanese culture. *Southwestern Journal of Anthropology*, 1948, *4*(4), 345-355.

Iga, Mamoru. Cultural factors in suicide of Japanese youth with focus on personality. *Sociology and Social Research*, 1961, *46*(1).

_____. Change in value orientations of Japanese Americans. Mimeographed, 1967.

_____. Japanese adolescent suicide and social structure. *In* E. S. Shneidman, ed. *Essays in Self Destruction.* New York: Science House, 1968.

Ikeda, Kazuyoshi. Morita's theory of Neurosis and its application in Japanese psychotherapy. Undated, mimeographed.

Inglis, James. *The Scientific Study of Abnormal Behavior.* Chicago: Aldine, 1966.

Ishii, Takezo. The increasing value of Morita therapy. Mimeographed, 1972.

————. Morita ryōhō: shudan gakushu no keiken (Morita therapy: The experience of group learning). Unpublished manuscript, 1974.

Iwai, Hiroshi, and Reynolds, David K. Morita therapy: The views from the West. *American Journal of Psychiatry,* 1970, *126,* 1031-1036.

Jacobsen, Avrohm, and Berenberg, Albert N. Japanese psychiatry and psychotherapy. *American Journal of Psychiatry,* 1952, *109,* 321-329.

James, William. *The Varieties of Religious Experience.* New York: Collier Books, 1961.

Johnson, Colleen L., and Johnson, Frank A. Interaction rules and ethnicity: The Japanese and Caucasians in Honolulu. Paper presented at American Anthropological Association meeting, Toronto, 1972.

Kahn, Herman. *The Emerging Japanese Superstate.* Englewood Cliffs, N.J.: Prentice-Hall, 1970.

Kapleau, Philip. ed. *The Three Pillars of Zen.* Tokyo: Weatherhill, 1965.

Kasahara, Y., and Sakamoto, K. Ereuthophobia and allied conditions. *In* S. Arieti, ed. *World Biennial of Psychiatry and Psychotherapy.* New York: Basic Books, 1970. Pp. 292-311.

Kato, Masaaki. Taijin Kyofu wo megutte (Concerning anthropophobia). *Seishin Igaku,* 1964, *6*(2), 107-112.

Kawai, Kiroshi, and Kondo, Kyoichi. Discussion on Morita therapy. *Psychologia,* 1960, *3*(2), 92-99.

Kelley, George A. *The Psychology of Personal Constructs.* Vols. 1, 2. New York: Norton, 1955.

Kelman, Harold. Psychotherapy in the Far East. *Progress in Psychotherapy,* 1959, *4,* 296-305.

————. Communing and relating. *American Journal of Psychotherapy,* 1960, *19, 70.*

Kerlinger, Fred N. Behavior and personality in Japan. *Social Forces,* 1953, *31,* 250-258.

Kierkegaard, S. *The Concept of Dread.* Trans. W. Laurie. Princeton: Princeton University Press, 1944.

Kiev, Ari, ed. *Magic, Faith, and Healing.* New York: Free Press, 1964.

Kiev, Ari. *Curanderismo.* New York: Free Press, 1968.

Kim, Jong He. Morita ryōhō to manabite (Understanding Morita therapy). *Arugamama,* 1967, no. 22, 17-24.

Kitano, Harry H. L. *Japanese-Americans.* Englewood Cliffs, N.J.: Prentice-Hall, 1969.

Kitsuse, John I. Moral treatment and reformation of inmates in Japanese prisons. *Psychologia,* 1965, *8,* 9-23.

————. A method of reform in Japanese prisons. *In* Maurice Schneps and Alvin D. Coox, eds. *The Japanese Image.* Tokyo: Orient/West, 1966, *2,* 1-7.

Kluckhohn, Florence R., and Strodtbeck, Fred L. *Variations in Value Orientations.* Evanston, Ill.: Row, Peterson, 1961.

Koestler, Arthur. *The Lotus and the Robot.* New York: Macmillan, 1961.

Kondo, Akehisa. Morita therapy: A Japanese therapy for neurosis. *American Journal of Psychoanalysis*, 1953, *13*, 31-37.

_____. Shinri ryōhō ni okeru chiryōsha kanja kankei Horney gakuha oyobi Morita ryōhō no tachibai kara (The therapist-patient relationship in psychotherapy from the standpoint of Horney's school and Morita therapy). *Seishin Bunseki Kenkyu*, 1961, 7(6), 30-35, 59-62.

Kondo, Kyoichi. A study of the socio-cultural background of anthropophobia. *Shinkeishitsu*, 1960, *1*(2), 47-65.

Kora, T. *Shinkei hakujaku no Honno to Chiryo (The Cause and Cure of Neurosis)*. Tokyo: Hakuyōsha, 1954.

_____. *Ningen no Seikaku (Human Character)*. Tokyo: Hakuyōsha, 1956a.

_____. *Taijin Kyofu no Naoshikata (A Way of Curing Anthropophobia)*. Tokyo: Hakuyōsha, 1956b.

_____. Morita therapy. In *Memorial Lectures for Professor Emeritus Kora*. Tokyo: Jikei University, 1964.

_____. Morita therapy. *International Journal of Psychiatry*, 1965, *1*(4), 611-640.

_____. Jibun wo shiru (Know thyself). NHK reprint of radio broadcast, March 6-8, 1967.

_____. Seishin ryōhō ni okeru shido no shikata (A method of instruction in psychotherapy). Nihi Iji Shimpō Special Publication number 2291, 1968. Trans. D. Reynolds. Repr. in *Jikeikai Medical Journal*, 1968, *15*(4), 315-325.

_____. Taijin kyofusho to nipponjin no rekishiteki shakaiteki kankyo (Anthropophobia and the social-historical milieu of the Japanese people). In *Memorial Collection in Honor of Emeritus Professor Shimoda*. Kyushu University, undated.

Kora, T., and Ohara, Kenshiro. Morita therapy. *Psychology Today*, 1973, 6(10), 63-68.

Kora, T., and Sato, K. Morita therapy: A psychotherapy in the way of Zen. *Psychologia*, 1958, *1*, 219-225.

Kumasaka, Y. Discussion. *International Journal of Psychiatry*, 1965, *1*(4), 641-642.

Lanham, Betty B. Aspects of child care in Japan: Preliminary report. *In* Bernard S. Silberman, ed. *Japanese Character and Culture.* Tucson: University of Arizona Press, 1962.

_____. The psychological orientation of the mother-child relationship in Japan. *Monumenta Nipponica*, 1966, *21*(3-4), 322-333.

Leighton, Alexander H. The therapeutic process in cross cultural perspective: A symposium. *American Journal of Psychiatry*, 1968, *124*(9), 1177-1178.

Leonhard, K. Die japanische Morita — Therapie aus der Sicht eigener psychotherapeutischer Vergahren. *Arch. Psychiat. Nervenkr.*, 1965, *207*, 185.

Leonhard, K. Trans. Kiroshi Iwai. Jiko no seishin ryōhō no shikaku yori mitaru Nippon no Morita ryōhō (Japan's Morita therapy from the viewpoint of my psychotherapeutic method). *Shinkeishitsu*, 1966, 6(2), 28-35.

Levy, Norman J. Discussion. *International Journal of Psychiatry*, 1965, *1*(4), 642-643.

Lifton, Robert J. *Thought Reform and the Psychology of Totalism.* New York: Norton, 1961.

Lilly, John C. *The Center of the Cyclone.* New York: Bantam, 1972.

London, Perry. *The Modes and Morals of Psychotherapy.* New York: Holt, Rinehart and Winston, 1964.

Mandler, George, and Watson, David L. Anxiety and the interruption of behavior. *In* Charles D. Spielberger, ed. *Anxiety and Behavior.* New York: Academic Press, 1966.

Marks, I. M. *Fears and Phobias.* London: Heineman, 1969.

Matsubara, Haruo. *Kaku Kazokujidai.* Tokyo: Nippon Hoso, 1969.

Matsumoto, Scott. *Contemporary Japan: The Individual and the Group.* Transactions of the American Philosophical Society, 1960.

Meerloo, Joost A. M. *The Rape of the Mind.* Cleveland: World, 1956.

Mills, C. W. Situated actions and vocabularies of motive. *American Sociological Review,* 1940, *5,* 904-913.

Mitchell, S. Wier. The evolution of the rest treatment. *Journal of Neurology and Mental Disease,* 1904, *31,* 368.

Miura, Momishige, and Usa, Shin-ichi. Morita therapy. *Psychologia,* 1970, *13*(1), 18-34.

Mizutani, Keiji. *Shincho de daitan na ikikata (A Prudent, Daring Way of Life)* Tokyo: Hakuyōsha, 1967.

Morita, Shōma. The true nature of shinkeishitsu and its treatment. In *Anthology of Theses Commemorating the 25th Anniversary of Professor Kure's Appointment to His Chair.* Tokyo: Jikei University, 1917.

Morita, Shōma, and Kora, Takehisa. *Sekimen Kyofu no Naoshikata (A Way of Curing Blushing Phobia.)* Tokyo: Hakuyōsha, 1953.

Morita, Shōma, and Mizutani, Keiji. *Sei no Yokubō (The Desire to Live Fully).* Tokyo: Hakuyōsha, 1956.

Mowrer, O. Hobart. The basis of psychopathology: malconditioning or misbehavior? *In* Charles D. Speilberger, ed. *Anxiety and Behavior.* New York: Academic Press, 1966.

Murase, Takao, and Reynolds, David. *Naikan Therapy.* Tokyo: Naikan Training Center Publication, 1974.

Murphy, Jane M. Psychotherapeutic aspects of shamanism on St. Lawrence Island, Alaska. *In* Ari Kiev, ed. *Magic, Faith, and Healing.* New York: Free Press, 1964.

Naka, Syuzo, and Kawakita, Yukio. Psychiatry in Japanese Culture. *Diseases of the Nervous System,* 1964, *25,* 298-304.

Naranjo, C. Present-centeredness. *In* Fagen, J., and Shepard, I. L., eds. *Gestalt Therapy Now.* New York: Harper and Row, 1970.

Nippon (tables 4-5, Japan's population by age-groups). Tokyo: Kokuseisha, 1966.

Nishizono, M. Japanese characteristics of the doctor-patient relationship in psychotherapy. *Proceedings of the 7th International Congress of Psychotherapy,* Wiesbaden. Basel and New York: Karger, 1968.

Nomura, A. Morita therapy, a psychotherapy developed in Japan. *Proceedings of the Joint Meeting of the Japanese Society of Psychiatry and Neurology and the American Psychiatric Association,* 1963.

Noonan, R. J. A note on an eastern counterpart of Frankl's paradoxical intention. *Psychologia*, 1969, *12*, 147-149.

Norbeck, Edward. *Changing Japan*. New York: Holt, Rinehart and Winston, 1965.

Northrop, F. S. C., symposium chairman, and Livingston, Helen H., ed. *Cross Cultural Understanding*. New York: Harper and Row, 1964.

Ohara, Kenshiro, Aizawa, S., and Iwai, H. *Morita Ryōhō* (*Morita Therapy*). Tokyo: Bunkodo, 1970.

Ohara, Kenshiro, et al. Morita ryōhō (nyuin shiki) no Genkyo (The present state of Morita therapy, inpatient treatment). *Seishin Igaku*, 1966*a*, *8*(3), 75-84.

Ohara, Kenshiro, et al. Shinkeishitsu Shiryo (*Shinkeishitsu* data). *Shinkeishitsu*, 1966*b*, *6*(2), 39-51.

Ohara, Kenshiro, and Reynolds, David K. Changing methods in Morita psychotherapy. *International Journal of Social Psychiatry*, 1968, *14*(4), 305-310.

————. Morita psychotherapy: Characteristics of a Japanese treatment for neurosis. Unpublished paper, 1973.

Okuda, Y. Autonomic nervous system reactions of mental patients. *Shinkeishitsu*, 1960, *1*(1), 43-64.

Ornstein, Robert E. *The Psychology of Consciousness*. San Francisco: W. H. Freeman, 1972.

Perls, F., Hefferline, R., and Goodman, P. *Gestalt Therapy*. New York: Dell, 1965.

Peterson, D. R. *The Clinical Study of Social Behavior*. New York: Appleton-Century-Crofts, 1968.

Phillips, Bernard, ed. *The Essentials of Zen Buddhism: An Anthology of the Writings of Daisetz T. Suzuki*. London: Rider, 1962.

Phillips, E., and Wiener, D. *Short Term Psychotherapy and Structured Behavior Change*. New York: McGraw Hill, 1966.

Plath, David William. *The After Hours*. Berkeley: University of California Press, 1964.

Prince, R. Indigenous Yoruba psychiatry. In Ari Kiev, ed. *Magic, Faith, and Healing*. New York: Free Press, 1964.

Raucat, T. *The Honorable Picnic*. New York: Modern Age Books, 1924.

Reynolds, David K. Morita therapy and the behavior therapies. *Anthropology UCLA*, 1969*a*, *1*(2), 33-43.

————. Directed behavior change: Japanese psychotherapy in a private mental hospital. Ph.D. dissertation, University of California, Los Angeles, 1969*b*.

————. Gaikokujin ni yoru gajoku no kosatsu (A foreigner considers isolated bed rest). *Ima ni Ikiru*, 1969*c*, *9*(2), 31-33.

————. Ningen to wa? (What is man?). *Seishin Ryōhō Kenkyu*, 1972, *4*(1), 51-54.

————. Experiential research and shadowing: Methodological innovations in the anthropological study of suicide. Paper presented at American Anthropological Association meeting, Mexico City, 1974*a*.

————. Naikan therapy: An experiential view. Submitted for publication, 1974*b*.

Reynolds, David K., and Farberow, Norman L. Experiential research: An inside perspective on suicide and social systems. *Life Threatening Behavior*, 1973a, *3*(4), 261-269.

————. The suicidal patient: An inside view. *Omega*, 1973b, *4*(3), 229-241.

————. Experiential research in a board and care setting. *In* Parad, H., Resnik, H., and Parad, L., eds. *Emergency Mental Health and Disaster Aid.* New York: Charles Press, 1975.

Reynolds, David K., and Kitano, H. H. L. A cross cultural study of neurotic symptomatology among college students. Unpublished manuscript, 1970.

Reynolds, David K., and Ohara, Kenshiro. Morita therapy and attempted suicide. *Anthropology UCLA*, 1969, *1*(2), 45-48.

Reynolds, David K., and Yamamoto, Joe. East meets West: Moritist and Freudian psychotherapies. *Science and Psychoanalysis*, 1972, *21*, 187-195.

————. Morita psychotherapy in Japan. *Current Psychiatric Therapies*, 1973, *13*, 219-227.

Rosenzweig, S. A dynamic interpretation of psychotherapy oriented towards research. *Psychiatry*, 1938, *1*(4), 521-526.

Sansom, G. B. *Japan: A Short Cultural History.* Rev. ed. New York: Appleton-Century-Crofts, 1962.

Santucci, P. S., and Winokur, G. Brainwashing as a factor in psychiatric illness. *A.M.A. Arch. Neurol. and Psychiat.*, 1955, *74*, 11-16.

Sargant, William. *Battle for the Mind.* London: Heinemann, 1957.

Sato, Koji. Psychotherapeutic implications of Zen. *Psychologia*, 1958, *1*, 213-218.

————. Introduction to articles on Naikan. *Psychologia*, 1965a, *8*, 1.

————. I. Yoshitomo: Forty years of Naikan. *Psychologia*, 1965b, *8*, 23-24.

Schein, Edgar H. *Coercive Persuasion.* New York: Norton, 1961.

————. Reaction patterns to severe, chronic stress in American Army prisoners of war of the Chinese. *In* Vinacke, W. E. et al., eds. *Dimensions of Social Psychology.* Chicago: Schot, Foresman, 1964.

Shinfuku, Naotake. Shinkeishitsu to shite no Morita setsu to Bunseki setsu to no kankei (The relationship between the Moritist and psychoanalytic theories of neurosis). *Seishin Igaku*, 1959, *1*(7), 475-488.

————. Shinri ryōhō: Morita ryōhō (Psychotherapy: Morita therapy). Tokyo: Jikei University, undated.

Sikkema, Mildred. Observations on Japanese early child training. *In* Douglas G. Haring, ed. *Personal Character and Cultural Milieu.* Rev. ed. Syracuse: Syracuse University Press, 1949.

Soseki, Natsume. *Kojin (The Wayfarer).* Trans. Beongcheon Yu. Tokyo: Tuttle, 1967.

Soskin, William F., and John, Vera P. The study of spontaneous talk. *In* Roger G. Barker, ed. *The Stream of Behavior.* New York: Appleton-Century-Crofts, 1963.

Storrow, H. A. Psychotherapy as interpersonal conditioning. *In* Jules Masserman, ed., *Current Psychiatric Therapies*, 1965, *5*, 76-86.

Stryk, Lucien, and Ikemoto, Takashi, eds. *Zen: Poems, Prayers, Sermons, Anecdotes, Interviews.* Garden City, N.Y.: Doubleday Anchor, 1965.

Suzuki, Tomonari. *Fuan no Kaiketsu (The Solution to Anxiety)*. Tokyo: Ikeda, 1956.

————. Shinkeishitsu no Morita ryōhō (The Morita therapy of *shinkeishitsu*). *Seishin Igaku,* 1959, *1*(7), 41-47.

————. Morita ryōhō to Zen (Morita therapy and Zen). *Seishin Igaku,* 1966, *8*(11), 55-60.

————. Morita ryōhō no tachibai kara (From the standpoint of Morita therapy). *Seishin Igaku,* 1967 *9*(7), 11-19.

Szasz, Thomas S. *The Myth of Mental Illness.* New York: Hoeber, 1961.

Takahashi, Y. A psychophysiological study of neurotic in-patients treated by Morita therapy. *Shinkeishitsu,* 1960, *1*(1), 21-42.

Takamizu, R. A medical view on insomnia. *Psychoanalysis* (Tokyo), 1952, *10*(3), 12-15.

Takano, Keitaro. P. F. test administered to neurotics. *Shinkeishitsu,* 1961, *2*(2), 27-42.

Takeuchi, Katashi. On "Naikan" method. *Psychologia,* 1965, *8*, 2-8.

Takeyama, T., et al. Shinkeishitsu Shiryō (1) (*Shinkeishitsu* data). *Shinkeishitsu,* 1966, *6*(1), 18-29.

Thompson, C., and Millahy, P. *Psychoanalysis: Evolution and Development.* New York: Hermitage House, 1950.

Ullman, Leonard P., and Krasner, Leonard, eds. *Case Studies in Behavior Modification.* New York: Holt, Rinehart and Winston, 1965.

U.S. Army Area Handbook for Japan. U.S. Government Printing Office. 2nd ed. 1964.

Vogel, Ezra F. *Japan's New Middle Class.* Berkeley and Los Angeles: University of California Press, 1963.

Walker, Richard L. *China under Communism.* London: Allen and Unwin, 1956.

Watts, Alan W. *The Way of Zen.* New York: Pantheon, 1957.

————. *The Spirit of Zen.* New York: Grove Press, 1958.

————. *Psychotherapy East and West.* New York: Random House, 1961.

Wendt, I. Y. Japanische Psychotherapie. *Z. Psychother. med. Psychol.,* 1958, *8*, 204.

————. Eine Japanische Klinik im Westen. *Schweiz Z. Psychol.,* 1965, *24*, 366.

Wetty, Paul Thomas. *The Asians: Their Heritage and Their Destiny.* Rev. ed. Philadelphia: Lippincott, 1963.

Wolpe, Joseph. Reciprocal inhibition as the main basis of psychotherapeutic effects. *In* H. J. Eysenck, ed. *Behavior Therapy and the Neuroses.* New York: Macmillan, 1960.

Wolpe, Joseph, Salter, Andrew, and Reyna, R. J. *The Conditioning Therapies.* New York: Holt, Rinehart and Winston, 1964.

Yamamoto, Tasuro. Recent studies in Japanese national character. *In* F. S. C. Northrop, symposium chairman, and Helen H. Livingston, ed. *Cross Cultural Understanding.* New York: Harper and Row, 1964.

Yokoyama, Keigo. Morita therapy and seiza. *Psychologia,* 1968, *11*(3-4), 179-184.

Yora, Ken. Shinkeishitsho no yogo ni taisuru rinjiteki kenkyu (A clinical study of the sequelae of neurosis). *Jikei University Medical Journal*, 1959, 75(2), 306-321.

Yoron Chosa (Public Opinion Research Magazine), 1973, 5(9).

Zilboorg, G., and Henry, G. *A History of Medical Psychology*. New York: Norton, 1941.

INDEX